DR. CHARLES BURNEY'S
CONTINENTAL TRAVELS

AMS PRESS
NEW YORK

Dr Charles Burney

After Reynolds

DR. CHARLES BURNEY'S
CONTINENTAL
TRAVELS

1770–1772

*Compiled from his Journals
and other Sources by*

CEDRIC HOWARD GLOVER

BLACKIE & SON LIMITED
LONDON AND GLASGOW
1927

Library of Congress Cataloging in Publication Data

Burney, Charles, 1726-1814.
    Dr. Charles Burney's continental travels.

    Reprint of the 1927 ed. published by Blackie, London.
    Original t.p.: "Compiled from his Journals and other
sources by Cedric Howard Glover."
    1. Europe—Description and travel—17th-18th centuries.
2. Music—Europe. I. Glover, Cedric Howard.
ML195.B967 1978   780'.92'4   74-26048
ISBN 0-404-12920-X

Reprinted from the edition of 1927, London
First AMS edition published in 1978
Manufactured in the United States of America

AMS PRESS INC.
NEW YORK, N.Y.

PREFACE

This book furnishes the reader with an account of Dr. Charles Burney's tours in Western Europe, and of the people whom he met during his travels. During the year 1770 Dr. Burney traversed France and Italy, penetrating as far south as Naples. The second expedition in 1772 covered a wide area in Germany and the Netherlands, and included visits to many of the capital cities in the constituent states of the Empire.

Our knowledge of the details of these journeys is derived mainly from two Journals published in each case soon after the return of the traveller to England, and from a manuscript journal of the Italian tour, which supplies valuable supplementary matter excised by the author from the published version. There are no English editions of the Journals later in date than the eighteenth century, and it is probable that the extracts peculiar to the manuscript journal, which are used in this volume, now appear in print for the first time.

The primary object of Dr. Burney's travels was the acquisition of material for the *General History of Music* which it was his ambition to compile, and his Journals are therefore mainly concerned with the results of his researches. However interesting to the public of his own day, there can be no question that the sections of his Journals devoted to purely musical matters are in the main responsible for the somewhat rapid decline in popular favour which his books experienced.

Yet embedded in accounts of interviews with long forgotten musicians, we can still find plenty to delight and entertain us.

The Journals contain graphic descriptions of encounters with many of the notable figures in the literary and musical history of that time—Voltaire and Rousseau, Mozart and Gluck, Laura Bassi, the lady professor of Bologna, and Sir William Hamilton, antiquarian and collector. Few Englishmen had the luck to hear Frederick the Great play the flute at Potsdam, or to watch Henry, Cardinal York, the last of the Stuarts, say vespers in Rome.

But it is not only the personal side of the Journals which arrests attention. There is much to interest us in Dr. Burney's adventures on the road. He gives us a striking picture of the devastation and misery caused by the Seven Years' War, of his own discomforts on the journey by river on a log raft from Munich to Vienna, and of the villainy in general of postboys and innkeepers. Finally there is the pleasure of watching the actions and reactions of an engaging personality. A man of his age, with no great complexity of character, Dr. Burney makes us share his pleasures even in the condescensions of the great. His insatiable curiosity is infectious; nothing is too trivial to enlist his sympathetic attention. His patience is unending especially towards tedious old men, like Quantz, flute instructor to Frederick the Great, who must have bored him with the minute trivialities of autobiography as much as his account of them wearies us.

Whilst the relation of Dr. Burney's travels remains the chief object of this book, there is the subsidiary intention of making the best portions of his Journals once more available and in such a form as may reasonably be expected to interest the general reader. To secure a consecutive narrative it has often been necessary to resort to drastic rearrangement of the material taken from the Journals, which were written loosely in diary form. Large sections have been disregarded altogether, the question of retention or omission of passages being governed, apart from the question of relevancy, by their potential interest for the average reader rather than for the specialist. The residuum, though of course largely concerned with music and musicians, carries an interest beyond its subject matter, whether biographical, historical or antiquarian, which it would hardly have possessed at the time when it was written.

As much, therefore, as possible of Dr. Burney's vivid and lively prose has been preserved, leaving him to tell his own story whenever feasible—an easier task in the German than in the Italian Journal. Spelling has as a rule been modernized, punctuation and italics for the most part retained as essential to preserve the author's meaning. In order to maintain the continuity of the narrative, the quotations from the Journals, with the exception of those embodied in the text itself, have been assimilated into the main structure of the book without further distinction than a change of type. This involves a constant and sudden transition, often within a sentence, from the third person to the first, and from the historic aorist to the present tense. Constant interchange from *oratio obliqua* to *oratio recta* was the alternative to lifeless paraphrasing. Indulgence is therefore asked of those possessing a strong sense of the unities, whose feelings may be outraged by such procedure; it is confidently anticipated that the end will be found to have justified the means, however heterodox.

The Journals have long played their part in the formation of musical history; the present volume sets out to win them the favour of a wider circle of readers than the musical lexicographers by bringing into prominence the many factors of varied interest contained in them; these, it is hoped, may prove a substantial contribution to the history of those remote days when Continental travelling required the courage and endurance now demanded of an Arctic explorer.

CONTENTS

PART ONE—FRANCE AND ITALY IN 1770

PART TWO—GERMANY AND THE NETHERLANDS IN 1772

CONTENTS

INTRODUCTION

The children of great men are usually overshadowed in renown by their fathers. The converse is more rarely encountered; few such children succeed in surpassing their parents in the race for fame; fewer still are so completely successful that they eclipse the reputation of the parent altogether, yet there can be no doubt that Fanny Burney has innocently been guilty of this unfilial act. Few of Dr. Burney's contemporaries could have foreseen that he, the friend of the great Dr. Johnson, a fellow of the Royal Society, and author of a prodigious *History of Music* from Tubal Cain downwards, would be dispossessed by his shy, retiring daughter, the anonymous author of *Evelina*, of fame so laboriously acquired. Yet of the thousands who know and love the work of Fanny Burney, how many have so much as heard of Dr. Charles Burney, her father? If they know his name, it is merely in the parental capacity, or owing to the letters addressed to him by Dr. Johnson and included in Boswell's biography, or to references in musical dictionaries and histories. Some may remember the descriptions of him and his circle in Macaulay's essay on his daughter, few will have ploughed through the egregious memoirs which Madame D'Arblay, as an act of filial piety, possibly by way of atonement, thought fit to perpetrate in her old age: that the memoirs richly merit the condemnation since pronounced against them may be proved ·by reference to the few extracts included in the present volume.

The fact remains that Dr. Burney, although devoid of the precocious and perhaps overrated genius of his daughter

Fanny, yet possessed qualities which singled him out even amid the brilliant constellation of literary and artistic luminaries in which he moved. He might reasonably have anticipated a lasting immortality for some at least of his literary work, though he could hardly have claimed it for his musical compositions. He would, no doubt, have been content to go down to posterity as a historian of his beloved art, but even this solace was denied him, and his great history in four ponderous volumes has become merely a happy hunting-ground for others who succeeded him in this capacity. He was, anyhow, spared the humiliating knowledge that the rival history of Sir John Hawkins, which appeared in the same year as his own, was to be reprinted seventy-seven years after, while his own was to languish unhonoured and in obscurity, neglected by all except the bibliophile or musical antiquary.

The story of Charles Burney's life is brief and uneventful: he was born at Shrewsbury on 7th April, 1726 (O.S.), and was educated at the free school founded by Queen Elizabeth in that city. He was afterwards removed to the public school in Chester, where he received his first instruction in music from a Mr. Baker, a pupil of Dr. Blow and organist of the cathedral. In 1741 young Burney had his first glimpse of Handel, who was passing through Chester on his way to Ireland. Later in the same year Burney returned to Shrewsbury, where he pursued his musical studies under the direction of his half-brother, James Burney, who filled the post of organist in Shrewsbury for a period of fifty-four years.

Three years later another famous composer, Dr. Arne, passed through Shrewsbury on his way from Ireland to London, whither he was going to assume command at Drury Lane Theatre: he met Charles Burney, took a fancy to the boy, and bore him off to London as an articled pupil. Burney played in the theatre orchestra, but otherwise did not derive much benefit from Arne's instruction, but the sister of his preceptor, Mrs. Cibber, the actress, took an interest in him, and at her house Burney met many of the celebrities of the day, including Handel and Garrick. For a short period Burney came under the patronage of Fulke Greville, the notorious fop, who paid Dr. Arne to cancel the indentures by which his pupil was bound. In 1749 Burney married his first wife and, having severed his connexion with Greville, soon after received the appointment of organist at St. Dionis Backchurch in Fenchurch Street. In 1750 or 1751, Burney's health having suffered from the confined atmosphere of the city, he was ordered to the country by his physician, and accepted the vacant post of organist at King's Lynn in Norfolk, which he held for ten years. We find the Burney family back in London again in 1760 and living in Poland Street, but in the following year the home was darkened by the tragic death of Mrs. Burney.

Burney soon began to build up a reputation as a composer, a performer, and a teacher of music. After a visit to Paris in 1764 to place his daughters, Esther and Susan, at school there, Burney made an adaptation of Rousseau's *Le Devin du Village*, at Garrick's suggestion, for the Drury Lane stage, which was performed in 1766 under the title of " The Cunning Man ". Burney graduated bachelor and doctor of music at Oxford University in the same year; it is in the handsome gown of a doctor of music that he sat to Reynolds for the fine portrait of which a reproduction forms the frontispiece of the present volume: we hear of Dr. Burney once more in connexion with the university, as it was at his instigation that Joseph Haydn was granted an honorary degree of doctor of music in 1791.

Dr. Burney married again in 1767, his second wife being a widowed lady with whom he had been acquainted at King's Lynn. The years 1770–1773 were occupied by the travels in search of information for the projected history of music and the publication of the two journals which are the basis of this book. In the year following Dr. Burney's return from Germany he was elected a fellow of the Royal Society, and from thence onwards until 1789 his leisure was devoted to the preparation of his great *History of Music*, of which the first volume appeared in 1776, the same year in which Sir John Hawkins's rival history was published. In 1784 Dr. Burney wrote an account of the first Handel Festival, and in 1796 he published a life of Metastasio, the Italian poet, whom he met in Vienna during the German tour.

The Burney family moved in 1774 from Poland Street to

Isaac Newton's house in St. Martin's Street, Leicester Square, and in 1783 into apartments in Chelsea College, where Dr. Burney had received the post of organist through the influence of Burke. He lived here until his death on 14th April, 1814, his last years being rendered immune from anxiety by a Government pension of £300, given to him by Fox in 1806.

Dr. Burney's name crops up continually in the literary history of the period, whether as a friend of Dr. Johnson, whose biography he nearly undertook, or as a visitor to Horace Walpole at Strawberry Hill.[1] When Haydn came to London in 1791, it was Dr. Burney who received him and recited the adulatory poem of welcome. Further, he possessed in no small measure the versatility of the age: he published an essay on comets in 1769, wrote a poem in twelve cantos on astronomy, and throughout his travels displayed the most omnivorous curiosity towards everything strange and novel which crossed his path. We find him in a position to discuss electricity on terms of equality with Laura Bassi in Bologna, and astronomy with Boscovich in Milan. Wedded to this curiosity was a real power of observation and a sincere love of knowledge, and above all a kindly temperament and benevolence, which seem to have endeared him to all with whom he came into contact.

An attempt, therefore, to restore Dr. Burney's Journals to their rightful position in English literature does not require any justification. However, apart altogether from the engaging personality of Dr. Burney himself and his associations with a famous literary coterie, the glimpses which we get in the journals of Europe in the 1770's are alone sufficient warranty for the present volume.

Superficial differences between the two periods, such, for instance, as that in locomotion, at once put the age in which Dr. Burney is writing at a considerable remoteness from our own. When we come to examine his tastes and judgments, the distance is intensified. We are bewildered by the space which he devotes to composers and singers of whom we know next to nothing; the latter, it is true, can never earn lasting fame, but the creative artist of merit might justifiably expect a small measure of immortality. Farinelli, padre Mar-

[1] Cf. Horace Walpole's *Letters*, 16th August, 1796, or 6th September, 1785.

tini, Jomelli, C. Ph. E. Bach are mere names to all but the avowed student of musical history. In Handel alone should we find a point of direct contact with Dr. Burney, and even here our admiration would have but little in common with his. On the other hand, Dr. Burney's lukewarm attitude towards J. S. Bach seems incomprehensible, until we recollect how little of the great composer's music was available in those days. More unreal still to readers of the present century must seem the acrimonious dispute regarding the comparative merits of French and Italian music, in which Dr. Burney displays an active partisanship.

Dr. Burney lived at the end of a period, political and musical. The old régime was doomed and the end in sight. The glimpses which we get in the Journals of the wanton extravagance of the little German courts and of Central Europe, devastated by the Seven Years' War, are all damning evidence of the failure of the prevalent state of society. In Italy, it is true, conditions were a little better: Dr. Burney admits that the Italians

may, perhaps, be accused of cultivating music to excess; but whoever continues a short time in any of their principal cities, must perceive that other arts and sciences are not neglected: and even in travelling through the country, if the Ecclesiastical State be excepted, the natural fertility of the soil does not appear to be the only source of abundance in the necessaries of life; for I can venture to affirm that, throughout Lombardy and Tuscany, agriculture is carried on with such art and activity, that I never remember to have seen lands better laid out, or less frequently suffered to lie idle: the poor, indeed, are oppressed and rendered worthless by the rigour of government; but were they less so under their Gothic tyrants, when arts and sciences were not only neglected but extirpated from among them? Perhaps the cultivation of the peaceful arts may contribute as much to the happiness of the present inhabitants of Italy, and, indeed, of the rest of the world, as the conquering kingdoms did to that of their martial ancestors; who, when they were not busied in cutting the throats of each other, employed all their time and talents in plundering and enslaving mankind.

Music, the youngest of the arts, was in a stage of transition. The long supremacy of Italy had been challenged, and was on the wane: C. Ph. Emanuel Bach and Joseph Haydn were together laying the foundations of the German ascendancy, which was to last throughout the following century. At the time when Dr. Burney was travelling, the pianoforte was still in a rudimentary condition; the technical limitations of its predecessors, the harpsichord and clavichord, acted as a curb on the aspirations of the composers of keyboard music. The orchestra was in an even more primitive state; the potentialities of the different mediums employed were hardly realized, the wind department in particular suffering from ill-constructed instruments, upon which the players could with difficulty even play in tune. In one point alone did the eighteenth century surpass its successors: it was the day of the great singer, and naturally music, to its detriment, came to play a subordinate rôle to the dazzling virtuosity of the executive artist. Music was indeed an aristocratic pursuit, maintained by the petty courts and rich noblemen everywhere existing; musicians were in a menial position; even Dr. Burney is unduly conscious of the condescension of the noblemen whom he meets on his travels. In extreme cases, as at the court of the notorious Archbishop Hieronymus of Salzburg, in whose service languished the great composer Mozart, the musicians were but little better than the scullions, who were often brought up to reinforce the orchestra when extra help was required. The composition of music was a craft not an art in those days; a composer was an essential member of every great household, and was expected to produce a constant supply of new music and pieces for special occasions whenever required to do so. The amount of music, therefore, composed during the eighteenth century reaches almost incredible proportions; the bulk, however, possesses neither value nor interest for posterity, and its existence, even in its own day, was completely ephemeral. There were, of course, outstanding figures, composers and executants alike, whose music or whose performances achieved international repute. But the difficulties with which an aspirant composer had to contend would seem almost insurmountable. A student of music had largely to rely on manuscript copies, and was handicapped by all the faults inherent in this unsatisfactory medium of reproduction; printed music was just beginning to be a commercial proposition, but few composers could hope to attain to print. Difficulties of dissemination and cost of production were therefore paramount obstacles to fame, coupled with which was a general apathy towards music except as a means for technical display.

It was therefore essential for Dr. Burney to collect for himself the materials for his projected *History of Music*. He tells us how he had consulted numberless books on the subject, which were

such faithful copies of each other, that he who reads two or three, has the substance of as many hundred. In hopes, therefore, of stamping on my intended history some marks of originality, or at least of novelty, I determined to allay my thirst of knowledge at the source, and take such draughts in Italy, as England cannot supply. It was there I determined to hear with my *own* ears, and to see with my *own* eyes; and, if possible, to *hear* and *see* nothing but *music*. . . .

I found the shortest and best road to such information as I wanted, was to talk with the principal professors, wherever I went. Learned men and books may be more useful as to ancient music, but it is only *living* musicians that can explain what *living music* is. This method, however, where I had no letters of recommendation, cost me a little money, some assurance, and a great deal of trouble.

So successful were Dr. Burney's endeavours that, in addition to a large quantity of manuscripts, he brought back from Italy alone nearly four hundred scarce books on music, and arranged for a correspondent in every important town, who was to keep him advised of all fresh local developments subsequent to his visit which ought to find a place in the *History of Music*.

The Journal of the Italian Tour, which appeared in 1771, was entitled:

THE
PRESENT STATE

OF

MUSIC

IN

FRANCE and ITALY:

OR,

The JOURNAL of a TOUR through those Countries, undertaken to collect Materials for

A GENERAL HISTORY OF MUSIC

By CHARLES BURNEY, Mus.D.

Ei cantarono allor si dolcemente,
Che la dolcezza ancor dentro mi suona.

DANTE, Purg. Canto 2do.

LONDON
Printed for T. BECKET and Co. in the Strand
MDCCLXXI

The Journal soon reached a second edition, and became one of the popular books of the day, its success being no doubt in some measure due to the interviews with famous singers like Farinelli, whose names were still household words among the older members of English polite society; the world has always shown a strong partiality for details of the private lives of its actors and singers, and, as we have already seen, the hero worship of the opera star was as strong in the eighteenth century as it is to-day.

Dr. Burney's original intention had been to temper the technicalities of his researches into music with accounts of things " miscellaneous of observation or of anecdote ", but against his better judgment and in deference to the opinion of Garrick and others, " who conjointly believed that books of general travels were already so numerous, and so spread, that their merits were overlooked from their multiplicity ", he ruthlessly excised from his Journal large portions, which would doubtless have assisted in staving off the oblivion to which it was later to be consigned. Fortunately the manuscript of the Journal in its original form has been preserved, and may be inspected in the manuscript room of the British Museum (Add. MSS. No. 35,122). A small square volume of 360 closely covered pages, the manuscript journal, in spite of the rambling style in which it is written, and the many irrelevancies which mar it, possesses in some way the spirit which is wanting in the published version. The criticisms of Dr. Burney's friends were no doubt justified: the manuscript journal is far too long and hopelessly diffuse; the author lacked the genius of Sterne. Yet had he known it, the little commonplaces of daily existence, and the unimportant incidents of the journey, would have possessed an interest for posterity far surpassing the specifications of organs and the careers of opera singers. The standard of values has completely changed. We search the journals to-day for just those features which to contemporary readers seemed of little account; we skip with a yawn those barren tracts in which Dr. Burney reports " the present state of music " in the countries which he visited.

Long after the Italian journal had lost all significance for the general public, it survived as an important " source book " for the musical historian; modern musical histories and dictionaries are heavily indebted to it for authoritative information regarding the period. Though from time to time references and short extracts have appeared in the press and in periodicals, it was not until 1921 that any extended portion of the work became again available to the general reader, who had not access to one of the early editions. A prophet is indeed not without honour save in his own country! In this year appeared the entire Italian section of the first Journal, translated into Italian by Virginia Attanasio under the title *Viaggio Musicale in Italia*, and published in the *Collezione settecentesca* of Remo Sandron. The original French translation, which appeared in 1809, was used as a basis for the text—" La difficoltà di procurarci la rara edizione inglese di quest' opera ci ha fatto ricorrere alla versione che ne fece il Brack." The volume is furnished with notes and illustrated with plates from Dr. Burney's *General History of Music*, including the Reynolds portrait, and pictures of the people whom he met, and the places which he visited; among the former are two pictures of Nelson's Emma, the editor evidently being guilty of a pardonable confusion between the two wives of Sir William Hamilton.

The Journal of the German Tour was published in two volumes in 1773, with a title similar to that of the previous Journal, except for the quotation, which in this case reads as follows:

Auf Virtuosen sei stolz, Germanien, die du gezeiget;

In Frankreich und Welschland sind grössere nicht.

ZACHARIÄ.

The book was " printed for T. Becket and Co. Strand; J. Robson, New Bond Street; and G. Robinson, Paternoster Row ". The fly-leaf of the second volume contains an invitation to subscribe for the *General History of Music*. The success of these two volumes surpassed even that of their predecessor, as Dr. Burney, yielding to his personal inclination and the judgment of several of his friends whose opinion he had reason to respect, intermixed (as he tells us in the advertisement to the second volume) " with his account of music and musicians, a few miscellaneous memorandums ". The disparity in size between the sections occupied by the two Journals in the present volume needs no further explanation.

No greater encomium could have been bestowed on Dr. Burney's two Journals than the tribute of Dr. Johnson, who had so high an opinion of them that he paid the author the flattering compliment of imitating his methods in his own Hebridean tour. It is difficult to conceive how Dr. Johnson, who was quite unmusical, could have waded through the technicalities of his friend's books; yet Madame D'Arblay is able to report the following conversation (*Memoirs of Dr. Burney*, Vol. II, page 78):

The *Tour to the Hebrides* being then in hand, Dr. Burney enquired of what size and form the book would be. " Sir," he replied, with a little bow, " you are my model!"

Impelled by the same kindness, when the Doctor lamented the disappointment of the public in *Hawkesworth's Voyages*,—" Sir," he cried, " the public is always disappointed in books of travel;—except yours!"

And afterwards, he said that he had hardly ever read any book quite through in his life; but added: " Chamier and I, Sir, however, read all your travels through;—except, perhaps, the description of the great pipes in the organs of Germany and the Netherlands!——"

which, needless to add, is omitted from the present volume.

The disappearance of the Journals from our bookshelves is nevertheless not surprising, and it is hardly conceivable, in spite of the new Italian edition, that either will ever be re-printed in its original form. Comparison with Arthur Young's *Travels in France* in the year 1787 is inevitable. Young set out to do for agriculture that which his brother-in-law and friend, Burney, had already done for music. Both differed in every respect from the conventional English tourist of the century. The Grand Tour had been a commonplace in Eng-

lish life since the days of John Evelyn; it was usually undertaken by the rich young man of the period as the last stage of
a liberal education. Burney and Young belonged to a different
grade of society; they undertook these journeys solely as
investigators with a very definite purpose in view, to which
their itineraries and plans were closely subordinated. Burney
frankly admitted that he would never have undertaken a
journey which had been attended " with much fatigue, expense, and neglect of other concerns ", had he not been compelled by lack of material for his *History*. It is therefore
reasonable to ask how Young's book should have succeeded
in maintaining its position, while Burney's Journals, dealing
with music, a subject of much greater general interest than
agriculture, should have signally failed to do so. A cursory
examination of the two books shows that it is a case of the
survival of the fittest. Both by nature of their quest were
naturally better equipped for shrewd observation than the
ordinary traveller. Young gave his powers free rein and kept
agriculture in the background—no one would to-day catalogue his book as a work on agriculture. Dr. Burney's
Journals, on the other hand, in their original form, could
come under no other category than that of musical history,
and those sections of his books which deal specifically with
music can make little appeal to-day except to the student of
the musically jejune age in which he was writing. But apart
from any questions of intrinsic merit, Young secured an important, though quite fortuitous, advantage over Burney, by
reason of the period during which his travels took place. His
journeys across France were made on the eve of the Revolution
and it was his picture of the country in the last days of the
old régime which set the seal of immortality on his work.
Burney travelled at a time of comparative peace; he tells us
of rumours of wars and revolutions, but he was eye-witness
of no event of historical importance. He found, however,
plenty of scope for his powers of description in the normal
incidents of everyday life. It is by the study of such commonplaces that we can most accurately reconstitute the environ-
ment in which our ancestors lived. A belief in the value of
such reconstruction was the main incentive to the compilation
of this book.

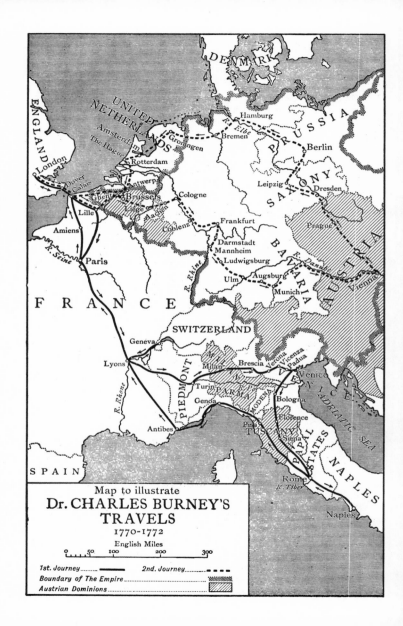

Map to illustrate
Dr. CHARLES BURNEY'S
TRAVELS
1770–1772

English Miles

0 50 100   200   300

1st. Journey............   2nd. Journey............
Boundary of The Empire............
Austrian Dominions............

PART ONE

France and Italy
in 1770

THE
EXPEDITION OF 1770

CHAPTER I

Paris and Geneva

The story of Dr. Burney's first expedition begins with his arrival in Dover on Tuesday, 5th June, 1770. For information regarding his experiences on the outward journey to Paris, we have to rely almost exclusively upon the manuscript journal. From this source we learn that Dr. Burney was detained in Dover

by a foolish accident which happened on the road, for having left my sword, that necessary passport for a gentleman on the Continent, I thought it of consequence enough to remain at Dover till I recovered it, which was not till Wednesday night.

This period of waiting was spent in seeing Dover Castle and wandering about the town. On Thursday, 7th June, Dr. Burney embarked, this being the third occasion on which he had crossed from England to France; he proceeded

with a fair wind and arrived at Calais without any other accident then the very common one of being intolerably ill during the whole passage. This in all my passages to and from France ever deprives me of a pleasure, which others enjoy in examining the two shores when equidistant from both. . . .

At Calais the ceremonial of the custom house gives a specimen at once of pride and meanness. The chief *commis*, or clerk there, was sitting in a velvet suit of clothes with every other appurtenance of the dress and appearance of a gentleman, or indeed rather of a man of fashion and quality; who, when he had signed my passport, being asked what there was to pay—" Ah! monsieur—ça c'est que la politesse "—and more compliments: and upon giving him a " pièce de 24 sous ", equal to a shilling English, his eyes sparkled, and he seemed as pleased as a man of equal appearance in England would have been with a place at court or a regiment.

Dr. Burney's route to Paris was by Lille and Cambrai, a different itinerary from that of Sterne, who in *The Sentimental Journey* travelled by Montreuil and Amiens.[1] Dr. Burney travelled by chaise from Calais to Lille, which cost him, with horses and attendance, just four guineas for the eighty miles; the night was spent at St. Omer, but he arrived after the gates were shut and was forced to stay at a miserable inn outside the city, where he " had not the courage to undress for fear of bugs and damp bedclothes ". He was unable to procure meat for his supper and had to content himself with " stale mackerel, a salad with rancid oil and an omelette made of addled eggs ".

The gates of St. Omer opened at 4 a.m., and soon after Dr. Burney drove through the town, past Bethune—" more strongly fortified and guarded than any (city) in French Flanders "—and so to Lille, arriving on 8th June. He had

---

[1] In connexion with the choice of route, Dr. Burney writes:

The French ambassador, M. du Chatelet, was expected to travel this way to-night or to-morrow morning from England, and this will make this road fashionable. The fat landlady endeavoured to persuade me that it was the nearest, though at least thirty miles about. However it is by far the best road.

missed the Paris diligence by one day, and had to wait until 10th June for the next. His thirst for musical knowledge gave him no rest, but neither at Lille nor at any other town on the way to Paris did he discover anything of consequence.

The diligence from Lille to Paris cost nearly three guineas and spent two days on the road, the passengers being boarded all the way.

The Lille diligence, in which I travelled, set out at 4 o'clock with only myself in it. At about a league's distance from the town, a young Strasbourgoise was taken up—she began to be very communicative, and to tell her story and adventures before we reached Douai; but upon the entrance of another *female* passenger, she was silenced and remained a mystery all the way. Women are always and everywhere more afraid of each other than of the men. I could perceive these two taking every opportunity to peruse each other. I was surprised at this among the French, who are in general so easy and well bred: if a new female entered among people that were before intimate and loquacious, in the provinces, a sudden silence ensued, which seemed wholly spent in the contemplation and study of the new object.

The third female passenger, whom we took up at Douai, was rather turned of 30, as handsome as her fat would allow. Upon her entrance into the vehicle, which even with my assistance she found to be rather a difficult feat of activity, she cries out, with a good natured laugh: " Ah! que je suis *Flamande!*"—the Flemish women having ever been remarkable for the " weary load under which they groan and sweat ". This sally seemed to promise well, but the conversation was spoilt till we reached Cambrai, where we dined. Here an outside passenger, a poor unfortunate tar, a young man seemingly worn out with labour and adversity, . . . joined us. He spared no folly in age, sex or condition, and all this was rather acrid than rude. He said some things at dinner about the English, which a little mortified me, but before we got up from table, my national pride was gratified by his declaring that he thought them the first people in the world for learning and probity, and, what made this eulogy more palatable was his having been a long while our prisoner during the last war.

The diligence passed through Cambrai, Senlis, and Peronne. A great part of Peronne was in ruins:

at present its only garrison is custom house officers; for at the entrance into this town all travellers and even its inhabitants, are visited and very narrowly searched, and this, to prevent the bringing into France the productions of Flanders, which are subject to a very high duty, such as the laces of Valenciennes, Lille, Dunkirk, cambrics of St. Quentin, Arras, Douai and above all Cambrai.

Tobacco was two-thirds cheaper outside Peronne than in the city itself!

At Cambrai several officers of the Irish brigade, who have quitted the service, live, I suppose, for cheapness and the convenience of being near their countrymen, who serve and are usually stationed in Flanders. They still wear the English red and blue uniform with some difference of button and cuff. These troops and the Swiss guards are, I believe, the only corps in the French service who are clothed in red: the rest are white, except the French guards which are in blue with silver trimmings.

There we took up an officer of the Irish brigade, who was going to Corsica, a well-bred, agreeable man, with whom by the time we reached Peronne, I became very well acquainted. He had been six months in England, being related to many of the Catholic nobility there as well as in Ireland. At first I took him and the officers I saw and heard speak English at Cambrai to be in the English service, for their uniform has undergone very little change since they quitted it with James the second. At present it is only the officers of these brigades that are Irish; the common men are Liegeois, Germans, of all other countries except France, but the words of command are still English, though no more intelligible to the men than the beat of drum: it is the number of syllables with metrical distinctions of long and short in the one and the strokes of the drumstick in the other, which direct their motions.

The party partook of dinner at Pont-Sainte-Maxence:

We had by this time added to our number another internal and external passenger. The dinner revived us all. The conversation became very lively and interesting. There were some religious points discussed by my fellow travellers, with more freedom than is usual in mixed companies that are wholly strangers to each other, even in England. On this occasion I was totally silent, and a mere bystander, which was not the case with the seaman, who showed himself to be a man of great reading, and a profound thinker. The new inside female passenger was an agreeable woman with certain indications of having lived in the world with good company. She was as ill all the morning as if at sea in a storm, but at dinner and afterwards bore a very intelligent part in the conversation. She was the wife of an officer in Champagne to whom she was going. Though a little *passée*, she had an extremely fine skin and great delicacy of features, not in the least overloaded in the Flemish way, her muscles being hardly enough covered.

Dr. Burney arrived in Paris on 12th June, soon after the marriage of the Dauphin and Marie Antoinette. During his visit he inspected the Place de Louis XV,

the late scene of so much blood, the account of the killed and wounded there at the playing of the fireworks for the marriage of the Dauphin increases every day: it is now said to surpass 1000.

He spent his first evening in Paris on " the Boulevard ".

The Boulevard is a place of public diversions, without the gates of Paris. It is laid out in walks, and planted. In the middle is a wide road for carriages, and at the sides are coffee-houses, conjurers, and shows of all kinds. Here every evening, during summer, the walks are crowded with well-dressed people and the road with splendid equipages; and here I saw the new Vauxhall, as they call it, but it is no more like ours,[1] than the emperor of China's palace. Nor is it at all like Ranelagh [2]; though, at the first entrance, there is a small rotunda, with galleries round it well lighted up, and decorated. Next to this is a quadrangle in the open air, where they

---

[1] The famous Vauxhall Gardens existed from 1660–1859, and were at the zenith of their popularity about the time Burney was writing.

[2] Not the Ranelagh at Barnes, but a wooden rotunda, holding 6000 people, erected in Chelsea in 1742. The adjacent tea-gardens were frequented by all the great wits of the age. It was shut up in 1804.

dance in warm weather; it is illuminated, and has galleries, which are continued to another room, which is square, and still larger than the first, with two rows of Corinthian pillars ornamented with festoons and illuminations. This is a very elegant room, in which are *minuets*, *allemandes*, *cotillons* and *contre danses*,[1] when the weather is cold, which was now the case in the extreme. However, here was a great crowd of well-dressed people. From the name of this place it was natural to look for a garden, but none was to be found.

In the coffee-houses on the Boulevard, which are much frequented, there are bands of music and singing, in the Sadler's-Wells [2] way, but worse. The women who perform there, go about with a plate to collect a reward for their trouble. Here, though they often sing airs *à l'Italienne*, original sin, in the expression, sticks as close to them as to us, at such places, in England.

Dr. Burney remained in Paris until 23rd June, and into these short ten days he succeeded in arranging meetings with most of the important musicians of the day, in addition to visits to the libraries in search of material for his history, and conversation with the librarians on such diverse subjects as Greek accents and the music of the ancients.

He was likewise assiduous in his attendance at operas, concerts, and theatres. His description of the reception of a comic opera at the Théâtre Italien is amusing:

[1] The *minuet* was a slow dance in triple time and was in common use as a contrasting middle movement in the classical sonata before Beethoven supplanted it with the *scherzo*. The *allemande* here mentioned is a German national dance in duple time and has no connexion with the suite movement, similarly styled, commonly used by Bach and Handel. This *cotillon* likewise has no relation to the modern dance of the same name. It is here used of a simple French dance much in vogue in the sixteenth and seventeenth centuries. The *contre-danse* is of English origin (" country dance ") and was imported into France at the beginning of the eighteenth century.

[2] Another famous eighteenth century house of entertainment in Pentonville which was particularly associated with music. The theatre, which formed part of the gardens, still survives in a derelict condition, and is now being restored.

this piece was as thoroughly damned as ever piece was here. I used to imagine that a French audience durst not hiss to the degree I found they did upon this occasion. Indeed quite as much, mixed with horse laughs, as ever I heard at Drury Lane, or Covent Garden. In short, it was condemned in all the English forms, except breaking the benches and the actors' heads; and the incessant sound of *hish* instead of *hiss*.

French music at the time at which Burney was writing was undoubtedly at a low ebb. The great days of Couperin and Rameau had passed and no prophets had arisen in their place. The rehabilitation of French music at the hands of Gluck, Méhul, and Cherubini was, however, not far distant. Burney, with a strong bias towards the so-called Italian style of composition introduced into England by Handel, could hardly be expected to evince sympathy with the mediocre performances of mediocre music to which he was treated in Paris. He thus sums up the whole position:

the style of composition is totally changed throughout the rest of Europe; yet the French, commonly accused of more levity and caprice than their neighbours, have stood still in music for thirty or forty years: nay, one may go still further, and assert boldly, that it has undergone few changes at the great opera since Lulli's time, that is to say, in one hundred years. In short, notwithstanding they can both talk and write so well, and so much *about it*, music in France, with respect to the two great essentials of melody and expression, may still be said to be in its infancy.

There is much else in the same strain. It is noteworthy in this connexion that of the musicians and composers whom Burney mentions only two are of any note: Couperin, the organist of St. Gervais and nephew of the great organist to Louis XIV of the same name, was one of the long line of Couperins, stretching from the middle of the sixteenth century to the beginning of the nineteenth, who served this church. Grétry (1741–1813) was at this time a young man, fresh from Italy, and even so described by Burney as "the most fashionable composer of the comic opera ".

Burney, however, found much to interest him in Paris apart from the search for material for his history. He gives us several little sketches of the Parisians of that age, of which the following is a specimen:

Thursday 14. This being *Fête Dieu*, or *Corpus Christi* Day, one of the greatest holidays in the whole year, I went to see the processions, and to hear high mass performed at Notre Dame. I had great difficulty to get thither. Coaches are not allowed to stir till all the processions, with which the whole town swarms, are over. The streets through which they are to pass in the way to the churches, are all lined with tapestry; or, for want of that, with bed-curtains and old petticoats: I find the better sort of people (*les gens comme il faut*) all go out of town on these days, to avoid the *embarras* of going to mass, or the *ennui* of staying at home. Whenever the host stops, which frequently happens, the priests sing a psalm, and all the people fall on their knees in the middle of the street, whether dirty or clean. I readily complied with this ceremony rather than give offence or become remarkable. Indeed, when I went out, I determined to do as other people did, in the streets and church, otherwise I had no business there; so that I found it incumbent on me to kneel down twenty times ere I reached Notre Dame. This I was the less hurt at, as I saw it quite general; and many much better dressed people than

myself almost prostrated themselves, while I only touched
the ground with one knee.   At length I reached the
church, where I was likewise a *conformist*; though here
I walked about frequently, as I saw others do, round the
choir and in the great aisle.

Another interesting function which he attended on the
same day was the *Concert Spirituel* in the great hall of the
Louvre. This began at five o'clock in the afternoon, the programme consisting of three motets, an oboe concerto, a violin
concerto, and a solo by a Mademoiselle Delcambre, " screamed
out . . . with all the power of lungs she could muster ". Burney
reserves his praise for the instrumental part of this formidable
programme and is unhesitating in his condemnation of the
vocal portions, which were received by the audience with
delirious rapture. Of the final chorus, he writes:

But the last chorus was a *finisher* with a vengeance!
It surpassed, in clamour, all the noises I had ever heard
in my life. I have frequently thought the choruses of
our oratorios rather too loud and violent; but, compared
with these, they are *soft music*, such as might sooth and
lull to sleep the heroine of a tragedy.

Dr. Burney describes the organs of several of the churches
which he visited. He was very enamoured of a harpsichord
shown him by M. Balbastre, one of the organists of Notre
Dame, which the owner had

had painted inside and out with as much delicacy as the
finest coach or even snuff box I ever saw in Paris. On
the outside is the birth of Venus; and on the inside of the
cover the story of Rameau's most famous opera, Castor
and Pollux; earth, hell, and Elysium are there represented: in Elysium, sitting on a bank, with a lyre in
his hand, is that celebrated composer himself; the

portrait is very like, for I saw Rameau in 1764.[1]

We learn from the manuscript journal that poor Dr. Burney was compelled to waste a considerable amount of his valuable time in Paris in trying to present four letters entrusted to him by Garrick, the recipients being continually absent from home when he called. He plaintively remarks that two of the letters were

full of commissions for him (Garrick) and Mrs. G., which hang upon my mind and plague me more than all I have to do for myself.

From the same source we glean a few interesting details regarding the journey from Paris to Lyons, which were omitted from the published version:

At 4.0 on Sunday morning the 24th June I left Paris in the diligence; unluckily once a week the vehicle of that name, which goes to Lyons has ten passengers (a late regulation—it used to have but eight) and this it was my lot to go in—such a pack of legs, &c.—so squeezed together and so swelled my legs, that it made it very fatiguing and disagreeable.

There were no female passengers on this occasion. Dr. Burney's fellow-travellers consisted of a captain with two cadets under his charge, a chevalier de St. Louis, a gentleman of Provence, a young officer, an old wine merchant, the Duke of Parma's surgeon, and a merchant of Amsterdam, who was a native of Milan.

The journey passed without incident. At Rouvray

we saw the first pretty girl we had met with since we left Paris and the whole company, as if electrified, was

[1] Jean Philippe Rameau (1683–1764) composed this opera, his masterpiece, in 1737. Dr. Burney was in Paris in 1764 with his daughters, Esther and Susan, who were to be placed at school there.

so struck with the novelty of the sight that they all at the
same instant applauded her by clapping hands violently.

At Chalons-sur-Saône the party left the diligence and
boarded a " passage boat ", where they had more room for
their feet. The remainder of the journey

we read, slept, played at cards, told stories, &c., as is so
usual in the like situation that it is hardly worth men-
tioning.

Conversation, however, was endless, so long as either the
chevalier or the gentleman of Provence was awake.

From Lyons Dr. Burney passed on to Geneva. As was his
custom, he sought out the musicians in both towns, but in
neither place did he discover much material of value for his
purpose. Of Geneva indeed he writes: " There is but little
music to be heard in this place as there is no play-house allowed;
nor are there organs in the churches, except two, which are
used for psalmody only, in the true purity of John Calvin."

While staying at Geneva Dr. Burney went to see Voltaire,
who had retired to his country house in the vicinity in 1755,
shortly after he had broken with Frederick the Great. The
veneration with which Dr. Burney regards Voltaire may strike
the reader as disproportionate in comparison with the normal
attitude of cordiality adopted towards men like Diderot and
J. J. Rousseau, both of whom Dr. Burney met in Paris on his
return journey. Voltaire's international fame among his
contemporaries certainly surpassed that of the other two
great French writers, but in addition he had spent three years
in exile in England (1726–1729), where he had met with considerable success among the literary men of the day. This
sojourn in England may well have given rise to a local tradition, which would naturally be stimulated by subsequent
literary triumphs in France and Voltaire's association with
Frederick the Great. Dr. Burney and the literary circle in
which he moved would have been heirs to this tradition and
have watched the career of the great sceptic with added
interest.

Dr. Burney in the course of his investigations had paid a visit to a certain M. Fritz, the only composer of whom Geneva could boast. He thus proceeds with his narrative:

My going to M. Fritz, broke into a plan I had formed of visiting M. de Voltaire at the same hour, with some strangers, who were then going to Ferney. But, to say the truth, besides the visit to M. Fritz being more *my business*, I did not much like going with these people, who had only a bookseller to introduce them; and I had heard that some English had lately met with a rebuff from M. de Voltaire, by going without any letter of recommendation, or anything to recommend themselves. He asked them what they wanted? Upon their replying they wished only to see so extraordinary a man, he said— " Well, gentlemen, you now see me—did you take me for a wild beast or monster, that was fit only to be stared at as a show?" This story very much frighted me; for not having any intention of going to Geneva, when I left London, or even Paris, I was quite unprovided with a recommendation: however I was determined to see his place (which I took to be—*Cette maison d'Aristippe, ces jardins d'Epicure*: to which he retired in 1755, but was mistaken). I drove to it alone, after I had left M. Fritz. His house is three or four miles from Geneva, but near the lake. I approached it with reverence, and a curiosity of the most minute kind. I enquired *when* I first trod on his domain; I had an intelligent and talkative postilion, who answered all my questions very satisfactorily. His estate is very large here, and he is building pretty farm-houses upon it. He has erected on the Geneva side a quadrangular *justice*, or gallows, to show

that he is the *seigneur*. One of his farms, or rather
manufacturing houses (for he is establishing a manufacture upon his estate) was so handsome that I thought
it was his *château*. We drove to Ferney, through a charming country, covered with corn and vines, in view of the
lake and mountains of Gex, Switzerland and Savoy. On
the left hand, approaching the house, is a neat chapel
with this inscription:

DEO

EREXIT

VOLTAIRE

M DCC LXI

When this building was constructed, M. de Voltaire
gave a curious reason for placing upon it this inscription. He said that it was high time to dedicate
one church to God, after so many had been dedicated to
Saints.

I sent to enquire whether a stranger might be allowed
to see the house and gardens, and was answered in the
affirmative. A servant soon came, and conducted me
into the cabinet or closet where his master had just been
writing, which is never shewn when he is at home; but
having walked out, I was allowed that privilege. From
thence I passed to the library, which is not a very large
one, but well filled. Here I found a whole length figure
in marble of himself, recumbent, in one of the windows;
and many curiosities in another room; a bust of himself,
made not two years since; his mother's picture; that of
his niece, Mademoiselle Denis; his brother, M. Dupuis;
the Calas family, and others. It is a very neat and elegant

house, not large, or affectedly decorated. I should have
said, that close to the chapel, between that and the house,
is the theatre, which he built some years ago; where he
treated his friends with some of his own tragedies: it is
now only used as a receptacle for wood and lumber,
there having been no play acted in it these four years.
The servant told me his master was seventy-eight [1], but
very well. "*Il travaille*," said he, "*pendant dix heures
chaque jour.*" He studies ten hours every day; writes
constantly without spectacles, and walks out with only
a domestic, often a mile or two—"*Et le voilà, là bas!*"—
and see, yonder where he is.—

He was going to his workmen. My heart leaped at the
sight of so extraordinary a man. He had just then quitted
his garden, and was crossing the court before his house.
Seeing my chaise, and me on the point of mounting it,
he made a sign to his servant, who had been my *Cicerone*,
to go to him, in order, I suppose, to enquire who I was.
After they had exchanged a few words together, he
approached the place where I stood, motionless, in order
to contemplate his person as much as I could when his
eyes were turned from me; but on seeing him move
towards me, I found myself drawn by some irresistible
power towards him; and, without knowing what I did,
I insensibly met him half way. It is not easy to conceive
it possible for life to subsist in a form so nearly composed of mere skin and bone, as that of M. de Voltaire.
He complained of decrepitude, and said he supposed
I was curious to form an idea of the figure of one walking
after death. However his eyes and whole countenance

[1] Hardly accurate, as Voltaire, having been born in 1694, was only 76 in 1770.

are still full of fire; and though so emaciated, a more lively expression cannot be imagined. He enquired after English news, and observed that poetical squabbles had given way to political ones; but seemed to think the spirit of opposition as necessary in poetry as in politics. " *Les querelles d'auteurs sont pour le bien de la littérature, comme dans un gouvernement libre, les querelles des grands, et les clameurs des petits sont nécessaires à la liberté.*" (Disputes among authors are of use to literature; as the quarrels of the great, and the clamours of the little, in a free government, are necessary to liberty.) And added, " When critics are silent, it does not so much prove the age to be correct as dull." He enquired what poets we had now; and I told him we had Mason and Gray. They write but little, said he, and you seem to have no one who lords it over the rest like Dryden, Pope and Swift. I told him that it was, perhaps, one of the inconveniencies of periodical journals, however well executed, that they often silenced modest men of genius, while impudent blockheads were impenetrable, and unable to feel the critic's scourge: that Mr. Gray and Mr. Mason had both been illiberally treated by mechanical critics, even in newspapers; and added, that modesty and love of quiet seemed in these gentlemen to have got the better even of their love of fame. During this conversation, we approached the buildings he was constructing near the road to his *château*. These, said he, pointing to them, are the most innocent, and, perhaps, the most useful of all my works. I observed that he had other works, which were of far more extensive use, and would be much more durable than those. He was so obliging as to shew me several farm-houses he had built, and the plans of others; after which I took my leave, for fear of breaking in upon his time, being unwilling to rob the public of things so precious as the few remaining moments of this great and universal genius.

Mr. Gray is of course the author of the *Elegy*, and among his most severe critics was Dr. Burney's great friend, Dr. Johnson. William Mason (1724–1797) was Gray's biographer: the " illiberal treatment " meted out is in his case fully justi-fied. Dr. Burney gave Mason a presentation copy of his book, probably in view of the allusion to him contained in this extract.

CHAPTER II

Turin and Milan

The bulk of the Journal of this present tour is devoted to Dr. Burney's musical investigations in Italy. For the cultured musician in the eighteenth century Italy, with a glorious musical inheritance and a virtual monopoly for two hundred years, set the standard in much the same way as Germany did in the nineteenth. Dr. Burney's scathing denunciations of French musicianship are the direct result of a self-satisfaction nurtured by the pure milk of the Italian tradition through Handel. Disillusionment, however, awaited the pilgrim almost from the moment when he set foot in Italy. Italian music was in truth at the beginning of that long decadence from which it has only just begun to recover—the subservience of the composer to the singer was everywhere marked. A few survivors endeavoured to maintain the high standard of instrumental music which had made Italy the pattern for the whole world, but the days of Vivaldi, Corelli, Domenico Scarlatti, and Tartini had passed, never to return.

Of the Italian section of his Journal, the author modestly writes as follows:

I cannot dissemble my fears that the reader will think it prolix; as, upon revising my journal, I am sorry to find that the further I advanced into that country, the more loose is the texture of my narrative; for in proportion as I had more to hear and to see, I had less time to spare for reflection and for writing: indeed, the mere matters of fact concerning musical exhibitions, will, I doubt, afford but small entertainment to the reader; for they are so much the same, that an account of one is, in many particulars, an account of all; so that a circumstantial narrative of things, perhaps not very interesting in themselves, might be tiresome even in spite of variety: all I have to urge in my defence, is, that the relation is faithful, and that, if the places through which I passed had afforded more entertaining incidents, they would have been given to the public.

After leaving Geneva Dr. Burney proceeded on his journey southwards and reached Turin about 10th July. Turin was at this period a city of the Kingdom of Sardinia. As was his custom, he divided his attention between the musical institutions of the city and the prominent musicians who lived in it. There was a fine university or royal library in the town,

where there are fifty thousand volumes, and many manuscripts, the catalogue of which fills two volumes in folio. The access to these books is easy, both before and after dinner, every day, holidays excepted.

Here " the distributer of the books " received Dr. Burney with every politeness and showed him some of the oldest manuscripts in the library.

Dr. Burney was introduced to Padre Beccaria [1], the scientist, who

through choice, lives up six pair of stairs, among his observatories, machines, and mathematical instruments; and there does everything for himself, even to making his bed, and dressing his dinner. . . .

He is not above forty; with a large and noble figure, he has something open, natural, intelligent, and benevo-

[1] Giovanni Battista Beccaria (1716–1781) was a physicist and early pioneer in electrical research. He was appointed professor of experimental physics in Turin in 1748. He was elected a Fellow of the Royal Society of London in 1755.

lent in his countenance, that immediately captivates. We had much conversation concerning electricity, Dr. Franklin [1], Dr. Priestley [2], and others. He was pleased to make me a present, finding me an *amateur* (which should be always translated a *dabbler*), of his last book, and the syllabus of the *Memoire* he lately sent to our Royal Society. . . . Mr. Martin, the banker here, came after me to Signor Beccaria's; and this great mathematician is so little acquainted with worldly concerns, especially money matters, that he was quite astonished and pleased at the ingenuity and novelty of a letter of credit. Mr. Martin desiring to look at mine, in his presence, in order to know how he might send my letters after me, the good father could hardly comprehend how this letter could be *argent comptant*, ready money, throughout Italy.

Dr. Burney visited the great opera house,

which is reckoned one of the finest in Europe. It is very large and elegant; the machinery and decorations are magnificent. I was carried into every part of it, even to the tailor's workshop. Here are six rows of boxes above the pit, both larger and deeper than those of the other theatre: the king is at the chief expense of this opera. Those who have boxes for the season, pay, in a kind of fees only, two or three guineas; money at the door being only taken for sitting in the pit.

There were performances here of serious opera every day

[1] Benjamin Franklin (1706–1790), the American statesman and scientist.
[2] Joseph Priestley (1733–1804), chemist and Nonconformist minister, became a Fellow of the Royal Society in 1766. Both Franklin and Priestley did important experimental work in the early days of electrical science.

except Friday from 6th January, the King's name-day, until Lent, but from October until Christmas, and during the summer, comic operas and plays were performed at another theatre every night except Friday.

I went thither the evening after my arrival; there was not much company; the boxes, or *palchetti*, are all engaged by the year, so that strangers have no place but in the pit; which, however, is far more comfortable than the *parterre*, or pit, at Paris, where the company stand the whole time; and even than that at London, where they are much crowded; but there are backs to the benches in this theatre, which are of double use, as they keep off the crowd behind, and support those who fill them. This theatre is not so large as that at Lyons, but pretty, and capable of holding much company: it is *dislungato*, or of an oblong form, with the corners rounded off. There are no galleries in it, but then there are five rows of boxes, one above another, twenty-four in each row: and each box will contain six persons, amounting in all to seven hundred and twenty; there is one stage box only on each side. The farce was truly what it promised, except the laughing part, as it did not produce that effect.

The performance, moreover, was indifferent and the singing poor, though Dr. Burney maliciously adds that " it would have been very good in France ". However,

the Italians themselves hold these performances in no very high estimation: they talk the whole time, and seldom attend to anything but one or two favourite airs, during the whole piece: the only two that were applauded were encored; and I observed that the performer does not take it as such a great favour to be applauded here as in England; where, whenever a hand is moved, all illusion is destroyed by a bow or a curtsy from the performer, who is a king, a queen, or some great personage, usually going off the stage in distress, or during the emotions of some strong passion. If Mr. Garrick, in some of his principal characters, was to submit to such a humiliating practice, it would surely be at the expense of the audience; who would every instant be told, that it was not Lear, Richard, or Macbeth they saw before them, but Mr. Garrick.

Dr. Burney adds:

I shall have frequent occasion to mention the noise and inattention at the musical exhibitions in Italy; but music there is cheap and common, whereas in England it is a costly exotic, and more highly prized.

Dr. Burney twice visited the King's chapel during the service, where

there is commonly a symphony played every morning, between eleven and twelve o'clock, by the King's band, which is divided into three orchestras, and placed in three different galleries; and though far separated from each other, the performers know their business so well that there is no want of a person to beat time, as in the opera and *concert spirituel* at Paris. The King [1], the royal family, and the whole city seem very constant in their attendance at mass; and all their devotion is silently performed at the *Messa Bassa*, during the symphony. [2] . . .

[1] Charles Emmanuel III, who reigned from 1730 to 1773.
[2] The morning service of the church here is called *Messa Bassa*, when the priest performs it in a voice so little louder than a whisper that it cannot be heard through the instruments (Dr. Burney's note).

The organ is in the gallery which faces the King, and in this stands the principal first violin.

In the service of the King of Sardinia were three instrumental soloists, who performed in the chapel on festivals:

Their salary is not much above eighty guineas a year each, for attending the chapel royal; but then the service is made very easy to them, as they only perform solos there, and those just when they please.

The violinist of this trio was Gaetano Pugnani (1727–1803), who played a concerto during one of Dr. Burney's visits to the chapel. He was a performer of international reputation and one of the last of the long line of great Italian players. His name has once again come into prominence by reason of the popularity among violinists of a fine transcription by Kreisler of one of his compositions. Dr. Burney's comment on his performance is as follows:

I need say nothing of the performance of Signor Pugnani, his talents being too well known in England to require it.[1] I shall only observe, that he did not appear to exert himself; and it is not to be wondered at, as neither his Sardinian majesty, nor any one of the numerous royal family, seem to pay much attention to music. There is a gloomy sameness at this court, in the daily repetition of state parade and prayer.

Dr. Burney was always particularly interested in the music of the people, and listened with sympathy to the itinerant players who swarmed over Italy in those days. The standard maintained by them was on the whole a high one, and the fact that they were usually able to sing in parts spoke well for the musical talent of the nation:

[1] Pugnani had been in London fifteen years or so previously; he had led the orchestra at the opera house and was therefore a well-known figure in the town.

The itinerant musicians, Anglicé, ballad singers, and fiddlers, at Turin perform in concert. A band of this kind came to the *Hôtel, la bonne femme*, consisting of two voices, two violins, a guitar, and bass, bad enough indeed, though far above our scrapers. The singers, who were girls, sung duets very well in tune, accompanied by the whole band. The same people at night performed on a stage in the *grande place* or square, where they sold their ballads as our quack doctors do their nostrums, but with far less injury to society. In another part of the square, on a different stage, a man and a woman sung Venetian ballads, in two parts, very agreeably, accompanied by a dulcimer [1].

Proceeding by way of Vercelli, Dr. Burney arrived in Milan about 16th July, and remained there eight or nine days. His chronology is almost invariably inaccurate or doubtful, and complete certainty regarding the length of time spent on the various stages of his journey is therefore impossible.

In Milan there was much to interest Dr. Burney, but most of his time was spent in the Ambrosian library in fruitless investigations into the origins of the Ambrosian Chant. He found occasion, however, for visits to the Duomo and to the opera, and attended several concerts. Needless to say, Dr. Burney came into contact with all the musicians in the city, where, according to his own statement, the composers were innumerable. He also made arrangements, as was his custom wherever he went, for a regular correspondent, who should keep him advised of the progress of music when he was in England. Of the composers whose names he recites, Giovanni Battista Sammartini is alone remembered to-day, and he was of particular interest to Dr. Burney in virtue of his relationship to the celebrated oboe player in Handel's orchestra, who had settled in England about 1729.

Although Dr. Burney's time was so largely occupied with

---

[1] A prototype of the modern pianoforte, still in use among the Hungarian peasants. The sound was produced by the player striking the strings with a small hammer.

matters musical, he lost no opportunity of conferring with the prominent men of science who were working in the cities through which he passed. While in Milan he made the acquaintance of the Jesuit father Boscovich, the famous mathematician and astronomer.[1]

A gentleman of Parma, with whom I had travelled from Paris, having a letter from M. Messier [2] to Padre Boscovich, giving him an account of a new comet which he had discovered on the eleventh of June, I had the pleasure of accompanying my friend in his visit to this father at the Jesuits College, who received us both with great courtesy; and being told that I was an Englishman, a lover of the sciences, and ambitious of seeing so celebrated a man, he addressed himself to me in a particular manner. He had several young students of quality with him, and said he expected that morning three persons of distinction to see his instruments, and invited me to be of the party; I gladly accepted the proposal, and he immediately began to shew and explain to me several machines and contrivances which he had invented for making optical experiments, before the arrival of the *Signori*, who were a Knight of Malta, a nephew of Pope Benedict XIV [3] and another *Cavaliere*. He then went on, and surprised and delighted us all

[1] Roger Joseph Boscovich (1711–1787) was born at Ragusa. After entering the Society of Jesus, he became an instructor in philosophy and mathematics at the Collegium Romanum in Rome. He was in London in 1760 and became professor at Pavia four years later. After the dissolution of the Society of Jesus in 1773, Boscovich went to Paris and became director of optics in the French navy. Later he returned to Milan and eventually lost his reason. His chief contribution to astronomical science was the discovery by means of sun-spots of the length of time in which the sun rotates. Dr. Burney's interest in astronomy was by no means a superficial one: in the year prior to his journey he had published a small popular book on comets, entitled *An Essay towards the History of Comets*.

[2] Charles Messier (1730–1817), an astronomer, who lived in Paris and was famous for his work on nebulæ.

[3] 1675–1758: he was elected pope in 1740.

very much, particularly with his *Stet Sol*, by which he can fix the sun's rays, passing through an aperture or a prism, to any part of the opposite wall he pleases: he likewise separates and fixes any of the prismatic colours of the rays. Shewed us a method of forming an aquatic prism, and the effects of joining different lenses, all extremely plain and ingenious. He has published a Latin dissertation on these matters at Vienna. Then we ascended to different observatories, where I found his instruments mounted in so ingenious and so convenient a manner, as to give me the utmost pleasure. He was so polite as to address himself to me always in French, as I had at first accosted him in that language, and in which I was at this time much more at my ease than in Italian. M. Messier had told him the comet had very little motion, being almost stationary; but Padre Boscovich afterwards found it so rapid as to move fifty degrees in a day. *Mais la comète, monsieur, lui dis-je, où est-elle à présent? Avec le soleil, elle est mariée.* The late Duke of York [1] made him a present of one of Short's twelve-inch reflectors, of twenty guineas price; but he has an achromatic one, by the same maker, which cost one hundred. The expense of his observatory, which is defrayed by himself, must have been enormous. He is university professor at Pavia, where he spends his winters. If any new discoveries are to be made in astronomy, they may be expected from this learned Jesuit; whose attention to optical experiments for the improvement of glasses, upon which so much depends; and whose great number of admirable

---

[1] Edward, Duke of York, second son of Frederick, Prince of Wales, and brother of George III. He died in 1767.

instruments of all sorts, joined to the excellence of the climate, and the wonderful sagacity he has discovered in the construction of his observatory and machines, form a concurrence of favourable circumstances, not easily to be found elsewhere. He complained very much of the silence of the English astronomers, who answer none of his letters. He was seven months in England, and during that time was very much with Mr. Maskelyne [1], Dr. Shepherd [2], Dr. Bevis [3], and Dr. Maty [4], with whom he hoped to keep up a correspondence. He had, indeed, lately received from Mr. Professor Maskelyne the last *Nautical Almanac*, with Mayer's Lunar Tables [5], who gave him hopes of reviving their literary intercourse. He is a tall, strong-built man, upwards of fifty, of a very agreeable address. He was refused admission into the French academy, when at Paris, though a member, by the parliament, on account of his being a Jesuit [6]: but if all Jesuits were like this father, making use only of superior learning and intellects for the advancement of science, and the happiness of mankind, one would have wished this society to be as durable as the world. As it is, it seems as if equity required that some discrimination should be made in condemning the

[1] Nevil Maskelyne (1732–1811) was at this time the Astronomer Royal. He was one of the fathers of modern astronomy and compiled a standard catalogue of the stars. The *Nautical Almanac* was started under his supervision in 1767.

[2] Dr. Antony Shepherd (1721–1796) was Plumian Professor of Astronomy at Cambridge University.

[3] Dr. John Bevis (1693–1771) was an astronomer and had travelled in France and Italy.

[4] Dr. Maty (1745–1787) was the principal secretary of the Royal Society and principal librarian of the British Museum. He was a friend of Dr. Burney, and after his death Dr. Burney undertook the education of his son.

[5] Tobias Mayer (1723–1762) was a professor at Göttingen University. His Lunar Tables first appeared in 1755.

[6] The Jesuits were expelled from France in 1762.

Jesuits; for though good policy may require a dissolution of their order, yet humanity certainly makes one wish to preserve the old, the infirm, and the innocent, from the general wreck and destruction due only to the guilty.

Dr. Burney gives several interesting details regarding operatic enterprise in Milan. It was symptomatic of the condition of musical Italy at this time that the season of serious opera in a town of Milan's importance was confined to the carnival time. The remainder of the year was occupied with light opera and burlesques of the most ephemeral nature, some of which are described by Dr. Burney.

The opera was carried on by thirty noblemen, who subscribed sixty zechins each (equivalent at that time to £27), and for this sum each subscriber was provided with a box. The remainder of the boxes were hired out for the year at fifty zechins (about £22, 10s.) for the first row, forty (£18) for the second, and thirty (£13, 10s.) for the third, and so on. The only seats which could be booked at the door were those in the pit and gallery. Performances took place every night except Friday.

The theatre [1] here is very large and splendid; it has five rows of boxes on each side, one hundred in each row; and parallel to these runs a broad gallery, round the house, as an avenue to every row of boxes: each box will contain six persons, who sit at the sides, facing each other. Across the gallery of communication is a complete room to every box, with a fireplace in it, and all conveniences for refreshments and cards. In the fourth row is a *faro* table, on each side the house, which is used during the performance of the opera. There is in front a very large box, as big as a common London dining-

---

[1] This was not the magnificent La Scala Theatre, but its predecessor, which was burnt down in 1776. The new theatre, built on the site of the church of S. Maria della Scala, was opened two years later.

room, set apart for the Duke of Modena, governor of Milan, and the *Principessina* his daughter, who were both there.[1]   The noise here during the performance was abominable, except while two or three airs and a duet were singing, with which every one was in raptures: at the end of the duet, the applause continued with un-remitting violence till the performers returned to sing it again, which is here the way of encoring a favourite air. . . . In the highest story the people sit in front; and those for whom there are no seats, stand behind in the gallery: all the boxes here are appropriated for the season, as at Turin. Between the acts the company from the pit come upstairs, and walk about the galleries.

Dr. Burney found time for a visit to the Palazzo Simonetto, a mile or two outside Milan, where there was a famous echo:

The *Simonetto* palace is near no other building; the country all around is a dead flat, and no mountains are nearer than those of Switzerland, which are upwards of thirty miles off. This palace is now uninhabited and in ruin, but has been pretty; the front is open, and sup-ported by very light double Ionic pillars, but the echo is only to be heard behind the house, which, next to the garden, has two wings. . . .

Now, though it is natural to suppose that the opposite walls reflect the sound, it is not easy to say in what manner; as the form of the building is a very common one, and no other of the same construction, that I have ever heard of, produces the same effects. I made experiments of all

---

[1] The reigning duke at this time was Francis III (1698–1780), but it seems more probably that Dr. Burney saw his successor, who became Hercules III, with his daughter, Maria Beatrice, who married Archduke Ferdinand, the son of Maria Theresa, on 15th October, 1771 (see Appendix, footnote 1).

kinds, and in every situation, with the voice, slow, quick; with a trumpet, which a servant, who was with me sounded; with a pistol, and a musket, and always found agreeable to the doctrine of echoes, that the more quick and violent the percussion of the air, the more numerous were the repetitions; which, upon firing the musket, amounted to upwards of fifty, of which the strength seemed regularly to diminish, and the distance to become more remote. . . . One blow of a hammer produced a very good imitation of an ingenious and practised footman's knock at a London door, on a visiting night. A single *ha!* became a long horse-laugh; and a forced note, or a sound overblown in the trumpet, became the most ridiculous and laughable noise imaginable.

CHAPTER III

Padua—Venice—Bologna

Dr. Burney passed on his way through Bergamo to Brescia, which, he informs us in the manuscript journal,

was almost wholly destroyed last September by a thunder-storm: had I known this last night I should not perhaps, dare-devil as I am, have slept so sound. The town walls, gates, palaces, houses, &c., now lie in rubbish without end, though many are patched up.

He was in Brescia one day, which was devoted to the usual routine of investigation and sight-seeing. On 28th July, two days later, he reached Verona and witnessed the *commedia dell' arte* " in true Italian purity ", performed in the famous Roman amphitheatre, which had been recently repaired. " The inhabitants say that it will contain sixty thousand persons, which is more than twice the number at present in Verona."

At Vicenza Dr. Burney fell in with

a great number of pilgrims, young men, who were going to Assisi to visit the tomb of St. Francis [1]; they used to

[1] Dr. Burney refers to this incident again in the Journal of the German Tour (*vide* Part II, Chapter V); " like the pilgrims that I heard in Italy, who were going to Assisi ". It is not clear, however, why the substitution of Assisi for Loretto should satisfy the requirements of the senate, as Assisi was not within the territory of the republic, and therefore presumably just as objectionable from the official point of view as Loretto. The first edition has " Venice " instead of " Assisi "; this mistake was corrected in the second edition.

go to Loretto once a year, but the senate has forbidden them to go out of the Venetian territories.

Here, during dinner, he was entertained with

a kind of vocal music which I had not before heard in Italy: it consisted of a psalm, in three parts, performed by boys of different ages, who were proceeding from their school to the cathedral, in procession, with their master, a priest, at their head, who sung the bass. There was more melody than usual in this kind of music; and though they marched through the street very fast, yet they sung very well in time and tune. These boys are a kind of religious *press-gang*, who seize all other boys they can find in their way to the church, in order to be catechized.

Dr. Burney went on to Padua and remained there some time. The death of the great violinist and composer, Tartini, a few months prior to his arrival in the town, was an immense disappointment to him. However, he consoled himself by visits to the house where Tartini had lived, and closely investigated " everything, however minute and trivial, which could afford . . . the least intelligence concerning his life and character, with the zeal of a pilgrim at Mecca ". In relating the facts of Tartini's life, he quotes verbatim from de Lalande's *Voyage d'un Français* the account which the author of this work received from the lips of Tartini himself regarding the origin of the " Trillo del diavolo " violin sonata. This story is now a commonplace of musical history, and its original version is therefore of interest:

" He (Tartini) dreamed one night, in 1713, that he had made a compact with the Devil, who promised to be at his service on all occasions; and during this vision everything succeeded according to his mind; his wishes were prevented, and his desires always surpassed by the assistance of his new servant. In short, he imagined he gave the Devil his violin, in order to discover what kind of a musician he was; when, to his great astonishment, he heard him play a solo so singularly beautiful, and executed with such superior taste and precision, that it surpassed all he had ever heard or conceived in his life. So great was his surprise, and so exquisite his delight upon this occasion, that it deprived him of the power of breathing. He awoke with the violence of this sensation, and instantly seized his fiddle, in hopes of expressing what he had just heard, but in vain; he, however, then composed a piece, which is, perhaps, the best of all his works, (he called it the Devil's Sonata) but it was so inferior to what his sleep had produced, that he declared he should have broken his instrument, and abandoned music for ever, if he could have subsisted by any other means."

Foremost among the friends and pupils of Tartini, whom Dr. Burney met in Padua, is Nardini, whose name is still honoured by the violinists of to-day for his compositions in the style of his great master. Nardini played Dr. Burney a number of Tartini's best compositions, and the excellence of his performance is the subject of particular comment.

Dr. Burney's next halt was at Venice, where he arrived on 3rd August. Venice was a city after his own heart, and he finds much to praise there and little to blame. Musically the Republic stands out pre-eminent in the Journal, and is only equalled by Rome and Naples.

Dr. Burney devoted much of his time to the four music conservatorios [1] for girls for which the city was famous.

---

[1] Ospidale della Pietà, Mendicanti, Incurabile, and the Ospidaletto a S. Giovanni e Paolo. Only the Pietà survived the débâcle of 1797, when the Republic came to an end.

Each was a species of " Foundling Hospital for natural children, under the protection of several nobles, citizens, and
merchants, who, though the revenue is very great, yet contribute annually to its support. These girls are maintained here
till they are married, and all those who have talents for music
are taught by the best masters of Italy." The conservatorios
had for many years past been directed by musicians of international repute, who had succeeded in maintaining a very
high standard of proficiency. At the time of Dr. Burney's
visit, Galuppi (1706–1785) reigned supreme in Venice. He
was director of music at St. Mark's and head of the Incurabili,
and famous throughout Europe as a composer of operas.

There are many instances of love of music among the
Venetians, and the excellence of their singing and playing:

The first music I heard here was in the street, immediately on my arrival, performed by an itinerant band
of two fiddlers, a violoncello, and a voice, who, though
as unnoticed here as a small-coalman or oyster-woman
in England, performed so well, that in any other country
of Europe they would not only have excited attention,
but have acquired applause, which they justly merited
. . . but I shall not mention all the performances of this
kind which I met with here; as they happened so frequently, the repetition would be tiresome.

And again:

The people here, at this season, seem to begin to live
only at midnight. *Then* the canals are crowded with
gondolas, and St. Mark's Square with company; the banks
too of the canals are all peopled, and harmony prevails in
every part. If two of the common people walk together
arm in arm, they seem to converse in song; if there is
company on the water, in a gondola, it is the same; a
mere melody, unaccompanied with a second part, is not

to be heard in this city: all the ballads in the streets are sung in duo. Luckily for me, this night, a barge, in which there was an excellent band of music, consisting of violins, flutes, horns, basses, and a kettle-drum, with a pretty good tenor voice, was on the great canal, and stopped very near the house where I lodged; it was a piece of gallantry, at the expense of an *inamorato* in order to serenade his mistress. Shakespeare says of nocturnal music,

> " Methinks it sounds much sweeter than by day,
>   Silence bestows the virtue on it—I think
>   The nightingale, if she should sing by day,
>   When every goose is cackling, would be thought
>   No better a musician than the wren." [1]

Whether the time, place and manner of performing this music, gave it adventitious and collateral charms, I will not pretend to say; all I know is, that the symphonies *seemed* to me to be admirable, full of fancy, full of fire; the passages well contrasted; sometimes the graceful, sometimes the pathetic prevailed; and sometimes, however strange it may be thought, even noise and fury had their effect.

Dr. Burney was evidently of a somewhat sentimental turn of mind, and such rhapsodizing is frequent in his book. He was affected to tears by the service at S. Giovanni e Paolo, when the Doge attended in state, and his feelings undoubtedly ran away with his judgment on many occasions.

Among the many musical amateurs with whom Dr. Burney came into contact in Venice was a member of the Thurn and Taxis family, who was superintendent-general of the German and Venetian post office and had been a great friend of Tartini.

[1] *The Merchant of Venice*, Act V, line 100 *seq.*

He possessed " a very curious keyed instrument which was made at Berlin, under the direction of his Prussian Majesty ", and which, in respect of its potential metamorphosis into allied keyboard instruments, bears some resemblance to the Emmanuel Moor pianoforte. In passing it is interesting to note that it was at the court of this same Prussian Majesty that Bach had years before been introduced to the new Silbermann pianofortes; we have here, therefore, additional testimony to the interest of Frederick the Great in experiments of this nature. Dr. Burney describes the instrument in the following terms:

It is, in shape, like a large clavichord [1], has several changes of stops, and is occasionally a harp, a harpsichord, a lute, or pianoforte; but the most curious property of this instrument is, that by drawing out the keys the hammers are transferred to different strings, by which means a composition may be transposed half a note, a whole note, or a flat third lower at pleasure, without the embarrassment of different notes or clefs, real or imaginary.

Dr. Burney was particularly impressed by the activity of the Venetian printers and by the number of booksellers in " the fine street called *Merceria* ". In this connexion he makes some illuminating remarks regarding the printing of music in the eighteenth century and the power of the vested interest of the copyists:

The art of engraving music there (in Venice) seems to be utterly lost, as I was not able to find a single work printed in the manner we print music in England. In the first place there is no such thing as a music *shop* throughout Italy, that I was able to discover. Indeed

[1] One of the immediate forerunners of the pianoforte, the other being the harpsichord or spinet. The clavichord was a soft-toned, sensitive instrument, greatly affected by J. S. Bach. The harpsichord was loud-toned but incapable of any sustained expression. The mechanical differences between the two were considerable.

M. di Castro, a spirited bookseller . . . has published a proposal for printing music with types, in the manner attempted by Mr. Fought, but has met with small encouragement, having only published one book of little duets and trios. Musical compositions are so short-lived in Italy, such is the rage for novelty, that for the few copies wanted, it is not worth while to be at the expense of engraving, and of the rolling-press. Indeed there, as in Turkey, the business of a transcriber furnishes employment for so many people, that it is cruel to wish to rob them of it, especially as that trade seems more brisk and profitable than any other.

Dr. Burney attributes the flourishing artistic life in the Republic to the fact that the normal activities of mankind, walking, riding, and the like, are denied the Venetians. The Gondoliers had a free *entrée* to all the theatres and performed the service of the modern " deadhead ":

When a box belonging to a noble family is disengaged, and likely to remain empty, the opera manager permits the Gondolieri to occupy it, rather than a report should prevail that the performance drew but little company.

The wholesome influences of the numerous theatres and of the four conservatorios resulted in a far more widespread cultural development in every division of society in Venice than was the case in the other Italian cities which Dr. Burney visited.

Dr. Burney's next halt was at Bologna, whither he went with the express purpose of visiting Farinelli, one of the most romantic figures in the musical and political history of the eighteenth century, and Padre Martini, who was engaged on a similar task to that which occupied Dr. Burney himself, the production of a history of music from the earliest times.

Padre Martini (1706–1784) was a Franciscan monk, and is

more famed for his musical erudition than for his talent for composition. He was at this time " far advanced in years, and . . . of an infirm constitution, having a very bad cough, swelled legs, and a sickly countenance ". In him Dr. Burney, of course, found a kindred spirit, though they evidently differed fundamentally in their methods. Dr. Burney's envy was in particular roused by Padre Martini's library of 17,000 volumes, which was housed in four rooms, and he comments on the great price which had been paid for some of the scarcest books and MSS., one of which, a Spanish book printed in Naples in 1613, had actually cost a hundred ducats, about twenty guineas!

Farinelli (1705–1782) was the greatest singer of the century, and the memory of the three years during which he had been in England (1734–1736) was still cherished, when he was visited by Dr. Burney, who told him " that in England there were still many who remembered his performance so well, that they could bear to hear no other singer; that the whole kingdom continued to resound his fame ". Farinelli was at this time living in a country house about a mile outside Bologna. He had left off singing, but still played on the harpsichord and the viol d'amore. He had a large collection of keyboard instruments, which he called after the names of great Italian painters, the favourite being a pianoforte, made in Florence in 1730, and inscribed in gold letters with the name *Rafael d'Urbino*; others were christened Correggio, Titian, Guido, &c. He also possessed a harpsichord, made under his own direction in Spain, with movable keys, similar to the one which had been shown to Dr. Burney by Count Thurn and Taxis in Venice, on which mechanical transposition was possible. It was made chiefly of cedar wood, the " white notes " being black and the black notes covered with mother-of-pearl.

Dr. Burney's visit to Bologna happened to coincide with that of Leopold Mozart and his young son Wolfgang, at this time a boy of fourteen and at the height of his fame. Mozart's astonishing talents were well known to Dr. Burney, as the boy had been in London in 1764. Dr. Burney met the Mozarts at the annual festival of the Bologna Philharmonic Society in the church of S. Giovanni in Monte, where he " had the advantage of sitting to hear the music ", with Raphael's St. Cecilia on one side of him and· Domenichino's Madonna of the Rosary on the other. Dr. Burney's account of his meeting with one of the greatest geniuses of the world is quite consistent with contemporary opinion of Mozart. His " premature and almost supernatural talents . . . when he had scarce quitted his infant state ", were admired, but the enduring qualities of his great creative ability were hardly recognized at all. Dr. Burney dismisses the interview in thirteen lines—a meagre allotment compared with the thirty-eight pages which he devotes to the life-history and opinions of a nonentity like Quantz, flute instructor to Frederick the Great. Some further particulars regarding the Mozart family, obtained by Dr. Burney from a correspondent, will be found in the Appendix to this volume.[1]

Despite the presence of so much talent in Bologna, Dr. Burney has little good to say of the musical activities of the city. He missed the " Brav' Orbi ", or blind fiddlers of the city:

All the masters admire them, in their way, very much, particularly Jomelli [2], who always sends for them, when in the same town, to play to him. They travel about in summer to Rome, Naples, and elsewhere: one plays on the violin, the other on the violoncello, and is called *Spacca Nota*, or Split Note.

There was no opera in Bologna at the time of Dr. Burney's visit, but he was present at the performance of an Italian tragedy called *Tomire*, " but soon grew tired of the ·long speeches and declamation ":

[1] The account in the manuscript journal is worth recording:

" Among the rest, whom should I spy there but the celebrated little German, Mozart, who 3 or 4 years ago surprised everybody in London so much by his premature musical talents. I had a great deal of talk with his father. I find they are at prince Pallavicini's. The little man is grown a good deal but still a little man—he is engaged to compose an opera for Milan—his father has been ill here these 5 or 6 weeks."

[2] Jomelli (1717–1774), one of the most important Italian composers of that day, whom Dr. Burney subsequently met in Naples.

Thomyris, Queen of the Amazons, came on dressed in a very equivocal manner; for, in order to give her a martial look, she had her petticoats trussed up in front above her knees, which were very discernible through her black breeches. However strange this appeared to me, the audience clapped violently, as they did constantly at the worst and most absurd things in the piece. There was a great deal of religion in it, and such anachronisms that they talked of Jesus Christ and the Trinity, nor were Freewill and Predestination forgotten; and when Cyrus is dying of the wound he received in battle, he is examined by a Jewish priest (a principal character in the play) as his confessor, concerning his religious principles, and he makes to him a *profession of faith.*

Dr. Burney had again occasion to comment on the behaviour of the audience:

The inattention, noise, and indecorum of the audience too, are quite barbarous and intolerable. The silence which reigns in the theatres of London and Paris, during representation, is encouraging to the actor, as well as desirable to the hearer of judgment and feeling. In Italy the theatres are immense, and, in order to be heard through space and noise, the actors seem in a perpetual bawl. Each sentence, thus pronounced, is more like the harangue of a general at the head of an army of a hundred thousand men, than the speech of a hero or heroine in conversation; this allows of but few modulations of voice; all the passions are alike noisy, the tender and the turbulent.

Although Dr. Burney encountered disillusionment on every side, it was only with reluctance that he abandoned the traditional faith in Italy as the home of the arts, and he attempts to excuse the mediocrity of the performance described above by the obsession of the Italians for operas, which was incompatible with true tragedy and comedy. He still cherished a belief that " when they apply all their powers to the sock and buskin, and the writer and actor are obliged to make use of every resource with which the national language and genius abound; they will probably surpass the rest of Europe in the dramatic, as well as in the other arts ".

Dr. Burney was the bearer of an introduction, given him by Padre Beccaria of Turin, to the Dottoressa Madame Laura Bassi [1], who was working in the University of Bologna; he describes her as a woman of between fifty and sixty, and " though learned, and a genius, not at all masculine or assuming ". After a discussion on general matters, the talk soon veered round to electricity, the all-absorbing scientific topic of the day, and one in which Dr. Burney throughout manifests particular interest, with the following qualification: " Electricity is universally allowed to be a very entertaining and surprising phenomenon, but it has frequently been lamented that it has never yet, with much certainty, been applied to any very useful purpose."

She showed me her electrical machine and apparatus: the machine is simple, portable and convenient; it consists of a plain plate of glass, placed vertically; the two cushions are covered with red leather; the receiver is a tin forked tube; the two forks, with pins at the ends, are placed next the glass plate. She is very dexterous and ingenious in her experiments, of which she was so obliging as to shew me several. She told me that Signor Bassi, her husband, immediately after Dr. Franklin had proved the identity of electrical fire and lightning [2], and published

---

[1] Laura Bassi (1711–1778), surnamed Veratti, professor of philosophy. It is recorded that she had twelve children and that she did her own housekeeping, in spite of her great learning. Veratti, her husband, was a physician.

[2] Benjamin Franklin (1706–1790) invented a lightning-conductor known as " Franklin's rod " in 1753, for which he received the Copley Medal of the Royal Society.

his method of preserving buildings from the effects of it, by iron rods, had caused conductors to be erected at the Institute; but that the people of Bologna were so afraid of the rods, believing they would bring the lightning upon them, instead of the contrary, that he was forced to take them down. Benedict XIV[1], one of the most enlightened and enlarged of the popes, a native, and in a particular manner the patron, as well as sovereign of Bologna, wrote a letter to recommend the use of these conductors; but it was so much against the inclination of the inhabitants of this city, that Signor Bassi desisted entirely, and they have never since that time been used here.

Dr. Burney visited the Institute, where there was a room allocated for electricity, though the machines were old-fashioned and inferior. The university was apparently in low water; the salaries were small, and the money allocated to its support was all appropriated.

Dr. Burney left Bologna for Florence on the 31st of August. He paid a farewell visit to Farinelli, who played to him so long and so exquisitely on " Raphael " that he was in danger of being shut out of the city of Bologna, the gates being locked at dark. He also bade adieu to Padre Martini, who gave him many letters of recommendation and copies of certain two-part canons for which he had manifested a liking.

[1] 1675–1758: elected pope in 1740.

CHAPTER IV

Florence—Rome (first visit)

Dr. Burney arrived in Florence during the first days of September and appears to have spent just under a fortnight there. His time was mainly occupied in visiting the churches and Florentine musical notables, of whom he speaks in high terms. He heard Nardini, the violinist and pupil of Tartini, and his little pupil, Thomas Linley, then a boy of fourteen, with whom Mozart had struck up a close friendship. This was at the house of an English gentleman, who played the flute, "improving the tone very much, by inserting a piece of sponge into the mouth-piece, through which the wind passes ". He attended the *salon* of Signora Morelli, who had a "wonderful talent of speaking verses *extempore* upon any given subject " — an almost unknown accomplishment in these days, but a common enough *tour de force*, like the kindred faculty of musical extemporization, in the eighteenth century. Another musical Englishman, resident in Florence, gave Dr. Burney an essay, which he had written, " on the capacity and extent of the violoncello, in imitating the violin, flute, French horn, trumpet, oboe, and bassoon "—an amazingly unprofitable line of research, but very characteristic of the eighteenth century! He attended the last performance of the season at the opera and comments on the good humour of the audience:

the crowd and applause were prodigious; printed sonnets, in praise of singers and dancers, were thrown from the slips, and seen flying about the house in great numbers, for which the audience scrambled with much eagerness, and at the close of all, it was rather acclamation than applause.

Dr. Burney was much interested in the *Laudisti*, or Psalm Singers. The company of *Laudisti* had been founded in Florence at the beginning of the fourteenth century and gradually spread throughout Italy. For the use of the *Laudisti* poetry and music were furnished by the most celebrated writers and composers of the age, which were later collected into volumes of Sacred Songs and published. Of the company of *Laudisti*, Dr. Burney writes:

It is now called *La Compagnia*, and the morning after my arrival in Florence, between six and seven o'clock, they passed by the inn where I lodged, in grand procession, dressed in a whitish uniform, with burning tapers in their hands. They stopped at the *duomo*, or great church, just by, to sing a cheerful hymn, in three parts, which they executed very well. In this manner, on Sundays and holidays, the tradespeople and artisans form themselves into distinct companies, and sing through the streets, in their way to church. Those of the parish of S. Benedetto, we are informed by Crescimbeni, were famous all over Italy; and at the great Jubilee, in the beginning of this century, marched through the streets of Rome, singing in such a manner as pleased and astonished everybody.

On another occasion,

just as it was growing dark, I met in the streets a company of *Laudisti*: they had been at Fiesole, and were proceeding in procession to their own little church. I had the curiosity to follow them, and procured a book of the words they were singing. They stopped at every church in their way, to sing a stanza in three parts; and when they arrived at their own church, into which I gained admission, there was a band of instruments to receive them, who, between each stanza that they sung, played a symphony.

Dr. Burney's most interesting experience, while he was staying at Florence, was his visit to Figline, which is worth quoting *in extenso*:

M. de Maupertuis [1], in his voyage to the polar circle, was told by the Laplanders of a monument which they regarded as the most wonderful thing in their country: upon the merits of this report only, he says, he was almost ashamed to confess that he undertook a very fatiguing and dangerous journey to see it. Something of the same kind happened to me: in going to the opera, a second time, I was surprised to find the theatre almost empty; and, upon enquiry into the reason of it, I was told that the chief musicians, and the best company of Italy, were assembled at Figline, a town in the Upper Val d'Arno, about thirty miles from Florence, to celebrate a kind of jubilee, in honour of Santa Massimina, the protectress of that place; and I am almost ashamed to confess, that, without enquiring of persons well informed, I took upon trust this report, and travelled all night, in order to be present at these games the next day.

I arrived at the place of action about seven o'clock in the morning, and found the road and town very full of country people, as at a wake in England, but saw very

---

[1] De Maupertuis (1698–1759), a famous French explorer and disciple of Newton. He led an expedition to measure an arc of the meridian near the equator. He was for some time president of the Academy of Sciences in Berlin, receiving the appointment from Frederick the Great.

few carriages, or persons of rank and fashion; however, considerable preparations were making in the great square, for the diversions of the evening.

At eleven high mass was performed in the principal church, which was very much ornamented, and illuminated with innumerable wax tapers, which, together with the greatest crowd I ever was in, rendered the heat almost equal to that of the black-hole at Calcutta, and the consequences must have been as fatal, had not the people been permitted to go out as others pressed in; but neither religious zeal, nor the love of music, could keep any one long in the church who was able to get out. In short, the whole was a struggle between those whose curiosity made them strive to enter the church, and others whose sufferings and fear made them use every means in their power to get out.

By permitting myself to drive with the stream, I at length was carried to a tolerable place near one of the doors, where I had perseverance sufficient to remain during the whole service, as I was in constant expectation of being rewarded for my sufferings, by the performance of some great singer, whom I had not heard before; but in this I was disappointed, as all the vocal performers, except one, were very indifferent: the music, however, was very pretty; full of taste and fancy. . . .

At four o'clock in the evening, the games began in the great square, which is a large piece of ground of an oblong form. There were 1500 peasants of the neighbourhood employed upon this occasion, who had been three months in training: they had the story of David and Goliath to represent, which was done with the most minute attention to the sacred story, and the *costume* of the ancients. The two armies of the Israelites and Philistines met, marching to the sound of ancient instruments, such as the *crotolo* or cymbal, the systrum [1], and others: they were all dressed *à l'Antique*, even to the common men; the kings, princes, and generals, on both sides, were sumptuously clad, and all on horseback, as were several hundreds of the troops.

The giant, Goliath, advanced and gave the challenge: the Israelites retreated in great consternation, till, at length, little David appears, and entreats Saul to let him be his champion, which request, after some time, is granted; the rest of the story was well told, and it was so contrived, that after Goliath was stunned by the stone from David's sling, in cutting off his head with the giant's own great sword, a quantity of blood gushed out, and many of the spectators shrieked with horror, supposing it to be the blood of the person who represented the champion of the Philistines. After this, there was a pitched battle between the two armies, and the Israelites, being victorious, brought David in triumph, at the head of the prisoners and spoils of the enemy, mounted on a superb chariot, in the ancient form.

At Vespers I heard the same story *sung* in an oratorio . . . during this performance, the whole town was illuminated in an elegant manner, and there were very ingenious fireworks played off in the great square; and, in justice to the pacific disposition of the Tuscans, I must observe, that though there were at least 20,000

---

[1] Defined by Dr. Burney in the *General History of Music* as " An Egyptian instrument of sacrifice ", still used in Abyssinia, whilst singing psalms of thanksgiving. It was shaken by one priest " in a very threatening manner at his neighbour ".

people assembled together on this occasion, without guards, yet not the least accident or disturbance happened. This may perhaps be owing, in some measure, to the peculiar sobriety of the Italians, as I do not remember to have seen one drunken person during the whole time I was in Italy.

It being impossible to procure a bed, if I would have paid eight or ten zechins for it, and the night being very fine, I set out at eleven o'clock for Florence, where I arrived at four the next morning: and though the musical performance at Figline was not what I had been made to expect, yet the rest was very superior, and what I was not likely to meet with elsewhere; so that, upon the whole, I did not think the time spent in this excursion entirely lost.

From Florence Dr. Burney passed on to Siena on his way to Rome, halting at Montefiascone to pay a visit to Guarducci, a famous singer. He arrived in Rome on 20th September, and remained there until 14th October. The account of his experiences in Rome is rather disappointing to the general reader. He was fêted by the English colony, and private concerts in his honour were arranged on all sides. Much of his time, naturally, was spent in the Vatican library, which was at this period in a pitiful state of confusion. There was no regular catalogue of the books and MSS., and but for the help of a kindly librarian, who spent five or six days in making a catalogue for Dr. Burney of the works which were likely to be useful to him, he would have fared badly. This same librarian undertook to have extracts made for Dr. Burney from the books which he selected.

Four days after Dr. Burney's arrival,

there was a grand *Funzioni* at the *Santi Apostoli*, on account of the reconciliation of the Pope and the King of Portugal.[1] It was at this church that I first saw his Holiness [2], and a great number of Cardinals, and heard *Te Deum*. There were two large bands of music, and an immense crowd. . . .

In the evening the outside of the cupola, church, and colonnade of St. Peter, together with the Vatican palace, were finely illuminated, which affords a spectacle to the inhabitants of Rome, not to be equalled in the universe. And in the balconies, next to the street, at the palaces of most of the Cardinals, besides illuminations, there were concerts of very numerous bands of instrumental performers; but chiefly at the residence of the Portuguese Ambassador, where the hands employed amounted to above a hundred, and these continued their performance all night. However, this music, though in the open air, was too noisy for me, and I retreated from it early, in order to have my ears soothed with more placid sounds at the Duke of Dorset's concert.

Dr. Burney went to the Duke of Dorset's [3] house nearly every night, and there made the acquaintance of all the best performers in Rome; as the theatres were shut, it might have been otherwise difficult for him to have seen them.

The Sistine chapel was of course a source of the greatest interest to Dr. Burney, and he made great friends with Santarelli (1749–1790), the Pope's Maestro di Cappella, who was

---

[1] Diplomatic relations between Portugal and the Holy See had been broken off as long before as 1764 in consequence of the execution of the Jesuit Malagrida. In 1769 the life of Joseph Emmanuel, the King of Portugal, was attempted, and the complicity of the Jesuits was alleged. Shortly afterwards the Vatican had to give way on the question of the Society of Jesus, and the order was suppressed.

[2] At this time Clement XIV, born 1705, who was elected pope in 1769 and died five years later.

[3] This was the third holder of the title. Born in 1745, he succeeded to the dukedom in 1769. He was afterwards ambassador at the French court and died in 1799. His chief claim to the interest of later generations lies in the fact that he was an early patron of cricket, and one of the committee which drew up the original laws of the Marylebone Club.

the author of a learned work on Church music. Santarelli
gave Dr. Burney a copy of the famous " Miserere " of Allegri
(1580–1652), and furnished him with full particulars regarding it:

This piece, which, for upwards of a hundred and fifty
years, has been annually performed in Passion Week at
the Pope's chapel, on Wednesday and Good Friday, and
which, in appearance, is so simple as to make those, who
have only seen it on paper, wonder whence its beauty
and effect could arise, owes its reputation more to the
manner in which it is performed, than to the composition:
the same music is many times repeated to different words,
and the singers have, by tradition, certain customs,
expressions, and graces of convention, which produce
great effects; such as swelling and diminishing the
sounds altogether; accelerating or retarding the measure
at some particular words, and singing some entire verses
quicker than others. . . .

However, some of the great effects produced by this
piece, may, perhaps, be justly attributed to the time,
place and solemnity of the ceremonials, used during the
performance: the Pope and conclave are all prostrated
on the ground; the candles of the chapel, and the
torches of the balustrade, are extinguished, one by
one; and the last verse of this psalm is terminated by
two choirs; the *Maestro di Cappella* beating time slower
and slower, and the singers diminishing or rather *ex-
tinguishing* the harmony, by little and little, to a perfect
point.

It is likewise performed by select voices, who have
frequent rehearsals, particularly on the Monday in Passion

Week, which is wholly spent in repeating and polishing the performance.

This composition used to be held so sacred, that it was imagined excommunication would be the consequence of an attempt to transcribe it.[1] Padre Martini told me there were never more than two copies of it made by authority, one of which was for the late King of Portugal, and the other for himself: this last he permitted me to transcribe at Bologna, and Signor Santarelli favoured me with another copy from the archives of the Pope's chapel.

Dr. Burney concludes his account of the Allegri " Miserere " with the following anecdote, communicated to him by Santarelli:

The Emperor Leopold the first [2], not only a lover and patron of music, but a good composer himself, ordered his ambassador, at Rome, to entreat the Pope [3] to permit him to have a copy of the celebrated *Miserere* of Allegri, for the use of the Imperial chapel at Vienna; which being granted, a copy was made by the *Signor Maestro* of the Pope's chapel, and sent to the Emperor, who had then in his service some of the first singers of the age; but, notwithstanding the abilities of the performers, this composition was so far from answering the expectations of the Emperor and his court, in the execution, that he concluded the Pope's *Maestro di Cappella*, in order to keep it a mystery, had put a trick upon him, and sent him

---

[1] Mozart in this actual year (1770) had astounded Rome by writing down the ' Miserere " from memory, after hearing it once performed. He was only fourteen at the time. Mendelssohn performed a similar feat in 1830.

[2] 1640–1705.

[3] Innocent XI, born 1611, elected pope in 1676, and died in 1689.

another composition.   Upon which, in great wrath, he
sent an express to his Holiness, with a complaint against
the *Maestro di Cappella*, which occasioned his immediate
disgrace, and dismission from the service of the papal
chapel; and in so great a degree was the Pope offended,
at the supposed imposition of his composer, that,
for a long time, he would neither see him, nor hear
his defence; however, at length, the poor man got one
of the cardinals to plead his cause, and to acquaint his
Holiness, that the style of singing in his chapel, particularly in performing the *Miserere*, was such as
could not be expressed by notes, nor taught or trans-
mitted to any other place, but by example; for which
reason the piece in question, though faithfully transcribed, must fail in its effect, when performed elsewhere.
His Holiness did not understand music, and could hardly
comprehend how the same notes should sound so dif-
ferently in different places; however, he ordered his
Maestro di Cappella to write down his defence, in order
to be sent to Vienna, which was done; and the Emperor,
seeing no other way of gratifying his wishes with respect
to this composition, begged of the Pope, that some of
the musicians in the service of his Holiness, might be
sent to Vienna, to instruct those in the service of his
chapel how to perform the *Miserere* of Allegri, in the same
expressive manner as in the Sistine chapel at Rome,
which was granted.   But, before they arrived, a war
broke out with the Turks[1], which called the Emperor
from Vienna; and the *Miserere* has never yet, per-

---

[1] Under Mahomet IV. The war culminated in the siege of Vienna, which was
raised by John Sobieski, King of Poland, on 12th September, 1683.

haps, been truly performed, but in the Pope's chapel.

Dr. Burney had been warned that he must not expect too much of the Vatican choir, which had suffered greatly owing to the competition of the opera houses and the consequent withdrawal of the best vocal talent elsewhere. Inadequate salaries and the general decline of interest in church music at this time were contributory causes. At the time of Dr. Burney's visit the establishment of the Vatican choir was thirty-two: eight sopranos, eight altos, eight tenors, and eight basses, not a very happy balance of parts. At high festivals assistance was given by famous opera singers, and the numbers were doubled. The singing was invariably unaccompanied, and the singers dressed in a kind of purple uniform.

It would be wearisome to retail Dr. Burney's accounts of his meetings with various prominent musicians in Rome; their names would in every case be unfamiliar to the present-day reader. For the most part they were singers and violinists, one of the latter being in possession of a very fine Steiner [1] fiddle. The dearth of keyboard executants is very remarkable in a country which produced Domenico Scarlatti. Dr. Burney states categorically that he never met a great harpsichord player or an original composer for the instrument during his whole tour. In fact it was little used, except for accompaniments. This curious neglect of the most universal instrument of the century is accounted for as follows:

To persons accustomed to English harpsichords, all the keyed instruments on the Continent appear to great disadvantage. Throughout Italy they have generally little octave spinets to accompany singing, in private houses, sometimes in a triangular form, but more frequently in the shape of our old virginals [2]; of which the keys are so noisy, and the tone so feeble, that more wood

[1] Jacob Steiner, or Stainer (1621–1683), the first German violin maker who worked on Italian models. He was reputed to have been a pupil of the great Nicholas Amati.
[2] A generic term for all keyboard instruments in which the sound was produced by the string being struck by a quill; it was thus generally synonymous with the terms " spinet " and " harpsichord ".

is heard than wire. . . . I found three English harpsichords in the three principal cities of Italy, which are regarded by the Italians as so many phenomena.

The following quotation from Dr. Burney's account of his conversation with an old Neapolitan composer, Rinaldo di Capua, is cited merely to demonstrate the unchanging character of human nature. It is curious to think that, even in 1770, when music was so young, there were the old musical " diehards " who decried the innovations of their successors, and who imagined that the last word was said when they and their contemporaries ceased to write. Even this old man had been an inventor in his youth—he was erroneously credited with having been the first to use accompanied recitatives: in actual fact, he only claimed to be among those who first made use of the orchestra to play long passages in " the recitatives of strong passion and distress, which express or imitate what it would be ridiculous for the voice to attempt ". Dr. Burney's account is as follows:

Though a good-natured man, his opinions are rather singular and severe upon his brother composers. He thinks they have nothing left to do now, but to write themselves and others over again; and that the only chance they have left for obtaining the reputation of novelty and invention, arises either from ignorance or want of memory in the public; as everything, both in melody and modulation, that is worth doing, has been often already done. He includes himself in the censure; and frankly confesses, that though he has written full as much as his neighbours, yet out of all his works, perhaps not above *one* new melody can be found, which has been wire-drawn in different keys, and different measures, a thousand times. And as to modulation, it must be always the same, to be natural and pleasing;

what has not been given to the public being only the
refuse of thousands, who have tried and rejected it, either
as impracticable or displeasing. The only opportunity a
composer has for introducing new modulation in songs,
is in a short second part, in order to *fright* the hearer
back to the first, to which it serves as a foil, by making
it comparatively beautiful. He likewise censures with
great severity the noise and tumult of instruments in
modern songs.

What would the poor old man think of Strauss's " Helden-
leben "! The folly of prophecy could not be more aptly
demonstrated. The story has a pathetic ending. With a
touching faith in the fickle public,

when he found old age coming on, he collected together
his principal works, such as had been produced in the
zenith of his fortune and fancy; thinking these would
be a resource in distressful times. These times came;
various misfortunes and calamities befell him and his
family, when, behold, this resource, this sole resource,
the accumulated produce of his pen, had, by a graceless
son, been sold for waste paper!

. . . .

Having heard the most eminent performers; conversed
with the principal theorists and composers, found many
of the books, manuscripts, and antiquities I had sought;
and explained my wants with regard to the rest, to several
friends at Rome, who kindly promised me their assistance
in supplying them during my absence; I set off for
Naples on Sunday evening, the fourteenth of October.

Thus Dr. Burney, on quitting the Eternal City.

CHAPTER V

Naples

Dr. Burney arrived in Naples on 16th October full of high hopes and great expectations. Naples had been the cradle of most of the great Italian composers, and had nurtured men like the two Scarlattis, Pergolese, and Farinelli, the great singer. He was as usual destined to disappointment. Naples was living on a great reputation, but musical life there was being vitiated, as in all the other Italian cities which Dr. Burney visited, by an indiscriminate rage for novelty, a foolish preoccupation with the performer and indifference to the music played. In spite of such evident signs of decadence, the Neapolitans as a whole were musical to the finger-tips. Their popular music was peculiar and full of strange modulations; their methods of singing " noisy and vulgar ", but the violin and guitar accompaniments excellent. Dr. Burney, who was so much interested in the music of the people—an uncommon trait in those days—one evening invited into his room a party of musicians who were performing in the street under his window. Their music proved, however, better at a distance, and the singing was coarse and out of tune:

It is a very singular species of music, as wild in modulation, and as different from that of all the rest of Europe as the Scots, and is, perhaps, as ancient, being among the common people merely traditional. However, the violin player wrote down the melody of the voice part for me, and afterwards brought me something like the accompaniments; but these parts have a strange

appearance when seen on paper together. I heard these
musicians play a great number of Neapolitan airs, but
all were different from other music.

Dr. Burney then makes some interesting reflections on
Italian folk-song:

A little before Christmas, musicians of this sort come
from Calabria to Naples, and *their* music is wholly different from this; they usually sing with a guitar and
violin, not on the shoulder, but hanging down. . . . Another sort is peculiar to Apulia, with which the people
are set a-dancing and sweating, who either have, or
would be thought to have been bitten by the tarantula.
Of this music Dr. Cirillo procured me a specimen.
Signor Serrao, in a dissertation on the subject, and Dr.
Cirillo, who has made several experiments, in order to
determine the fact, are both of opinion that the whole
is an imposition, practised by the people of Apulia, to
gain money: that not only the cure but the malady
itself is a fraud. Dr. Cirillo assured me that he had
never been able to provoke the tarantula either to bite
himself or others upon whom he had repeatedly tried
the experiment. However, the whole is so thoroughly
believed by some innocent people in the country, that,
when really bitten by other insects or animals that are
poisonous, they take this method of dancing, to a particular tune, till they sweat; which, together with their
faith, sometimes makes them whole. They will continue
the dance, in a kind of frenzy, for many hours, even till
they drop down with fatigue and lassitude.

This dance, known as the " tarantelle ", became better

known during the next century, its popularity being due to the many imitations produced by composers of the lighter kind of music.

Naples was chiefly famous for its three schools of music, which rivalled those of Venice, already described. The Venetian schools were for the education of girls and specialized in the training of singers, the Neapolitan schools, on the other hand, were exclusively for boys, and they enjoyed a reputation second to none as nurseries for young composers, though a thorough grounding in vocal and instrumental playing was imparted to the pupils. Dr. Burney's visit fortunately coincided with the eight-day musical festival at the Franciscan church; it was in consideration of their services at this annual festival that the "Conservatorios" held their charters, and they were also exempted from all taxes on food and wine. Dr. Burney gleaned some interesting particulars regarding these historic institutions from Piccinni, the great composer and rival of Gluck, whom he was fortunate enough to meet in Naples.[1] Saint Onofrio held some ninety scholars, La Pietà a hundred and twenty, and Santa Maria di Loreto two hundred. The boys were admitted between the ages of eight and twenty, and the younger pupils were bound for the space of eight years; older boys could only obtain admission if they showed exceptional talent. There was a system of superannuation for those whose proficiency did not justify further instruction: some were taken as paying pupils, and these were not subject to the eight years' agreement. The masters included two *Maestri di Cappella* for each school, one for composition and the other for singing, and assistant masters, termed *Maestri Secolari*, for each instrument. Old pupils were often retained in this capacity. The boys of the Pietà wore a blue uniform, those of Santa Maria di Loreto a white uniform with a black sash, and those of St. Onofrio a white uniform. Dr. Burney heard performances by pupils of all three institutions, but found only further examples of the general decadence which he was experiencing wherever he went:

[1] When he returned to London after the German tour, Dr. Burney formulated a scheme for the establishment of a school of music at the Foundling Hospital, similar in constitution to those which he had inspected in Venice and Naples. *A Plan for a Music School* was published in 1774, but, in spite of much discussion, it was never adopted, much to Dr. Burney's disappointment.

These seminaries, which have heretofore produced such great professors, seem at present to be but low in genius. However, since these institutions, as well as others, are subject to fluctuations, after being languid for some time, like their neighbour Mount Vesuvius, they will, perhaps, blaze out again with new vigour.

Dr. Burney was introduced to a young Englishman, named Oliver, who was studying at St. Onofrio, and made a thorough inspection of the buildings and the rooms where the boys lived:

On the first flight of stairs was a trumpeter, screaming upon his instrument till he was ready to burst; on the second was a French horn, bellowing in the same manner. In the common practising room there was a *Dutch concert*, consisting of seven or eight harpsichords, more than as many violins, and several voices, all performing different things, and in different keys: other boys were writing in the same room; but it being holiday time, many were absent who usually study and practise in this room. The jumbling them all together in this manner may be convenient for the house, and may teach the boys to attend to their own parts with firmness, whatever else may be going forward at the same time; it may likewise give them force, by obliging them to play loud in order to hear themselves; but in the midst of such jargon, and continued dissonance, it is wholly impossible to give any kind of polish or finishing to their performance; hence the slovenly coarseness so remarkable in their public exhibitions; and the total want of taste, neatness, and expression in all these young musicians, till they have acquired them elsewhere.

The beds, which are in the same room, serve for seats to the harpsichords and other instruments. Out of thirty or forty boys who were practising, I could discover but two that were playing the same piece; some of those who were practising on the violin seemed to have a great deal of hand. The violoncellos practise in another room; and the flutes, oboes, and other wind instruments, in a third, except the trumpets and horns, which are obliged to fag, either on the stairs, or on the top of the house.

There are in this college sixteen young *Castrati*, and these lie upstairs, by themselves, in warmer apartments than the other boys, for fear of colds, which might not only render their delicate voices unfit for exercise at present, but hazard the entire loss of them for ever.

The only vacation in these schools, in the whole year, is in autumn, and that for a few days only: during the winter, the boys rise two hours before it is light, from which time they continue their exercise, an hour and a half at dinner excepted, till eight o'clock at night; and this constant perseverance, for a number of years, with genius and good teaching, must produce great musicians.

Granted—but it must have been a survival of the fittest. Yet a large number of the greatest composers of those early days of music had received their training at one of the schools, men such as Scarlatti, Porpora, Pergolesi, or Cimarosa; Stephen Storace, the brother of Nancy Storace, and well known both for his light operas and his associations with Drury Lane, was educated at St. Onofrio, and Michael Kelly, the Irishman, at Santa Maria di Loreto, though he lived with the principal and did not have to wear the uniform or perform any duties. Michael Kelly's remarks on his first introduction to Santa Maria di Loreto are worth quoting, as they exactly corroborate Dr. Burney's account:

He (i.e. Finaroli, the principal) took me to see his Conservatorio, in which there were between three and four hundred boys; they studied composition, singing, and to play on all instruments. There were several rooms, but in the great school-room, into which I was introduced, there were some singing, others playing upon the violin, oboe, clarionet, horn, trumpet, &c., &c., each different music, and in different keys. The noise was horrible; and in the midst of this terrific Babel, the boy who studied composition was expected to perform his task, and harmonize a melody given him by his master. I left the place in disgust, and swore to myself never to become an inmate of it. . . . On or after the 17th of October, the boys of the three Conservatorios are obliged to attend morning and evening, for nine days, at the Franciscan Church in their dresses. It is by attending this festival, and performing without remuneration, that they are exempt, by the King's permission, from all taxes on provision and wine, which are paid by every other class of inhabitants.[1]

There are constant allusions besides the above throughout Dr. Burney's Journals to the artificial male sopranos and altos who abounded in Europe during the seventeenth and eighteenth centuries, and for many years were even members of the Vatican choir. The great male singers of the century, men like Farinelli and Senesino, whose names were household words in England, belonged to this class, and it was only towards the end of the century, when Dr. Burney was writing,

[1] *The Reminiscences of Michael Kelly*, Vol. I, p. 42 (London, 1826). Kelly was writing of the year 1779, and seems on internal evidence to have refreshed these memories of forty-seven years' standing by reference to Dr. Burney's book.

that the public conscience became awakened to the enormity of this horrible custom, whereby young boys, at the instigation of their parents, were mutilated in the hope of mercenary gain. His remarks on this subject are therefore of much interest, as they indicate the change of attitude which had come over Europe since the great days of Handel's operas, when the male sopranos and altos were at the height of their popularity:

I enquired throughout Italy at what place boys were chiefly qualified for singing by castration, but could get no certain intelligence. I was told at Milan that it was at Venice; at Venice, that it was at Bologna; but at Bologna the fact was denied, and I was referred to Florence; from Florence to Rome, and from Rome I was sent to Naples. The operation most certainly is against law in all these places, as well as against nature; and all the Italians are so much ashamed of it, that in every province they transfer it to some other.

> " Ask where 's the North? At York, 't is on the
>   Tweed;
> " In Scotland, at the Orcades; and there,
> " At Greenland, Zembla, or the Lord knows where."
>   POPE's *Essay on Man.*

However, with respect to the Conservatorios at Naples, Mr. Gemineau, the British consul, who has so long resided there, and who has made very particular enquiries, assured me, and his account was confirmed by Dr. Cirillo, an eminent and learned Neapolitan physician, that this practice is absolutely forbidden in the Conservatorios, and that the young *Castrati* came from Lecce in Apulia; but, before the operation is performed, they are brought to a Conservatorio to be tried as to the probability of voice, and then are taken home by their parents for this barbarous purpose. It is, however, death by the laws to all those who perform the operation, and excommunication to everyone concerned in it, unless it be done, as is often pretended, upon account of some disorders which may be supposed to require it, and with the consent of the boy. And there are instances of its being done even at the request of the boy himself, as was the case of the Grassetto at Rome.[1] But as to these previous trials of the voice, it is my opinion that the cruel operation is but too frequently performed without trial, or at least without sufficient proofs of an improvable voice; otherwise such numbers could never be found in every great town throughout Italy, without any voice at all, or at least without one sufficient to compensate such a loss. Indeed all the *musici* in the churches at present are made up of the refuse of the opera houses, and it is rare to meet with a tolerable voice upon the establishment in any church throughout Italy. The *virtuosi* who sing there occasionally, upon great festivals only, are usually strangers, and paid by the time.

Dr. Burney further adds that the term *musico* in Italy was at this time almost exclusively applied to singers whose voices had been thus artificially preserved.

While at Naples Dr. Burney was fortunate enough to meet two of the foremost composers of the day, Piccinni and Jomelli. Piccinni (1728–1800), as we have already noted, gave him much useful information regarding the Neapolitan Conservatorios; he is chiefly remembered to-day as one of

[1] Dr. Burney heard him at a private concert in Rome. He had a very good voice and was " in other respects, a very pleasing singer ". Not only did he submit to the operation at his own request, but against the advice of his friends.

the protagonists in the great feud in Paris with Gluck—one
of the most famous of musical rivalries, and only comparable
with that between Handel and Buononcini for the fervour of
partisanship accompanying it. Dr. Burney went several times
to hear an opera of Piccinni which was running at the time.

> For want of dancing [1], the acts are necessarily so long,
> that it is wholly impossible to keep up the attention; so
> that those who are not talking, or playing at cards, usually
> fall asleep.

Piccinni, like Richard Strauss, was accused of using instruments to excess, and Dr. Burney relates how no copyist in
Italy would undertake the transcription of Piccinni's scores
without an extra remuneration of a zechin over and above
the customary rate.

Padre Martini had given Dr. Burney an introduction to
Jomelli (1714–1774). He was excessively corpulent, and reminded Dr. Burney of Handel, though he had better manners.
He was said to be suffering from a common complaint among
composers, writing for the " learned few, rather than for the
feeling many ", but nevertheless he was one of the greatest
of the old school of composers, which was then passing away.
Dr. Burney attended a brilliant *première* of a new opera by
Jomelli at the San Carlo opera house. He went as the
guest of Mr. Hamilton, the British Minister, in the latter's
box:

> It is not easy to imagine or describe the grandeur and
> magnificence of this spectacle. It being the great festival
> of St. Charles and the King of Spain's name-day [2], the
> court was in grand gala, and the house was not only
> doubly illuminated, but amazingly crowded with well-
> dressed company. In the front of each box there is a

---

[1] Dancing was only permitted at the San Carlo, the theatre royal.

[2] Charles III, who was King of Spain at this time, was the father of Ferdinand,
then King of Naples. When Charles III ascended the Spanish throne, his rights to
the kingdom of Naples devolved on Ferdinand, his second son.

mirror, three or four feet long, by two or three wide, before which are two large wax tapers; these, by reflection, being multiplied, and added to the lights of the stage and to those within the boxes, make the splendour too much for the aching sight. The King and Queen were present. Their Majesties have a large box in the front of the house, which contains in height and breadth the space of four other boxes. The stage is of an immense size, and the scenes, dresses, and decorations were extremely magnificent; and I think this theatre superior, in these particulars, as well as in the music, to that of the great French opera at Paris. . . . Yet with all this, it must be owned that the magnitude of the building, and noise of the audience are such, that neither the voices nor instruments can be heard distinctly. I was told, however, that on account of the King and Queen being present, the people were much less noisy than on common nights. There was not a hand moved by way of applause during the whole representation, though the audience in general seemed pleased with the music: but, to say the truth, it did not afford me the same delight as at the rehearsal; nor did the singers, though they exerted themselves more, appear to equal advantage: not one of the present voices is sufficiently powerful for such a theatre, when so crowded and so noisy.

Dr. Burney states elsewhere, on the authority of the leader of the orchestra at the opera house, that the orchestra consisted of eighteen first violins, eighteen second violins, five double basses, and only two violoncellos! The double bass was played so coarsely throughout Italy, that the sound produced resembled nothing better than the strokes of a hammer. This man dined with Dr. Burney and afterwards sang comic songs, accompanying himself on the violin and producing "the effects of a numerous band". Dr. Burney was amazed to see him arrive carrying his instrument in his hand:

It is very common in the great cities of Italy to see performers of the first eminence carry their own instruments through the streets. This seems a trivial circumstance to mention, yet it strongly marks the difference of manners and characters in two countries not very remote from each other. In Italy, the leader of the first opera in the world carries the instrument of his fame and fortune about him, with as much pride as a soldier does his sword or musket; while, in England, the indignities he would receive from the populace would soon impress his mind with shame for himself and fear for his instrument.

In one respect at any rate we rise superior to our ancestors of 150 years ago: the sight of a musician carrying a violin in the streets of London no longer affords provocation for a riot!

The remainder of Dr. Burney's stay in Naples was devoted to conversations with the musical and scientific notabilities of the town, attendance at operas and concerts, and the like. He was also present at the public baptism of two Turkish slaves who had been converted to Christianity. The ceremony took place at a neighbouring convent, and was graced by the presence of several bishops and the élite of Naples. He likewise revelled in the ancient instruments and manuscripts in the museum at Portici, and obtained a great deal of useful information for his projected *History of Music*.

Of the many friends whom Dr. Burney made in Naples, none were kinder than Sir William Hamilton (then Mr. Hamilton) and his wife. Sir William Hamilton (1730–1803) had been British Minister at the court of Naples since the year 1764. He was an antiquarian of European reputation, and his collections subsequently formed the basis of the present department of Greek and Roman antiquities in the British Museum. His first wife, who died in 1782, was an accomplished musician, and Dr. Burney agrees with Michael Kelly in assigning her a very high place as a harpsichord player. Burney's standard was of course rather low, as he adds: " Ladies, it must be owned, though frequently neat in execution, seldom aim at expression "—probably the ladies of his time would have considered such an aim in itself to be unladylike! At the Hamilton's country house, the " Villa Angelica " at the foot of Mount Vesuvius, Dr. Burney stayed three days, and after their return to Naples the Hamiltons arranged a large concert at their town house for him and invited all musical Naples. It is hardly necessary to add that Sir William Hamilton was in later years the husband of Emma, who played so great a part in the life of Lord Nelson.

Dr. Burney spent nearly a month in Naples, and, having completed his labours there, started on his homeward journey on 7th November.

CHAPTER VI

The Return Journey

On his return to Rome, Dr. Burney found sufficient work awaiting him to enable him to spin out his stay there to a duration of over ten days. To begin with, he had to visit those numerous friends who had undertaken transcriptions for him during his absence, in order to collect the results of their labours. There were also museums and churches which he had omitted to see during his previous stay, not to speak of numerous functions, musical and otherwise, which would naturally appeal to his eager curiosity. Among such, and chief in interest, was the ceremony at the convent of St. Ursula, at which a nun took the veil:

The company was very numerous, and composed chiefly of the first people of Rome, who were all in full dress. I was placed close to the altar, where I could see the whole ceremony, and hear every word that was uttered. The service was begun by saying mass, then cardinal de Rossi entered in great state; while the organ was playing, and the mass was singing: the music, both vocal and instrumental, was performed by the nuns and ladies of the convent, who were placed in the organ gallery. The composition was pretty, but ill executed; the organ was a bad one, and too powerful for the band: most of the best hands, as I was informed, were occupied in the convent with the internal ceremony, the external was all performed in the chapel.

When the cardinal was robed, the noviciate was led into the chapel by a lady of the first rank in Rome, and brought to the altar in exceeding high dress. Her hair was of a beautiful light brown, and curled *en tête de mouton* all over her head. Her gown was of the richest embroidered, and, I believe, embossed blue and silver, I ever saw. She had on a large stage hoop, and a great quantity of diamonds; the train of her robe dragged full two yards on the ground; she seemed rather a pretty sort of young person than a beauty. When she first appeared, she looked very pale, and more dead than alive; she made a most profound reverence to the cardinal, who was seated on the steps of the altar in his mitre and all his rich vestments, ready to receive her. She threw herself upon her knees at the foot of the altar, and remained in that posture some time, while other parts of the ceremony were adjusting; then she walked up to the cardinal, who said, *Figlia mia, che domandate?* My child, what is your request? She said, that she begged to be admitted into that convent as a sister of the order of St. Ursula: Have you well, said the cardinal, considered of what you ask? She answered, cheerfully, that she had; and was well informed of all she was about to do. Then she kneeled down again, and kissed the cardinal's hands, and received from him a little crucifix, which she also kissed; after which she retired again to the foot of the altar, where she threw herself on her knees, while the cardinal said mass, which was sung at the same time in the organ loft. After this, there was a sermon in the Italian language, and that being over, the cardinal led the nun-elect into the convent, where she was divested of all her gorgeous attire and worldly vanities, and had her hair cut off. She then came to the gate in her religious dress, to receive the white veil, with which she was invested by the lady abbess, the cardinal and the other assistants standing by.

After this there was more pretty music badly performed. The organ, by executing all the symphonies and accompaniments, overpowered the violins, and had a bad effect, though neatly played.

When her veil was on, the new sister came to the convent door, to receive the congratulations of her friends and of the company; but first, with a lighted taper in her hand, she went round the convent to salute all the nuns, who had likewise tapers in their hands. When she was at the door, with the veil and crown on, but her face uncovered, I, among the rest, went close to her, and found she was much prettier than I had before imagined. She had a sweet mouth, and the finest teeth in the world, with lively sparkling eyes, and a genteel shaped visage; she would, anywhere else, have been styled a very pretty woman; but here, so circumstanced, a beauty. At the altar she changed countenance several times, first pale, then red, and seemed to pant, and to be in danger of either bursting into tears, or fainting; but she recovered before the ceremony was ended, and at the convent door assumed an air of great cheerfulness; talked to several of her friends and acquaintance, and seemed to give up the world very heroically.—And thus ended this human sacrifice!

On the afternoon of this same Sunday, Dr. Burney visited the Chiesa Nuova in Rome to hear an oratorio, which he thought very commonplace. It was a lengthy affair: the service began with matins, then the " Salve Regina " was sung, and after this there were prayers,

and then a little boy, not above six years old, mounted the pulpit, and delivered a discourse, by way of sermon, which he had got by heart, and which was rendered truly ridiculous by the vehicle through which it passed,

and in between the parts of the oratorio, which followed, there was another sermon delivered by a Jesuit father!

Dr. Burney made a thorough inspection of the Sistine chapel, which appears to have been in a very dilapidated condition. " The Last Judgment ", Michael Angelo's greatest work, was badly discoloured, and the fine ceiling by the same master actually broken down in many places to a breadth of two or three feet. The whole chapel was very dusty and out of repair, and evidently a typical example of eighteenth century apathy and neglect.

He inspected the old organ in the church of St. John Lateran, which had been built in 1549, and, in spite of a recent overhauling, had not been fitted with a " swell ". In fact, according to Dr. Burney, the organs which he inspected in Italy and Germany were all deficient in this respect, though the swell had been a commonplace in England since the beginning of the century. He comments most unfavourably on the general inferiority of the action of the organs on the Continent, which, in spite of their immense size and innumerable stops, were coarser, and harsher in tone than those in England.

Dr. Burney's second visit to Rome coincided with the foundation festival at St. Peter's. The service was held in the large winter chapel on the left-hand side, which contained the largest organ in the cathedral. Two choirs were employed, and two of the best male singers of the city took the solo parts. The instrumental parts were sustained by two organs (one probably a small movable organ), four violoncellos, and two double basses. Vespers were said by Cardinal York, assisted by several bishops. This was the second son of the

Old Pretender, Henry Stuart (1725–1807), by the Jacobites styled " Henry IX ".

In the Veruspi palace, where Shelley afterwards lived (1819), there was a well-known collection of musical instruments in the so-called Podini gallery. Dr. Burney examined the instruments with great interest and found them, contrary to general report, in very poor order. The collection contained

a very fine harpsichord, to look at, but not a key that will speak: it formerly had a communication with an organ in the same room, and with two spinets and a virginal; under the frame is a violin, tenor, and bass, which, by a movement of the foot, used to be played upon by the harpsichord keys. The organ appears in the front of the room, but not on the side, where there seems to be pipes and machines enclosed; but there was no one to open or explain it, the old *Cicerone* being just dead.

This instrument was evidently a precursor of the modern Orchestrion.

There were seven or eight theatres in Rome at this time, two being appropriated to operas:

There are no public spectacles allowed in Rome, except during carnival time, which lasts from the seventh of January to Ash-Wednesday; nor are any women ever suffered to appear upon the stage, the female characters being represented by eunuchs, and frequently so well, from their delicacy of voice and figure, as to deceive persons unacquainted with this prohibition.[1]

---

[1] It is hardly necessary to remind the reader that the jurisdiction of the Sovereign Pontiff extended throughout the city and the surrounding country until 1870. These regulations were in strict accordance with ecclesiastical discipline, which controlled the whole city at that time.

Rome is the post of honour for composers, the Romans being the most fastidious judges of music in Italy. There is likewise in this city more cabal than elsewhere, and party runs higher. It is generally supposed that a composer or performer who is successful at Rome, has nothing to fear from the severity of critics in other places.[1] At the opening of an opera, the clamour or acclamation of the company frequently continues for a considerable time before they will hear a note. A favourite author is received with shouts of *Bravo! Signor Maestro. Viva! Signor Maestro.* And when a composer is condemned by the audience, it is with discrimination in favour of the singer, by crying out, after they have done hissing, *Bravo! pure, il Guarducci* [2] (Bravo! however, Guarducci), and on the contrary, if the performer displeases in executing the music of a favourite composer, after they have expressed their disapprobation of him, by hissing, they cry out *Viva! pure, il Signor Maestro.*

Among the social functions which Dr. Burney attended was a big concert at the house of a Russian general, Schovelhoffe, probably one of the Schouvaloff family. The company consisted almost entirely of his own countrymen, to the number of thirty. It was with much regret that he tore himself away from Rome, but he had urgent business awaiting him in England, and there was a war scare and the possibility that he might be kept a prisoner on the Continent.

The manuscript journal contains a long and entertaining account of the homeward journey into France, which is

[1] The approbation or condemnation of the Roman audiences was, however, no criterion of ultimate success. Rossini's most famous opera, "The Barber of Seville", was received with hissing and booing when it was produced in Rome in 1816.

[2] A famous singer whom Dr. Burney had visited at Montefiascone on his way from Florence to Rome. Dr. Burney states that he was admittedly the finest singer of the day. He had met with considerable success in London, and was now living in retirement, at times in Florence and otherwise at his birthplace, Montefiascone.

dismissed in a few lines in the printed edition. The hardships and difficulties of travelling were intensified by the incessant rainstorms "which had rendered the roads intolerable", particularly "over the tremendous mountains of Genoa". Dr. Burney passed through Pisa, where he was able to inspect the leaning tower ("beautiful not in its deformity of being all awry, but otherwise in its construction"):

In this one night we passed through five different states, from Pisa to Sarzana, namely the Tuscan, Lucchese, Tuscan again, Modena and Genoa. At Sarzana we dismounted from the chaise, and got on mules; our trunks and baggage with assistance did the same. I had no boots and was otherwise but ill prepared for riding on horseback; however there was no help for it—the orders of necessity are the easiest complied with.

Poor Dr. Burney received three or four terrible blows on the face and head from boughs of trees, and was kicked on the left knee and right thigh by the hind legs of his vicious mule, and finally knocked down.

Such bridges! such rivers! and such rocks! . . . however at length about 11.0 at night we arrived at a wretched inn or pigsty, half stable and half cowhouse, with a fire but no chimney, surrounded by boors and muleteers, all in appearance cut-throat personages, with no kind of refreshment but cold veal and some stinking eggs.

On arriving at Genoa, he learnt that

three ships had been lost near the port. Several English were waiting for horses, clothes, &c., from Nice, Antibes, Monaco, &c., without anything to appear in, and had been thus confined for near a fortnight to their rooms, unable to comfort or amuse themselves any other way

than by swearing, as I was told by the barber, mostly
d— G— G–d: D–n–tion bitch.

After leaving Genoa,

two days and two nights we were clambering up and
sliding or tumbling down these horrid mountains . . .
the night work was indeed most dreadful: the road always
on the very ridge of the mountain and the sea always
roaring beneath, with a strong land wind, which I often
thought would have carried me, mule and all, into it.
I was frequently obliged to alight, and hold by the opposite
side of the rock or mountain, and once the instant I was
got off, the mule's feet flew from under her, and she fell
with such violence that, if I had been on her back, I
must have been dashed to pieces.

From Final to Antibes Dr. Burney went by sea, arriving at
the latter place on 30th November. From Antibes he proceeded in the worst chaise in which he had ever travelled
to Lyons, which he reached on 3rd December. He went to
the theatre there, and was greatly disgusted by a performance,
so inferior to those he had attended in Italy—

so ill sung, with so false an expression, such screaming,
forcing and trilling, as quite made me sick.

Truth to tell, his habitual contempt for the French and
their music had reasserted itself again, and he had forgotten
how far Italy had fallen short of his expectations. He comments favourably, however, on the folk-songs of the country
people in these southern districts of France, and, wherever
he halted, he prevailed upon the peasants to sing to him.
The journey from Lyons to Paris occupied four days. In
Paris he conferred with many " men of letters of the first
class ", and was fortunate enough to obtain interviews with
both Diderot and Jean Jacques Rousseau.

Diderot (1713–1784) was the editor of the famous *Encyclopédie* and otherwise a writer of international reputation: of him Dr. Burney writes as follows:

With M. Diderot, I had the happiness of conversing several times; and I was pleased to find, that among all the sciences which his extensive genius and learning have investigated, there is no one that he interests himself more about, than music. Mademoiselle Diderot, his daughter, is one of the finest harpsichord-players in Paris, and, for a lady, possessed of an uncommon portion of knowledge in modulation; but though I had the pleasure of hearing her for several hours, not a single French composition was played by her the whole time, all was Italian and German; hence it will not be difficult to form a judgment of M. Diderot's taste in music. He entered so zealously into my views concerning the history of his favourite art, that he presented me with a number of his own MSS. sufficient for a volume in folio on the subject. These, from such a writer, I regard as invaluable; " Here, take them," says he, " I know not what they contain; if any materials for your purpose, use them in the course of your work, as your own property; if not, throw them into the fire." But notwithstanding such a legal transfer, I shall look upon myself as accountable for these papers, not only to M. Diderot, but to the public.

Perhaps Dr. Burney had occasion to modify this self-imposed obligation after he had examined Diderot's MSS. If the following trite specimen of Diderot's musical wisdom, which Dr. Burney quotes in his *History of Music*, is in any way typical of the whole, he must be acquitted of wanton negligence:

The division of a musical drama into three acts, says the late M. Diderot, has been fixed on very rational principles; as it furnishes a *beginning*, a *middle*, and an *end* to the narrative or event on which the plot is founded. (MS. Reflex.)

Jean Jacques Rousseau (1712–1778) wielded in the eighteenth century an extensive influence of a disruptive character, and his teaching was in no small measure responsible for the Revolution, which he did not live to see. By invitation of David Hume he had been in England for the four years prior to his meeting with Dr. Burney, but this was their first introduction to one another. Apart from the fact that he was author of the famous novel *La Nouvelle Heloïse*, Rousseau was an exceptionally interesting person to Dr. Burney, as he was also the compiler of a *Musical Dictionary* and had composed an opera, " Le Devin du Village ", which Dr. Burney had himself translated into English in 1766 under the title of " The Cunning Man ".

Of this visit he writes in the published Journal:

I regarded the meeting with M. Rousseau at Paris, as a singularly fortunate completion of my personal intercourse with the learned and ingenious on the Continent: I was so happy as to converse for a considerable time with him upon music, a subject which has received such embellishments from his pen, that the driest parts of it are rendered interesting by his manner of treating them, both in the *Encyclopédie*, and in his *Musical Dictionary*. . . .

The manuscript journal contains a detailed account of this interview. Rousseau lived up five pairs of stairs in a small house owned by a crayon-painter. Dr. Burney climbed the staircase in fear and trembling, fully aware of the morose character of the man and more than doubtful of the reception with which he would meet:

We got to the summit at last and entered a small room with a bed in it. Mademoiselle la Gouvernante was the first person we saw, at her needle, almost bent double. She took not the least notice of us, nor we of her. In a dark corner was the man mountain in a woollen night cap, great coat and slippers, for which he apologized and very civilly gave me the best place near the fire. The reception was far better than I expected, and I began immediately to tell him of my journey and errand into Italy and the account seemed to catch his attention. After a little time I told him that I was very much pleased to find his dictionary in all hands there, and that padre Martini in particular " en faisoit le plus grand cas "— he said he was very glad of that, as the Italians were the best judges of its merit (Gui printed it): after this I went all over Italy with him, discussed several curious points.

The conversation then turned upon musical theories and problems, but eventually reverted to personal matters:

It was I, who had given a translation of his pretty opera, I now ventured to say—I durst not attempt to flatter him before—and begged permission to send him a copy of the translation as soon as I got home. He said he should be very glad to see it, and asked if it was that which had been received on the stage a few years ago, and I answered in the affirmative. All this while we hit it off very well. He is a little figure with a very intelligent and animated countenance and black eyebrows. After this I had the courage to produce to him a copy of my plan in French, which had the appearance of great length, it having been copied wide by the abbé Morellet's secretary.

He said he never read, and seemed coy and afraid of it: however he took it in his hand, and began reading to himself, and, when he had got half way down the first page, he read aloud and seemed caught by it. . . . (He) went on with seeming eagerness to the end, and said several very civil things, which I dare not repeat. . . .

We parted exceeding good friends: he did not bite nor knock me down, but said he was very glad to have had the opportunity of conversing with one who loved and cultivated music so much, and was obliged to me for my visit and communication. So we parted; he came to the head of the stairs, whether I would or no. He showed me a very large print, (in) a splendid frame and glazed, close by the door, and asked me if I knew who it was—" c'est notre roi "—he nodded assent.

From Paris Dr. Burney travelled back to England through Amiens, Boulogne, where he arrived at midnight and left at 5 a.m. the following morning, and Calais, which he reached between 10 and 11:

I was hurried on board the packet in less than two hours' time without having leisure allowed me to dry or arrange my baggage, or even get any refreshments as it was expected the vessel would sail directly, but ere I had been on board half an hour, a storm, which had lasted several days, and had but just subsided, returned with redoubled violence, so that several ships, which had got out of harbour, were glad to return, and we all came on shore, where we continued without patience or hope of getting away from this dismal place, Calais, till Sunday the 23rd, at 3.0 in the morning, at which time we set sail with a tolerable fair wind, but it soon grew otherwise and we had a very disagreeable passage, being twelve hours at sea. However we arrived at Dover without accident on Monday evening. Next day, Christmas eve, to my great joy, I got home to my family and affairs in London, after an absence of near seven months.[1]

During this time he had amassed some 400 volumes of scarce books on music, and had established a correspondent in every important city which he had visited, who was pledged to keep him *au fait* with all the latest musical news.

His daughter Fanny, in her *Memoirs* of her father (1832), thus describes his home-coming:

With all the soaring feelings of the first sun-beams of hope that irradiate from a bright, though distant glimpse of renown; untamed by difficulties, superior to fatigue, and springing over the hydra-headed monsters of impediment that everywhere jutted forth their thwarting obstacles to his enterprise, Dr. Burney came back to his country, his friends, his business and his pursuits, with the vigour of the first youth in spirits, expectations, and activity.

Dr. Burney went down to Chessington to prepare his book for the press. Published in 1771, its reception was of the best, and orders flowed in from most of the great booksellers of the day, to be followed by letters in the most flattering terms from the author's fellow musicians. So content was Dr. Burney with the reception of his book, that he immediately resolved to undertake a similar tour in the Netherlands and Germany, the results of which we shall now proceed to examine.

[1] Manuscript journal.

PART TWO

Germany and The Netherlands
in 1772

THE EXPEDITION
OF 1772

CHAPTER I

Flanders and the Austrian Netherlands

Fortified with introductions from the Earl of Sandwich [1], Dr. Burney set off at the beginning of July, 1772, in " a travelling vehicle, which rapidly wheeled him back again to Dover ", for his second expedition in search of materials for the projected *History of Music*. Landing at Calais on the sixth of the month, he proceeded to St. Omer, intending to complete his survey of Flanders and the Austrian Netherlands before entering Germany. In no way disconcerted by the discomfort of his journey, Dr. Burney went straight to the dirty little town theatre to see a company of strolling players from Dunkirk act a tragedy and a comedy, and was very favourably impressed. There was apparently quite a considerable English colony in St. Omer at this time, and Dr. Burney met two or three families at the performance. There was, however, little to detain him here, and the only object in the town which excited his admiration was the organ in the abbey church of St. Bertin, the ruins of which were such a

---

[1] The notorious fourth Earl of Sandwich (1718–1792) was at this time First Lord of the Admiralty in Lord North's ministry. His name was a byword for political corruption, and is now chiefly remembered in connexion with the prosecution of Wilkes. He affected a patronage of the arts and was a collector of antiquities himself. Besides being a Fellow of the Royal Society, he was, though quite unmusical, a director of the Concert of Ancient Music, and hence his patronage of Dr. Burney

familiar sight to those who served in Flanders during the Great War. This organ was only five years old and had been built " by a country mechanic, who could neither write, read, nor play on his instrument when it was made ". The case and ornaments were particularly striking, and the movements fairly quiet for the period. Dr. Burney saw the mounting of the guard in the *Grande Place*: the band consisted of bassoons, oboes, and horns, with the now obsolete serpent—a very " reedy " combination. The serpent was a wooden instrument, encased in leather, with a compass of three octaves, deriving its name from its shape. It was constantly used on the Continent and in this country to support the voices in church services.

From St. Omer Dr. Burney passed on to Lille, which he had visited on his previous tour. He went to the theatre and saw Molière's " L'École des Maris ", which was followed by another play with incidental music by Grétry: the singing as usual evoked his severest censure. Having exhausted the resources of Lille on his previous journey, Dr. Burney had leisure for less serious things. He comments particularly on the improvement in the military bands, the marches played and musicians being chiefly German. The cymbals were used in the band, a custom adopted from the Turk. At the mounting of the guard, forty drums were in action, one half being employed to beat the march, while the other half accompanied them with continual rolls for several bars. The hereditary prejudice of the Englishman against France may be detected in the following remarks:

To persons who stay but a short time in French garrisoned towns, the military affords considerable amusement; there are not at present above four battalions, or two thousand men, quartered in the city; though it is usual for the garrison to consist of ten thousand. The mounting guard upon the *Grande Place*, or square, is, in itself, a gay and entertaining sight; yet it always gives me a melancholy, and painful sensation, to see the people out-numbered by the military. So many stout and robust fellows kept from the plough, and from manufactures, must be a great burden upon the community, and totally useless in time of peace, to anything but ambitious and oppressive views.

Dr. Burney sums up his impressions of French Flanders as follows:

In travelling through French Flanders, I could not help observing that the singing of the common people is strongly tinctured with the *plain-chant*, which they hear so frequently at church.

All the labouring people and *bourgeois* go to matins as soon as it is light on common days, and on Sundays and festivals two or three times in the course of the day; so that by their constantly hearing the priests, and singing with them, they acquire that kind of melody and expression which is used in the church, and apply it to their songs, in their work-shops, and in the street.

Though I omitted no opportunity of hearing all the instruments and performers I could, in my way through French Flanders, yet they furnished no new ideas or reflections concerning either the taste, or style, of French musicians. To describe them, therefore, would be only to repeat what I have already said on the subject, in my former musical tour through this country. I must, however, allow, and it would discover a total want of candour to be silent on the subject, that upon keyed instruments, particularly the harpsichord, the French, in point of neatness, precision, and brilliance of execution, are not excelled by the people of any other country in Europe; and it is but just to observe likewise, that the

French military music is now not only much better in itself, but better performed than it was a few years ago: and a very intelligent English officer, who was with me on the parade, remarked the same improvement in the discipline, dress, and appearance of the French troops in the same space of time. The men are now select, the manœuvres shortened, and there is some appearance both of the gentleman and the soldier, even in the common men.

At Courtrai Dr. Burney passed over into the Austrian Netherlands, where he experienced a sudden change in the manners, music, and language of the people. His efforts to make himself understood in French by the Flemish inhabitants (Dr. Burney calls them Walloon) were fruitless. It was at Courtrai that Dr. Burney had his first experience of the carillons or chimes, which exist throughout the Low Countries. When he arrived in Ghent he went up into the town belfry himself and examined the mechanism of the carillon there, and watched the carilloneur at work, " in his shirt with the collar unbuttoned, and in a violent sweat ". Performances were given in those days four times a week, on Sunday, Monday, Wednesday, and Friday, from 11.30 till midday. Dr. Burney admired the dexterity of the performer, but considered the whole affair " a Gothic invention, and perhaps a barbarous taste, which neither the French, the English, nor the Italians have imitated or encouraged . . . for by the notes of one passage running into another, everything is rendered so inarticulate and confused as to occasion a very disagreeable jargon ". He includes in this condemnation clockwork chimes, of which specimens can still be heard in England (for instance, at the Royal Exchange in London), and nothing in his opinion can be more tiresome— an opinion with which many people will heartily concur—

for, night and day, to hear the same tune played every hour, during six months, in such a stiff and unalterable manner, requires that kind of patience, which nothing but a total absence of taste can produce.

At Ghent Dr. Burney again found much to interest him in the garrison. There were two Walloon regiments stationed there, in the pay of Austria, and, though there was no general officer in the town, two bands played morning and evening on the Place d'Armes on parade. One was an extra band of professional musicians, and consisted of two oboes, two clarionets, two bassoons, and two French horns, a combination again rather lacking in brilliance when compared with that on which the military bands of to-day rely. The other band was composed of properly enlisted men and boys from the two regiments, to the number of twenty. This band was a much more brilliant affair, consisting of four trumpets, three fifes, two oboes, two clarionets, two tambourines, two French horns, cymbals, three side drums, and one big kettledrum.

Dr. Burney naturally visited the Ghent churches, and describes the organs in detail; he also conducted his customary researches in the principal libraries, hoping to find some tangible evidence of the statement that counterpoint had its rise in Flanders, but nothing was forthcoming.

Passing through Alost, Dr. Burney arrived by 15th July in Brussels, and straightway visited the opera, hearing another work of Grétry, which he criticizes in great detail. His report on the orchestra is of most interest, in view of the fact that it had an international reputation at this time. It gives the present-day music lover some idea of the sufferings which his eighteenth century predecessor must have endured from the imperfections of the rudimentary wind instruments of the day.

The orchestra was admirably conducted, and the band, taken as a whole, was numerous, powerful, correct, and attentive: but, in its separate parts, the horns were bad, and out of tune; which was too discoverable in the capital song of the piece, when they were placed at different distances from the audience, to imitate an echo, occasioned by the rocks, in a wild and desert scene. The first clarionet, which served as an oboe, was, though a very good one, too sharp the whole night; and the basses, which were all placed at one end of the orchestra, played so violently, that it was more like the rumbling reverberation of thunder, than musical sound. The four double basses, employed in this band, were too powerful for the rest of the instruments. There was no harpsichord, which, as there were but two pieces of recitative, and those accompanied, was perhaps not wanted.

On Friday evening, 17th July, Dr. Burney reached Antwerp, which was at this time at a very low ebb in its history, the Dutch having, by the Treaty of Westphalia (1648), gained command of the mouths of the Scheldt and blocked up the entrance to the harbour, and thus succeeded in transferring the greater proportion of the commerce of Antwerp to Amsterdam.

It is a city that fills the mind with more melancholy reflections concerning the vicissitudes of human affairs, and the transient state of worldly glory, than any other in modern times: the exchange, which served as a model to Sir Th. Gresham, when he built that of London[1], and which, though still entire, is as useless to the inhabitants, as the *Coloseo* at Rome: The Town-house (i.e. Hôtel de Ville), constructed as a tribunal, for the magistrates, at the head of two hundred thousand inhabitants, which are now reduced to less than twenty thousand: the churches, the palaces, the squares, and whole streets, which, not two hundred years ago, were scarce sufficient

---

[1] Not the present building, which was erected in 1858; the original, built in 1566, had been burnt down in 1666.

to contain the people for whom they were designed, and which are now almost abandoned: the spacious and commodious quays, the numerous canals, cut with such labours and expense, the noble river Scheldt, wider than the Thames at Chelsea-reach, which used to be covered with ships from all quarters of the world, and on which now, scarce a fishing boat can be discovered: all contribute to point out the instability of fortune, and to remind us that, what Babylon, Carthage, Athens, and Palmyra now are, the most flourishing cities of the present period, must, in the course of time, inevitably become!

Music in Antwerp was in a parlous condition. Dr. Burney examined the organs in the city, and not a single one was in tune! Instrumentalists were commonly employed at the church services; the violinists Dr. Burney dismisses as " mere scrapers ":

The bassoon players in common use, are worse than those nocturnal performers, who, in London, walk the streets during winter, under the denomination of *waits*; and for the *serpent*, it is not only over-blown, and detestably out of tune, but exactly resembling in tone, that of a great hungry, or rather angry, Essex calf.

Dr. Burney spent most of Sunday in attendance at the various church services. He was at first mass in the cathedral at 7 a.m. The music consisted chiefly of plain song, sung by voices supported by two bassoons and a serpent. There was also some singing in parts, in which a few violins took part with " mean effect ". At 9 a.m. high mass began, and lasted two hours. Before the service started, the canons and boys went in procession round the church, each with a lighted taper, chanting the psalms in four parts with the two bassoons and serpent assisting. In spite of a few sweet voices among the boys, the whole performance was so dissonant and false that

Dr. Burney derived no pleasure from it. It was evident to him that the richly abundant revenues of the church went in every direction except to the music. The establishment consisted of twenty-four canons at this time, with eight minor canons and a number of chaplains, seventy beneficed clergy in all; the vestments were gorgeous, and there was an almost innumerable quantity of candles constantly burning, and yet the services were conducted in such an inaccurate and slovenly manner that they totally lacked distinction.

Vespers at the church of Our Lady were no better. There were more instrumental players, but these

flourish and scrape with as much violence as at our theatre, when Richard the Third enters, or the King of Denmark carouses; which, in my opinion, betrays a barbarous taste, and total want of decency.

At 6 p.m. the same evening

a splendid procession passed through the streets, in honour of some legendary saint [1]: consisting of a prodigious number of priests, who sung psalms in *canto fermo* (i.e. plain song), and sometimes in counterpoint (i.e. in parts), all the way to the church, with wax tapers in their hands, accompanied by French horns, and *serpents*; a large silver crucifix, and a *Madonna* and child, as big as the life, of the same metal, decorated this solemnity.

The Spaniards have left this good people a large portion of pride and superstition; the former is shewn by the dress and inactivity of the nobles, and the latter by the bigotry and lively faith of the rest; there are more crucifixes and virgins, in and out of the churches here, than I ever met with in any other Roman Catholic town in Europe.

[1] Probably St. Margaret.

The procession above mentioned seemed to have been as much the occasion of riot and debauchery, among the common people, as. the *beer* and *liberty* with which an English mob is usually intoxicated on a rejoicing night in London; there were bonfires all over the town, and the huzzas, rockets, squibs, and crackers, were so frequent, and so loud, all night, in the *Place de Mer*, where I lodged, that it was impossible to sleep; and at two o'clock in the morning the mob was so vociferous and violent, that I thought all the inhabitants of the town had fallen together by the ears; and yet on other nights, no one of the citizens is allowed to walk in the streets later than half an hour after ten, without a particular permission from the governor.

The remainder of Dr. Burney's time was spent in interviews with the various organists in Antwerp and researches in the library of the Jesuits' College, where he discovered two fellow-countrymen. He was shown among other manuscripts a fine old copy of the Magna Charta.

In the Oostershuys, which was originally a warehouse of the Hanseatic merchants and had been used as barracks for two thousand men in the wars, Dr. Burney discovered some curious and interesting musical instruments. His account is worth quoting:

There are between thirty and forty of the common flute kind, but differing in some particulars; having, as they increase in length, keys and crooks, like oboes and bassoons; they were made at Hamburg and are all of one sort of wood, and by one maker; CASPER RAUCHS SCRATENBACH, was engraved on a brass ring, or plate, which encircled most of these instruments; the large ones have brass plates pierced, and some with

human figures well engraved on them; these last are
longer than a bassoon would be, if unfolded; The inhabitants say, that it is more than a hundred years since
these instruments were used, and that there is no musician,
at present, in the town who knows how to play on any
one of them, as they are quite different from those now
in common use. In times when commerce flourished in
this city, these instruments used to be played on every
day, by a band of musicians who attended the merchants,
trading to the Hansa towns, in procession to the exchange;
they now hang on pegs in a closet, or rather press, with
folding doors, made on purpose for their reception;
though in the great hall there still lies on the floor, by
them, a large single case, made of a heavy and solid dark
kind of wood, so contrived, as to be capable of receiving
them all; but which, when filled with these instruments,
requires eight men to lift it from the ground; it was of so
uncommon a shape, that I was unable to divine its use,
till I was told it.

Having exhausted the resources of Antwerp, Dr. Burney
returned to Brussels, where he spent the time in visiting
churches and going to plays and operas. On one occasion he
heard two French operettas given in Flemish; on another
evening he saw the Governor-General, Charles, Prince of
Lorraine (1712–1780) and his court in the theatre. Prince
Charles was the brother-in-law of Maria Theresa and the
hero of many battles during the Silesian and Seven Years'
Wars, though he was ultimately defeated by Frederick the
Great at Leuthen in 1757. At various periods of his life he
had served as Governor-General of the Austrian Netherlands,
and retired to Brussels in 1758 to resume his wise and liberal
administration, remaining there until his death.

From Brussels Dr. Burney passed on to Louvain, the last
town of importance in the Austrian Netherlands proceeding

eastwards from Brussels. The manuscripts in the famous library were in such disorder that he did not stop to research among them for material, as was his custom. He discovered, however, a fine violinist in the person of a certain Monsieur Kennis, and tells an amusing anecdote of a Homeric achievement of the local carilloneur, which is worth recording:

The solos he (i.e. Kennis) writes for his own instrument and hand, are so difficult, that no one hereabouts attempts them but himself, except M. Scheppen, the *Carilloneur*, who lately, piqued by the high reputation of M. Kennis, laid a wager, that he would execute upon the bells one of his most difficult solos, to the satisfaction of judges, appointed to determine the matter in dispute; and he gained not only his wager, but great honour by his success, in so difficult an enterprise.

Through Liège Dr. Burney proceeded to Maastricht, where he was entertained by the band of a Hessian regiment in Dutch pay, which played for some considerable time on the Place d'Armes, during the Retreat. The composition of this band is interesting. It consisted of oboes, clarionets, cymbals, big drum, side drums, and triangles; the quality of tone must have been very reedy and lacking in brilliance.

CHAPTER II

Up the Rhine

At Aix-la-Chapelle or Aachen, Dr. Burney heard German spoken for the first time on his tour, but otherwise there was nothing to interest him beyond the following ingenious method of decoration on the part of the inhabitants:

The passion for *carillons*, and chimes, seems here at an end; however, in the streets, through which a procession had lately passed, there were hung, to festoons and garlands, a great number of oblong pieces of glass, cut and tuned in such a manner, as to form little peals of four and five bells, all in the same key, which were played on by the wind. In walking under them, I was some time unable to discover from whence the sounds I heard proceeded; they are hung so near each other, as to be put in contact by the most gentle breeze, which may truly be called the *Carilloneur*.

On the way to Cologne, Dr. Burney was detained for a short time in a post-house at a place he calls Juliers, meaning thereby probably Jülich. Here he was much entertained by two vagabonds

who, in opposite corners of the room, imitated, in dialogue, all kinds of wind instruments, with a card and the corner of their hats, so exactly, that if I had been out of

101

their sight, I should not have been able to distinguish the copy from the original; particularly in the clarionet, French horn, and bassoon, which were excellent. After this they *took off* the bellowing noise of the Romish priests, in chanting, so well, that I was quite frightened; for, being in a Catholic town, where the inhabitants are very zealous for the honour of their religion, I thought it might be imagined that this *ludere sacra*, was at the instigation of the English heretic.

Dr. Burney did not tarry long in Cologne, though, of course, he inspected the organ in the half-finished cathedral, but proceeded on his way through Bonn, all unconscious of the existence of an eighteen-months old baby who was living there in humble circumstances, and was one day to become the great Beethoven. There was no music in Bonn owing to the absence of the Elector of Cologne; and in Coblenz, faring no better, he comments on the complete absence of music among the Sunday crowds, which was so contrary to his experiences in other Roman Catholic countries. He decided, therefore, to try his luck elsewhere, as so far his journey had produced nothing of importance. Crossing the Rhine, he successfully traversed " the terrible mountains of Wetteravia ", presumably the Taunus mountains, and arrived in Frankfurt-am-Main more exhausted even than he had been after crossing Mount Cenis.

Frankfurt, however, was similarly barren, though there was music to be heard in the streets:

In the streets, at noon, there was likewise a number of young students singing Hymns in three or four parts, attended by a chaplain; these are poor scholars designed for the church, who in this manner excite the benevolence of passengers, that contribute towards their clothing.

At the inn, called the Roman Emperor, where I lodged, after dinner there was a band of street musicians, who played several symphonies reasonably well, in four parts. All this happened on a day which was not a festival, and therefore it is natural to believe, that the practice is common.

Dr. Burney examined the organ in the great church of St. Bartholomew, which was vilely out of tune, " and the touch so heavy, that the keys, like those of a *carillon*, severally required the weight of the whole hand, to put them down ". It is interesting to note that this organ possessed a contrivance for transposing half a tone, a whole tone, or a minor third higher than its normal pitch. The choir in this church contained a number of girls, many of whom were Protestants, and, though the church belonged to the Roman Catholics, the steeple was in the possession of the Lutherans, who maintained a guard in it constantly,

a precaution, which, in peaceable times, *is said* to be used in order to give the alarm, in case of fire; but, in war, they make no scruple to confess, that it is to watch the motions of the Catholics, from whom they are in fear of a massacre.

The relations of the various religious bodies in Frankfurt at this time are difficult to comprehend. The Lutherans and Calvinists apparently assisted at the Roman Catholic services, in spite of the alleged purpose of the steeple guard. The Calvinists indeed were not allowed a place of worship in the city itself at all, but possessed a church at Bockenheim, some little distance away.

Dr. Burney soon went on his way through Darmstadt to Mannheim. As he was leaving his chaise in the former place the landgrave's guards came on parade. The band was one of the best he had ever heard: it consisted of four oboes, four clarionets, six trumpets, three on either side of the oboes and clarionets; on either side of the trumpets there were two bassoons, and in the rear a line of cornets and clarions; the cornets had no connexion with the modern brass instrument,

but were coarse-toned, leather-covered wooden instruments
of the Serpent family.   Naturally the effect produced was
considerably more brilliant than that of the bands which Dr.
Burney heard in St. Omer and Ghent, though he was surprised that the shrill and piercing tone of the trumpets and
clarions did not hurt his ears by the violent shock of sound.
This he attributes to the fact that the parade or square where
they mounted guard was so large that there was plenty of room
for the sound to expand.

It is not easy for us in the twentieth century to visualize
the inconveniences and discomforts of the traveller in the
eighteenth. The limitations of a journey in a post-chaise over
villainous roads are readily appreciated, but the perpetual
annoyance of constantly passing from one country into
another, with different monetary systems, exchanges, and
custom tariffs, is apt to be overlooked. The reference in the
following description to beggars reads strangely to those
who have been in modern Germany, where mendicancy is
or was conspicuously absent. For this the extravagance of
the small courts and the attendant miseries of the common
people, ground down by taxation, were directly responsible,
evidence of which will not be lacking in Dr. Burney's account
of his travels across Germany:

Before I proceed further in my musical narrative, I
must make two or three memorandums concerning the
villainous and rascally behaviour of postmasters and
postilions, in this part of the world; the effects of which
it is impossible to escape. In going over the mountains
of Wetteravia, under the pretence of bad roads, *three*
horses were tied to the hurdle, called a post-chaise, and
after I had once submitted to this imposition, I never
was allowed to stir with less. At Frankfurt I tried hard,
but in vain, though the innkeeper and his guests, who
were natives, all assured me, that they never had more
than two horses, when they travelled *extra post*; yet
here, though no mountains were to be crossed, the

sands were made a plea, notwithstanding the roads from Frankfurt to Mannheim are, in every particular, the least bad of any that I had yet travelled in Germany.

The women, among the common people in the country, are miserably ugly, not, perhaps, so much in feature, as from dress, and a total neglect of complexion. They entirely hide their hair, by a kind of a skull-cap, usually made of tawdry linen or cotton; they are hardly ever seen with shoes and stockings, though the men are furnished with both, such as they are.

I could wish to speak of these people with candour and temper, in despite of the bile which every stranger, travelling among them, must feel at work within him; but, as I neither mean to abuse nor flatter them, I must say, that the numberless beggars, clamorously importunate, though often young, fat, robust, and fit for any labour; the embarrassments of perpetual change and loss of money; the extortion, sullenness, and insolence of postmasters and postilions, are intolerably vexatious.

By 6th August we find Dr. Burney in Mannheim, but the Elector Palatine [1] was at Schwetzingen for the summer, and the town was therefore empty. Dr. Burney procured lodgings on the *Place d'Armes*, and the first music which he heard in Mannheim was the retreat played by drums and fifes, which provoked the following observation:

If I had had an inclination to describe, in a pompous manner, the effects of wind instruments in martial music, there had been no occasion to quit London; for at St. James's, and in the Park, every morning, we have now an excellent band; and hitherto, as I had not seen more

[1] Charles Theodore, who reigned from 1743 to 1799 and in 1778 became Elector of Bavaria.

soldierlike men in any service than our own, so the music and musicians, of other places, exceeded ours in nothing but the number and variety of the instruments; our military music at present must seem to have made great and hasty strides towards perfection, to all such as, like myself, remember, for upwards of twenty years, no other composition made use of in our footguards, than the march in Scipio [1], and in our marching regiments, nothing but side-drums.

During the absence of the Elector, a strolling company were permitted to provide entertainment for the citizens of Mannheim. Performances were given in a temporary booth, constructed of deal boards, in the market-place. The stage, however, was well decorated, and the scenery and dresses tasteful and elegant. On the night when Dr. Burney was present, a French opera, translated into German, was given. This was his first experience of the theatre in Germany, and he is enthusiastic in his praise of the singing, and considers the German language much better suited for music than the French. The orchestra, however, was very inferior, all the most eminent players having gone away with the Elector.

Dr. Burney was much impressed by the neatness and beauty of eighteenth century Mannheim, but he was aware of the rottenness under the veneer:

The expense and magnificence of the court of this little city are prodigious; the palace and offices extend over almost half the town; and one half of the inhabitants, who are in office, prey on the other, who seem to be in the utmost indigence.

After a day spent in the public library, where he found nothing of interest, Dr. Burney went on to Schwetzingen, where the electoral court was in residence. Here the Elector maintained one of those miniature imitations of Versailles,

[1] An opera of Handel, which appeared in 1726.

the relics of which may still be found scattered about near many of the old capital cities in Germany:

The going out from the opera at Schwetzingen, during summer, into the electoral gardens, which, in the French style, are extremely beautiful, affords one of the gayest and most splendid sights imaginable; the country here is flat, and naked, and therefore would be less favourable to the free and open manner of laying out grounds in English horticulture, than to that which has been adopted. The orangery is larger than that at Versailles, and perhaps than any other in Europe.

His electoral highness's suite at Schwetzingen, during summer, amounts to fifteen hundred persons, who are all lodged in this little village, at his expense.

To anyone walking through the streets of Schwetzingen, during summer, this place must seem to be inhabited only by a colony of musicians, who are constantly exercising their profession: at one house a fine player on the violin is heard; at another, a German flute; here an excellent oboe; there a bassoon, a clarionet, a violoncello, or a concert of several instruments together. Music seems to be the chief and most constant of his electoral highness's amusements; and the operas, and concerts, to which all his subjects have admission, form the judgment and establish a taste for music, throughout the electorate.

Into this musician's " El Dorado " Dr. Burney came with great expectations, for the electoral orchestra had an international reputation second to none. Under Stamitz and later under Cannabich, who was one of the principal violinists at the time of Burney's visit, the orchestra, formed largely of

celebrated virtuosi, achieved a height of perfection un-
paralleled in the eighteenth century.

The influence of the Mannheim orchestra on music cannot
be overestimated. The crude amateurishness of the average
eighteenth century orchestra, composed largely of domestic
servants or others engaged in menial occupations in the
houses of the great, imposed severe restrictions on composers
of that day. The Mannheim orchestra made possible the
finer subtleties of orchestral writing with which we are
familiar to-day, and on no one did its influence fall more
directly than on Mozart, who during the winter of 1777–1778
remained at the electoral court, revelled in its wonderful
orchestra, and made friends with Cannabich, the conductor,
and his colleagues. Mozart's letters to his father bear abundant testimony to the excellencies of the Mannheim orchestra,
of which Dr. Burney's account affords interesting corroboration.

His eagerness, however, to hear the Mannheim players perform made him forget the rigorous etiquette of the small
German courts. The first few days were spent in visiting and
receiving visits, and only then was there hope that his request
might be granted:

Travelling is not very common in this country; and
people here, like the English, are shy of strangers, and
wishing to shake them off. In France, and Italy, the
inhabitants are used to do the honours, and do them
well. As to my particular enquiries here, which, in fact,
concerned their honour more than my own, I gained but
little assistance; it was difficult to discover who *could*
afford me any, and much more to find those that *would*.
I sometimes wished to employ the town crier, at my
first entrance into a German city, to tell the musical
inhabitants who I was, and what I wanted; for it frequently happened, where His Majesty had no minister,
that I was on the point of quitting a place before this
was known.

Dr. Burney, however, attended a performance of an Italian comic opera in the Elector's theatre, adjoining the palace, the singers being with one exception all Italian, and was very well pleased with the performance, especially with the ballet:

The Elector, Electress,[1] and princess royal of Saxony, were present at this performance. The theatre, though small, is convenient; the decorations and dresses ingenious and elegant, and there was a greater number of attendants and figurers than ever I saw in the great opera, either of Paris or London: in the dance, representing a German fair, there were upwards of a hundred persons on the stage at one time; but this opera is very inconsiderable, compared with that at Mannheim, in the winter, which is performed in one of the largest and most splendid theatres of Europe, capable of containing five thousand persons; this opera begins the fourth of November, and continues generally, twice a week, till Shrove Tuesday.

I was informed that the mere illuminations of the Mannheim theatre, with wax lights, cost the Elector upwards of forty pounds, at each representation; and that the whole expense of bringing a new opera on this stage, amounted to near four thousand pounds. The great theatre, the ensuing winter, was to be opened with an opera composed by Mr. J. Bach [2], who was daily expected here from London, when I was at Mannheim.

---

[1] Frederick August III (1750–1827), who later became the first King of Saxony. He succeeded to the electorate in 1763. His consort was the Princess Mary Amelie of Zweibrucken. Dr. Burney was presented to the Elector and Electress during his stay in Dresden (see Chapter IX).

[2] Johann Christian Bach (1735–1782), eleventh son of the great Johann Sebastian Bach, is often called the "English Bach". He was sometime organist of Milan Cathedral, but eventually settled in London, where he became a friend of Dr. Burney. He was a well-known figure in London, and composed a number of popular operas.

I cannot quit this article, without doing justice to the orchestra of his electoral highness, so deservedly celebrated throughout Europe. I found it to be indeed all that its fame had made me expect: power will naturally arise from a great number of hands; but the judicious use of this power, on all occasions, must be the consequence of good discipline; indeed there are more solo players, and good composers in this, than perhaps any other orchestra in Europe; it is an army of generals, equally fit to plan a battle, as to fight it.

But it has not been merely at the Elector's great opera that instrumental music has been so much cultivated and refined, but at his *concerts*, where this extraordinary band has " ample room and verge enough ", to display all its powers, and to produce great effects without the impropriety of destroying the greater and more delicate beauties, peculiar to vocal music; it was here that Stamitz [1] first surpassed the bounds of common opera overtures, which had hitherto only served in the theatre as a kind of court crier, with an " O yes!" in order to awaken attention, and bespeak silence, at the entrance of the singers. Since the discovery which the genius of Stamitz first made, every effect has been tried which such an aggregate of sound can produce; it was here that the *Crescendo* and *Diminuendo* had birth; and the *Piano*, which was before chiefly used as an echo, with which it was generally synonymous, as well as the *Forte*, were found to be musical *colours* which had their *shades*, as much as red or blue in painting.

[1] Johann Karl Stamitz (1719–1761) is the most famous member of a renowned family of musicians. He entered the service of the Elector in 1745 as leading violin in the orchestra and remained there till his death. He was also a distinguished composer.

I found, however, an imperfection in this band, common to all others, that I have ever yet heard, but which I was in hopes would be removed by men so attentive and so able; the defect, I mean, is the want of truth in the wind instruments. I know it is natural to those instruments to be out of tune [1], but some of that art and diligence which these great performers have manifested in vanquishing difficulties of other kinds, would surely be well employed in correcting this leaven, which so much sours and corrupts all harmony. This was too plainly the case to-night, with the bassoons and oboes, which were rather too sharp, at the beginning, and continued sharper to the end of the opera.

My ears were unable to discover any other imperfection in the orchestra, throughout the whole performance; and this imperfection is so common to orchestras, in general, that the censure will not be very severe upon this, or afford much matter for triumph to the performers of any other orchestra in Europe.

The Elector, who is himself a very good performer on the German flute, and who can, occasionally, play his part upon the violoncello, has a concert in his palace every evening, when there is no public exhibition at his theatre; but when that happens, not only his own subjects, but all foreigners have admission gratis.

No wonder his poor subjects were in a state of indigence: the sums extorted from this small state to keep such a large

[1] This tranquil acceptance of the fact is striking evidence of the widely differing standards whereby the qualities of the old orchestras and those of to-day must be judged. It is evident from Dr. Burney's account that even the celebrated Mannheim orchestra would sound intolerable to a modern audience, unaccustomed to making allowances for the rudimentary condition of the wind instruments of the period.

organization in working order must have been considerable, and the Elector, at his people's expense, was by no means ungenerous to his musicians:

Many of the performers on the court list, are either superannuated or supernumeraries; but of the former, after having served the Elector for a number of years, if by sickness or accident they happen to lose their voice or talents, they have a handsome pension, which they enjoy as long as they live at Mannheim; and even if they choose to retire into their own country, or elsewhere, they are still allowed half their pension.

The Elector was evidently one of those princely patrons of the arts who, like Ludwig II of Bavaria, Wagner's patron, did not scruple to plunge his country into ruin to satisfy his passion for music.

From the Palatinate Dr. Burney passed into Würtemberg, deviating somewhat from the direct road to Vienna in order to visit Ludwigsburg, where the Duke of Würtemberg was said to be in residence:

The German courts are so much dazzled by their own splendour, as to be wholly blind to what is doing at the distance only of a day's journey among their neighbours; hence, I never found, in any of them, exactly what report had made me expect . . . alas! after being roasted alive, and jumbled to death, in a *wagon*, which the Germans call a post-chaise, for fourteen or fifteen hours, while I travelled seventy-five miles; when I came to Ludwigsburg, I found the information which I had received so far from exact, that the duke of Würtemberg was at Grafeneck, thirteen leagues off, and scarce a musician of eminence left in the town.

CHAPTER III

Ludwigsburg and Augsburg

Despite his disappointment in finding Ludwigsburg deserted, Dr. Burney was fortunate enough to meet Christian Schubart (1743–1797), at this time organist of the Lutheran church, who gave him a great deal of interesting information relative to his inquiries. Schubart is perhaps only known to-day as the author of the words which Franz Schubert used for some of his most famous songs, for instance, " Die Forelle ". His name, however, crops up constantly in the musical history of the day, and, although a man of genius, his life was characterized by wildness and excess which led him into conflict with the civil authorities and eventually to a long term of imprisonment, which he underwent some years after his meeting with Burney. Their manner of conversation was singular, Burney speaking in Italian, Schubart in Latin, which was a living language to him. When Dr. Burney gave him a German translation of the plan of his *History of Music*, he translated it at sight into Latin. Dr. Burney, however, did not essay to answer him in Latin, remarking that his pronunciation of this language, even had he been fluent in it, would have been unintelligible to Schubart. He also played a great deal to Dr. Burney on the harpsichord, organ, pianoforte, and clavichord, and showed him the sights of Ludwigsburg.

And, in the evening, he had the attention to collect together, at his house, three or four boors, in order to let me hear them play and sing *national music*, concerning which, I had expressed great curiosity.

Dr. Burney considered Schubart the first really great harpsichord player whom he had met in Germany—he was grounded on the Bach school and possessed a perfect double shake, " which is obtained but by a few harpsichord players ". Dr. Burney was more than ever well disposed towards him, because Schubart was likewise the first to think Dr. Burney's project a matter of national importance.

The composition of the duke's orchestra is of interest, orchestras being at this time in a transitional stage; it consisted of the following players:

eighteen violins	four oboes
six violas	two flutes
three violoncellos	three horns
four double-basses	two bassoons.

The balance of tone would hardly be satisfactory to a present-day listener, who would be aware of an excess of oboe tone and feel the absence of the clarionets.

The opera ballet consisted of thirty-two male and female dancers; the singers were, of course, of the best that Italy could produce.

Upwards of ninety persons are on the pension list for these operas; but many are kept in it long after they become unfit for service; and it is likewise swelled with the names of persons of no great importance, such as instrument carriers, copyists, and bellows-blowers. . . . The theatre is immense, and is open at the back of the stage, where there is an amphitheatre, in the open air, which is sometimes filled with people, to produce effects in perspective.

Charles Eugene, Duke of Würtemberg (1728–1793), himself a good harpsichord player, was even more prodigal in his expenditure on music than the Elector Palatine, but at the time of Dr. Burney's visit to Ludwigsburg the purse-strings had been considerably tightened. During the régime of the great Jomelli (1714–1774), whom Dr. Burney met in

Naples on his previous tour, the music at the duke's court had been for seven years the most renowned in Germany,

indeed the expense so far exceeded the abilities of his subjects to support, that the Germans say the duke of Würtemberg's passion for music was carried to such excess as to ruin both his country and people, and to oblige his subjects to remonstrate against his prodigality at the diet of the empire.

At present his highness seems economizing, having reformed his operas and orchestra, and reduced a great number of old performers to *half* pay: but, as most musicians have too great souls to live upon their *whole* pay, be it what it will, this reduction of their pensions is regarded, by the principal of those in the service of this court, as a dismission; so that those who have vendible talents, demand permission to retire, as fast as opportunities offer, for engaging themselves elsewhere. . . .

However, his economy is, I believe, more in appearance than reality; for at *Solitude*, a favourite summer palace, he has, at an enormous expense, established a school of arts, or Conservatorio, for the education of two hundred poor and deserted children of talents; of these a great number are taught music, and from these he has already drawn several excellent vocal and instrumental performers, for his theatre: some are taught the learned languages, and cultivate poetry; others, acting and dancing. Among the singers, there are at present fifteen Castrati, the court having in its service two Bologna surgeons, expert in this vocal manufacture. At Ludwigsburg there is likewise a Conservatorio for a hundred girls, who are educated in the same manner, and for the same purposes; the building constructed at *Solitude*, for the reception of the boys, has a front of six or seven hundred feet.

It is the favourite amusement of the duke of Würtemberg to visit this school; to see the children dine, and take their lessons. His passion for music and shows, seems as strong as that of the emperor Nero was formerly. It is, perhaps, upon such occasions as these, that music becomes a vice, and hurtful to society; for that nation, of which half the subjects are stage-players, fiddlers, and soldiers, and the other half beggars, seems to be but ill governed. Here nothing is talked of but the adventures of actors, dancers, and musicians.

The provision of music for their prince was not the only burden, which lay heavily upon the unfortunate Würtembergers:

The most shining parts of a German court, are usually its *military*, its *music*, and its *hunt*. In this last article the expense is generally enormous; immense forests and parks, set apart for a prince's amusement, at the expense of agriculture, commerce, and, indeed, the necessaries of life, keep vast tracts of land uncultivated, and his subjects in beggary.

The duke's sole economy was apparently in the provision of military music, no other instruments being employed except trumpets, drums, and fifes. What the soldiers lacked in this respect was, however, duly compensated for in every other direction:

The soldiery of this prince's present capital are so numerous, consisting never of less than six thousand in time of peace, that nothing like a gentleman can be seen in the streets, except officers. The soldiers seem disciplined into clockwork. I never saw such mechanical exactness in animated beings. One would suppose that the author of *Man a Machine* [1], had taken his idea from these men: their appearance, however, is very formidable; black whiskers, white peruques, with curls at the sides, six deep; blue coats, patched and mended with great ingenuity and diligence. There are two spacious courts, one before, and one within the palace, full of military.

Ludwigsburg was not, of course, the rightful capital of Würtemberg, but had been the residence of the sovereign for ten years prior to Dr. Burney's visit, Stuttgart being deserted:

It is no uncommon thing, in Germany, for a sovereign prince, upon a difference with his subjects, to abandon the ancient capital of his dominions, and to erect another at a small distance from it, which, in process of time, not only ruins the trade, but greatly diminishes the number of its inhabitants, by attracting them to his new residence: among the princes who come under this predicament, are the elector of Cologne, removed to *Bonn*; the Elector Palatine, removed from Heidelberg, to *Mannheim*; and the duke of Würtemberg, from Stuttgart to *Ludwigsburg*.

The ground upon which this town is built, is irregular and wild, yet it contains many fine streets, walks, and houses. The country about it is not pleasant, but very

---

[1] Attributed to Jean Baptiste de Boyer, Marquis d'Argens (1704–1771), " one of those writers who contributed to the general desolation of government, religion and morals ". *Man a Machine* was published in London in 1749, and D'Argens publicly repudiated authorship of the book by an advertisement in the *General Advertiser*, dated Potsdam 3rd October of that year (see Watt, *Bibliotheca Britannica*).

fertile, especially in vines, producing a great quantity of what is called Neckar wine.

Beyond the public library there was nothing in Ludwigsburg to detain Dr. Burney further, and the library contained little to interest him. He was, however, able to indulge his interest in astronomy, as the librarian showed him a wonderful orrery which the duke had recently purchased. It was invented and constructed by a certain M. Hahn, who was engaged for eighteen months in working upon it:

It is composed of three parts, that are put in motion by the weights of a common clock, which is wound up every eight days, and whose *pendulum* vibrates seconds.

In the middle part are three dials, placed perpendicularly.

The upper one simply marks hours and minutes.

The next, in which are fixed the signs of the Zodiac, indicates the hours of the day, the days of the week, and the days of the month, without its ever being necessary to regulate the index, for the unequal number of days in different months.

And the last dial, upon the great circle, on which are distinguished the centuries of 8000 years, has two principal indices, one of which points out the present century, and the other, the present year.

Of the two collateral parts of this machine, that on the right hand represents the Copernican system; and that on the left, the apparent course of the heavenly bodies. These parts are put in motion, by the principal spring of the clock in the middle, and correspond so perfectly, that no variation in their movements, or in the different aspects of the heavenly bodies has ever been discovered;

and both have been found constantly conformable to the calculations of the most exact ephemeris.

This whole machine is so constructed, that without any risk of putting it out of order, or spoiling it, the reciprocal positions of the planets and constellations, such as they *will* be in any future minute, or such as they *have* been, in any one that is past, may be seen; so that this machine takes in all time; the past, present, and future; and is, not only an orrery for these times, but a perpetual, accurate, and minute history of the heavens for all ages.

Dr. Burney proceeded on his journey by way of Ulm, his ultimate goal being Vienna. The nearest and cheapest way from Ulm to Vienna would have been down the Danube, a journey of six hundred miles, but, apart from his disinclination for this method of transit, he was anxious to visit Augsburg and Munich. He therefore crossed the Danube and arrived in Augsburg in the early morning of 15th August, after travelling through the night. Nothing daunted, however, he went straight to the cathedral and heard mass and part of the sermon, it being the festival of the Assumption. The playing of a difficult violin concerto pleased him well enough, but he was upset by the " crude, equivocal, and affected modulation " of the organist; he also disliked the " rude and barbarous flourish of drums and trumpets at the elevation of the Host ".

There was nothing to delay Dr. Burney in Augsburg. He was much struck by the architectural beauties of the place and the picturesque clothes of its inhabitants:

The head-dress of the women here is very singular; they wear a kind of gold skull-cap; some a broad border of gold lace, and the rest filled up by work in different colours, but mostly all gold embroidery; and here, as well as throughout Bavaria, the Roman Catholic women constantly walk the streets with a rosary in their hands, which is a fashion and ornament here as much as an implement of devotion.

The contrast between the free cities of the Empire, of which Augsburg was one, and those cities which were capitals of the small component states is very striking. The free cities were musically arid, and apart from the organist and the organ, both of which varied in quality, there was usually nothing of interest. The distinction has of course long since disappeared, and Dr. Burney's observations thereon are therefore interesting. The free cities

are not rich, and therefore have not the folly to support their theatres at a great expense. The fine arts are children of affluence and luxury: in despotic governments they render power less insupportable, and diversion from thought is perhaps as necessary as from action. Whoever therefore seeks music in Germany, should do it at the several courts, not in the free imperial cities, which are generally inhabited by poor industrious people, whose genius is chilled and repressed by penury; who can bestow nothing on vain pomp or luxury; but think themselves happy, in the possession of necessaries. The residence of a sovereign prince, on the contrary, besides the musicians in ordinary of the court, church, and stage, swarms with pensioners and expectants, who have however few opportunities of being heard.

In an amusing digression Dr. Burney thus describes an adventure which befell him at Augsburg:

I had sent my servant, and, at present, my interpreter, Pierre, a Liegeois, that I had brought with me from Antwerp, to enquire out, while the mass was performing, the habitation of M. Seyfurth, to whom I had been recommended by a friend at Hamburg. I had desired him to return to the church when he had executed his commission, in order to conduct me back to my inn. I waited patiently till ten o'clock, when all the music was over, but no Pierre! I walked about the church, till I was tired, and ashamed to stay any longer, but no Pierre! I walked round the church, and up and down the streets in sight of it, for I durst venture no farther, not knowing even the *name* of my inn; and I had, indeed, very little language in which to explain my situation to these cold, and, in appearance, surly people. What could I do, but return to the church and walk about again? This I did till past two o'clock, when I feared being suspected as a stranger, of a design to rob the church of some of its treasures; but no Pierre! at length I was compelled to take courage, and try to make my circumstances known: I perused every idle countenance to discover good nature in it. I accosted several in vain, till an old beggar-man applied to me for relief; I gave him two or three *kreuzers*, and thought that " one good turn deserved another ". I recollected the having been set down by the post-wagon, on my arrival, at a post-house: there are several in large German cities. *Welches ist der Weg nach dem Posthaus, guter Freund?* here was a gibble-gabble, which ended with, *die Briefe?* meaning, was it the post-house for letters? *Nein*, said I, *der Postwagen nach Ulm gehet hierab—Ja, ja, ich verstehe Sie.* At length we found this house; but then I knew not either what to say or do. I blundered out as well as I could, that I wanted the *Haus* where my baggage had been carried in the morning. But could not recollect the word *Wirths*, an inn; it turned out to be the Lamb, *das Lamm*, and when I found it, my joy was as great as that of a good Christian pilgrim would have been in a Pagan country, at the sight of an *Agnus Dei*. Where should the faithful Pierre, my honest Liegeois, have been all this while, but on his bed, comfortably and fast asleep? and I did not discover, till two months after, that he had never sought Mr. Seyfurth, to whom I had sent him, but had deemed it easier to find a bed, and to make me believe he was out of town, than to wear out his shoes in strolling about a strange place, after a person, with whom he had no business which concerned himself. But, in order to make the disappointment somewhat more palatable to me, he said, that the gentleman was only gone to Munich, for a few days, and that I should certainly find him there.

CHAPTER IV

Munich

From Augsburg Dr. Burney passed on to Munich, where he spent nine delightful days in the congenial society of fellow-musicians, and basked in the patronage of one of the most musical courts in the Germany of that day. On his arrival on 16th August, he presented letters of introduction to the British Minister at the electoral court, who immediately put him in touch with the people who would be of greatest service to him in his quest for knowledge. Dr. Burney counted himself particularly fortunate in meeting Guadagni and Mingotti, both singers of international repute and well known to the English public. Their views on the English opera audiences of the day are interesting. Guadagni cherished feelings of bitterness because he had been hissed for " going off the stage, when he was encored, with no other design than *to return in character* "—and this when he was giving his services at the performance for nothing! In some respects, at any rate, we can show an advantage over our ancestors.

Signora Mingotti says too, that she was frequently hissed in England, for having the toothache, a cold, or a fever, to which the good people of England will readily allow every human being is liable, except an actor or a singer. I know that the public are infidels in these matters, and with reason, as their hearts are hardened by repeated imposition; but, however, notwithstanding the many *pseudo* colds and fevers among theatrical performers, it is just possible for these people to have *real* disorders, otherwise they would bid fair for immortality.

Dr. Burney spent a whole morning with Signora Mingotti, and he relates at length the story of her life, which, interesting as it would have been to contemporary readers, is not of sufficient moment to warrant inclusion here.[1] She likewise had her harpsichord specially tuned so that she might sing to him, and thus entertained him for four hours, and further organized two private concerts at which the élite of Munich performed for Dr. Burney's delectation. And this was only typical of the reception with which our traveller met on all sides.

Dr. Burney's first day was naturally devoted to the electoral library, to which he was conducted by the British Minister himself, but, as always, the cataloguing of the library was unsatisfactory, and the whole time was spent in making a list, running into twenty large folio sheets of paper, of works on music. The evening was spent with Guadagni and two singer friends, who dined and supped with Dr. Burney and regaled him with trios " sung in such a way, as one never can hope to hear in public, and the chances are many against it in private ", and also took him to hear a comic opera at the little theatre, which was graced by the presence of the Elector and his family.

On the third day Dr. Burney went out to Nymphenburg to dine with Guadagni. The château, one of the many German imitations of Versailles, was situated three miles outside Munich: its gardens

are reckoned the finest in Germany, and are really as beautiful as they can be made, with innumerable fountains, canals, *jets d'eau*, cascades, alleys, bosquets, straight rows of trees, and woods, where " Grove nods at grove ", in the true French style.

The court was in residence at Nymphenburg, and thither

---

[1] See Grove's *Dictionary of Music and Musicians* under "Mingotti"; the article is largely based on Dr. Burney's account.

resorted the principal musicians to provide the nightly concert. Resident at the court at this time was Maria Antonia,
the Electress-Dowager of Saxony, a daughter of the Emperor
Charles VII, and sister to the reigning Elector of Bavaria.
She was a great patron of music and celebrated throughout
Europe for her proficiency in the art. Two Italian operas by
this talented princess had been printed in Leipzig, and were
frequently performed all over Germany. She was responsible
for words and music alike:

This is bringing about a reconciliation between music
and poetry, which have so long been at variance, and
separated. Among the ancients, the poet and musician
were constantly united in the same person; but modern
times have few examples of such a junction, except in
this princess, and in M. Rousseau, who was not only
author of the poetry, but of the music of his little drama,
the *Devin du Village* [1]:

This " reconciliation " was short-lived, and, with the important exception of Wagner, few composers have since had
the self-confidence to write libretti for their own operas.

Guadagni immediately informed Dr. Burney on his arrival
in Nymphenburg that he had mentioned him and his mission
to this talented princess and her brother, and that Dr. Burney
was to be presented to the princess before dinner, and to the
Elector and the rest of the family afterwards.

Accordingly, about half an hour past one, a page came
to acquaint us that the Electress-Dowager was ready to receive us; and I was conducted through a great number
of most magnificent apartments, by Signor Guadagni, to
an ante-chamber, where we waited but a very short time,
before the Electress entered the *Salle d'Audience*, into
which we were called, and I was very graciously received.

[1] Which, it will be remembered, Dr. Burney had himself translated into English.

I had enquired into the *Etiquette* of this ceremonial: I was to bend the left knee upon being admitted to the honour of kissing her hand; after this was over, her highness entered into conversation with me in the most condescending and easy manner imaginable; she was pleased to speak very favourably of my undertaking, and to add, "that it was not only doing honour to music, but to myself, as she believed I was the only modern historian who thought it necessary to travel, in order to gain information at the source, without contenting myself with second-hand, and hear-say accounts". This strong compliment, joined to her gracious and pleasing manner, took off all restraint; she was just returned from Italy, where, she said, that "By the great hurry and fatigue of travelling and talking loud, as is customary at the *Conversazioni* there, she had almost totally lost her voice, which had been much debilitated before, by having had a numerous family, and several severe fits of sickness ".

Dr. Burney eventually prevailed on the princess to converse with him in English, which she spoke well, though "she had learned it of an Irishman, who had given her a vicious pronunciation". After a talk on matters musical, Dr. Burney kissed the hand of the princess and retired. He dined with his friend Guadagni and then went into the "*grande salle*", where the Elector and his court were dining. After dinner the Electress-Dowager presented Dr. Burney to her brother and the other members of the royal family.

The Elector [1] is a very handsome and gracious prince, has an elegant appearance, and a figure, which is neither too fat, too lean, too tall, nor too short, if I was not too

[1] Maximilian Joseph III, succeeded 1745, and reigned till 1777.

much dazzled by his condescension, to see any of his defects. . . .

He told me that mine was a very uncommon journey, and asked, if I was satisfied with what materials I had hitherto found. This afforded me an opportunity of telling him, what was most true, that in point of books on my subject, and ancient music, I had as yet met with nothing equal to his electoral highness's library; and I had reason, from the reputation of the performers, and eminent musicians in his service, to expect great satisfaction, as to modern practical music. . . .

At this time some wild beasts were brought to the palace gates, which all the company running to see, put an end, for the present, to our conversation.

At eight o'clock the Elector's band began to assemble for the private concert, in which the Elector himself and his sister took part, while the Electress of Bavaria and the ladies of the court played cards. After the concert the court supped in the great hall where they had dined. Dr. Burney had a further opportunity for conversation with the Elector, and was honoured with the promise of specimens of the Elector's church music, on condition that he refrained from printing them. But the final honour which awaited him—so characteristic of the century's attitude towards musicians—must be described in his own words:

The lords in waiting offered us refreshments; and the Elector condescended to ask Guadagni, if he gave a supper to the Englishman, and his other company? . . .; he answered, that he should give us bread and cheese, and a glass of wine. " Here," cried the Elector, emptying two dishes of game on a plate, " send that to your apartments." His highness was implicitly obeyed. We supped together, after which I returned to Munich, abundantly flattered and satisfied with the events of the day.

The remainder of Dr. Burney's stay was fully occupied with visits to the opera, to the Academy, and to musical parties arranged in his honour. M. de Visme, the British Minister, personally took him to the Jesuits' college, where eighty children of eleven or twelve years of age and upwards were taught music, reading, and writing. They were boarded free but not clothed, and the instruction was given by outside masters and not by the Jesuits themselves. The boys, who remained in the college till they reached the age of twenty, had to play some instrument or know the rudiments of music to qualify for admittance to the school. Certain of their number, designated "poor scholars" and intended for the church, received instruction in languages, mathematics, and theology. The Jesuits played a large part in the musical education of the day. Dr. Burney frequently met these "poor scholars" during his travels in Germany, and was puzzled by their proficiency in music. Throughout the empire, wherever the Jesuits were established, they founded these music schools, where young people were taught to sing and play, and many eminent musicians owed their early training to the enterprise of the Society of Jesus in this respect. The "poor scholars" of the Munich school paid Dr. Burney a pretty compliment in return for his visit:

In going home from the opera, I heard a very good concert in the street; it was performed at the door of M. de Visme, by torch-light, and attended by a great crowd: after I returned to my lodgings, I heard the same performers at the inn door; upon enquiring who they were, I was told, that they were *poor scholars*; but I did not discover till the next day, that this concert was intended, as a regale, for M. de Visme and me, on account of our having been at their college to inform ourselves concerning their institution.

Dr. Burney heard the " poor scholars " on another occasion playing in the streets at night. The little band consisted of violins, oboes, French horns, a violoncello, and bassoon. These public performances in the streets were an obligation laid upon the scholars in order that the public, at whose expense they were maintained, might judge of the progress which they were making.

Amongst the many other services which M. de Visme rendered Dr. Burney was an introduction to a Polish refugee, Prince Sapieha, who was staying at the sign of the Golden Hart, as was also Dr. Burney. They had already established a nodding acquaintance, and the information which the prince subsequently gave Dr. Burney regarding Polish national music was of the greatest value to him. Dr. Burney later heard that the poor prince had suffered the confiscation of all his Polish estates, as he refused homage to the then Empress of Russia, Catharine, who had recently possessed herself of Polish territory at the first Partition in 1772.

Dr. Burney found time for a second visit to the court at Nymphenburg, and was again received by the Elector and his sister. He received confirmation of the promise of specimens of their work from both illustrious composers.

The Elector at first made some difficulty, lest I should publish it; as his *Stabat Mater* had been stolen, and printed at Verona, without his permission, and would have been published, had not his highness purchased the plates, and the whole impression; but upon my assuring him that without licence I should never make any other use of the piece, with which he should honour me, than to enrich my collection of scarce and curious compositions, he was pleased to give orders for its being transcribed.

The Electress-Dowager told me that her disposition, in this particular, was different from her brother's; for, instead of concealing what she was able to produce, she took as much care to have it known, as the birth of a legitimate child; and had, accordingly, printed and published her two operas in score.

On this occasion Dr. Burney was presented to the Duchess of Bavaria, sister-in-law of the Elector and sister of the Elector Palatine, who expressed regret that Dr. Burney, for want of somebody to introduce him, had not been presented to her brother in Schwetzingen, seeing that they had such a strong common interest.

It was with great reluctance that Dr. Burney left Munich. He had rarely on his travels been so fêted and fussed over. Even on the day of his departure, the indefatigable Signora Mingotti arranged a small concert at nine in the morning, in order that he might hear two pupils of Tartini play the violin, whom he would otherwise have missed. He voices his appreciation of Munich in the following terms:

The city of Munich is one of the best built, and most beautiful in Germany; I am ashamed to mention all the honours and favours, which were undeservedly conferred upon me, during my short residence there. All that I can add to this article is, that I quitted it with great regret; as I had so numerous an acquaintance, and so many protectors, that I lamented the not being able to spare more time, to avail myself of their kindness and good offices.

On the afternoon of 24th August, Dr. Burney quitted Munich and began his seven-day journey by water to Vienna.

CHAPTER V

From Munich to Vienna by River

We have now reached one of the most entertaining episodes in Dr. Burney's Journals; there is throughout but scanty reference to the journey and modes of travelling; much which would seem remarkable to us, would naturally appear a commonplace to the writer. It is, however, from the more personal of Dr. Burney's experiences that we are best able to gauge the idiosyncrasies of his character, and from none in a greater measure than that which is about to be related. As far as possible the tale of Dr. Burney's woes shall be told in his own vivid narrative. In passing, it is noteworthy that he gives no hint of his reason for selecting this unconventional method of reaching Vienna, and one can only conclude that his natural curiosity overcame his discretion or that he was the victim of bad advice, if not of a practical joke.

I went from Munich to Vienna, down the two rivers Isar and Danube; and as the musical incidents during this voyage are but few, and no itinerary or book of travels, that I remember to have seen, has described the course of these rivers, or the method by which persons are conveyed upon them, from one place to another, I shall not scruple to add to my few musical memorandums, such other remarks and observations as I find set down in my miscellaneous journal.[1]

[1] An interesting account of the same journey will be found on p. 98 *seq.* of *A Ramble among the Musicians of Germany*, which appeared anonymously in 1828, the author being Edward Holmes, the schoolfellow of Keats and biographer of Mozart; the book is closely modelled on Dr. Burney's Journals, but has an independent interest.

The Isar, upon which the city of Munich is situated, and which empties itself into the Danube, about a hundred miles below, though very rapid, is too much spread and scattered into different channels, to be sufficiently deep for a bark or any kind of passage-boat, that has a bottom to float upon it. The current of this river is even too rapid for anything to be brought back against it; but Bavaria being a country abounding with wood, particularly fir, rafts, or floats made of those trees, lashed together, are carried down the stream, at the rate of seventy or eighty miles a day. Upon these rafts, a booth is built for passengers in common; but if anyone chooses to have a cabin to himself, he may have it built for about four florins. I preferred this, not only to avoid bad company and heat, but to get an opportunity of writing and digesting my thoughts and memorandums, being at this time very much in arrears with my musical journal.

I quitted Munich at two o'clock in the afternoon. The weather was intensely hot, and I was furnished with no means of tempering it; a clear sky and burning sun, reflected from the water, having rendered my fir cabin as insupportable as the open air. It was constructed of green boards, which exuded as much turpentine as would have vanquished all the aromatics of Arabia.

As I was utterly ignorant of the country, through which I was to pass, and the accommodations it would afford, all that my foresight had suggested to me, in the way of furniture and provisions, were a mattress, blanket, and sheets; some cold meat, with bread, and a bottle of wine; there was water in plenty always at hand. But I soon found myself in want of many other things; and, if I were ever to perform this voyage again, which I hope will never happen, experience would enable me to render the cabin a tolerable residence, for a week or ten days.

In quitting Munich by water, the city is a beautiful object; but the country we passed through is a wretched one, to all appearance; there being nothing but willows, sedge, sand, and gravel in sight. The water was so shallow in several places, that I thought our float would have stuck fast. At six o'clock we arrived at Freising, the see and sovereignty of a prince bishop; his palace is placed on a high hill at a little distance from the town, which is on another hill, and looks very pretty from the water-side. I would not go on shore to pay for a bad bed and supper, with which I was already furnished in my cabin; my servant however went with the common company, which amounted to upwards of fifty persons, in order to get some fresh bread, but which the place did not afford.

There had been no rain in these parts of Germany for six weeks; but, when we arrived at Freising, I saw a little black cloud to the westward, which, in less than half an hour, produced the most violent storm of thunder, lightning, rain, and wind, that I ever remember to have seen. I really expected every moment, that the lightning would have set fire to my cabin; it continued all night with prodigious fury, so that my man could not get back, and I was left on the water, sole inhabitant of the float, which was secured by a hawser to a wooden bridge.

Two square holes were cut in the boards of my cabin, one on each side, by way of window; the pieces were to serve as casements, one of these was lost, so that I was forced to fasten with pins, a handkerchief against the hole, to keep out wind and rain; but it answered the purpose very ill, and moreover, it rained in, at a hundred different places; drop, drip, drop, throughout my little habitation, sometimes on my face, sometimes on my legs, and always somewhere or other. This, with the violent flashes of lightning and bursts of thunder, kept off drowsiness; luckily, perhaps, for I might have caught cold, sleeping in the wet. I had been told, that the people of Bavaria were, at least, three hundred years behind the rest of Europe in philosophy, and useful knowledge. Nothing can cure them of the folly of ringing the bells whenever it thunders, or persuade them to put up conductors to their public buildings; though the lightning here is so mischievous, that last year, no less than thirteen churches were destroyed by it, in the electorate of Bavaria. The recollection of this, had not the effect of an opiate upon me; the bells in the town of Freising were jingling the whole night, to remind me of their fears, and the real danger I was in. I lay on the mattress, as far as I could from my sword, pistols, watch-chain, and everything that might serve as a conductor. I never was much frightened by lightning before, but now I wished for one of Dr. Franklin's beds, suspended by silk cords in the middle of a large room.[1] I weathered it out till morning, without a wink of sleep; my servant told me, that the inn on shore was miserable; it rained into every room of the house, and no provisions could be found for these

---

[1] Benjamin Franklin was a prolific inventor, much interested in the prevention of damage by lightning; his inventions ranged from an improved type of domestic hearth to dishes for use on board ship, which would not spill in a storm.

fifty people, but black bread and beer, boiled up with two or three eggs.

At six, we got into motion, the rain and wind continuing with great fury, and from violent heat, the air grew so chill and cold, that I found it impossible to keep myself warm with all the things I could put on. For though I added to my dress a pair of thick shoes, woollen stockings, a flannel waistcoat, great coat and night cap, with all the warm garments in my possession, yet I was benumbed with cold.

We advanced for four hours through a dreary country, as far as I was able to descry, but the weather was so bad, that I could not often examine it. At ten o'clock some fir trees appeared, which enlivened the view, and at eleven, nothing else could be seen on either side. There was a very high and steep shore on the right, covered with firs, and on the left, trees scattered near the water, and groves at a distance. At eleven, the float stopped at Landshut, where the passengers dined. I stuck to my cabin and cold meat: if it had not rained in, I should have thought myself very well off; but, in my present circumstances, I was so uncomfortable, that I could not, for a long time, write a word in my journal books; the weather had so lowered my spirits, and stiffened my fingers; however, towards the afternoon, I made an effort, and transcribed many things from my tablets, which were full. At six o'clock, the float stopped at Dingolfing; in the evening I got a candle, which was a luxury denied to me the night before in the thunderstorm. Rain, rain, eternal rain, and wind made the water nothing less than pleasant.

The next morning was clear, but cold. The passengers
landed at Landau about ten; at one we entered the
Danube, which did not appear so vast a river here as I
expected. However, it grew larger as we descended: we
stopped at two o'clock at a miserable village, with a fine
convent in it, however. Here the wind became so violent,
that I thought every minute it would have carried away
both my cabin and myself; at three, it was determined
to stay here all night, as it was not safe to stir during
this wind; but as this seems, and is called, *Le Pays des
vents*, it was an exercise for patience to be stopped at a
place, where I had nothing to do. My provisions grew
short and stale, and there were none of any kind to be
had here!

I had suffered so much the night before, that I now
seriously set about contriving how to keep myself warm.
The blanket bought at Munich for me, by my knave, or
fool of a servant, and which I had not seen soon enough
to change, was a second-hand one, and so filthy, ragged,
and likely to contain all kinds of vermin, and perhaps
diseases, that hitherto I could not find in my heart to
touch it; however, cold and hunger will tame the proudest
stomachs. I put the blanket over the sheet, and was
gladdened by its warmth.

At three in the morning, the passengers were called,
and soon after the float was in motion; it was now a
huge and unwieldy machine, a quarter of a mile long,
and loaded with deals, hogsheads, and lumber of all kinds.
The sun rose very bright; but at six there was a strong
easterly wind, full in our teeth, and so great a fog, that
not a single object could be seen on either side the river.

When I agreed to live night and day, for a week, upon the water, I forgot to bargain for warm weather; and now it was so cold, that I could scarcely hold the pen, though but the 27th of August! I have often observed, that when the body is cold, the mind is chilled likewise; and this was now so much the case with myself, that I had neither spirits nor ideas for working at my musical journal.

At eight o'clock we stopped at Vilshofen, a sweet situation. Here is a wooden bridge, of sixteen arches, over the Danube. The hills on the opposite side of the town are covered with wood, and exceedingly beautiful. The fog was dissipated, and the sun now shone on them in great glory. There is a gentle visit here from the custom-house officers; the seals were cut off my trunk, being the last town in Bavaria. They threatened hard as to the severe examination I was to undergo upon entering Austria; however, I had little to lose, except time; and that was now too precious to be patiently parted with to these inquisitorial robbers.

At half an hour past nine we set off for Passau, in very fine weather, which revived my spirits, and enabled me to hold my pen. The Danube abounds in rocks, some above water, and some below, which occasion a great noise by the rapidity of the current, running over, or against them.

We met this morning a gang of boats, laden with salt, from Salzburg and Passau, dragged up the river by more than forty horses, a man on each, which expense is so great, as to enhance the price of that commodity above four hundred per cent. We did not seem to move so fast now as upon the Isar, which had frequent cascades; and sometimes the float dipped so deep, as to have three or four feet of water rush suddenly into my cabin.

On arriving at Passau, Dr. Burney disembarked in order to visit the cathedral, where he found much to interest him in the two organs. He was very impressed with the position of this imperial city:

This is the boldest, and at the same time the pleasantest situation, that I ever saw. The town is built on the side and summit of a steep hill, on the right of the Danube. There is a hill on the other side, answering to that on which the town is built; however, there are but few houses upon it. . . . At the end of this town is the confluence of three rivers; the Inn, on the right hand; the Ilz, on the left; and the Danube in the middle. After this junction, the Danube becomes more and more rapid: the shore on each side, for a considerable way below Passau, has hills and rocks as high as those at Bristol; but these are covered with spruce fir trees and box, and look much less terrible, though quite as high. These rocks deprived us of the sun at three in the afternoon. About four miles below Passau, Austria is on the left, and Bavaria on the right,[1] as far as Engelhardzsell, when we were fairly entered into Austria. Here is the custom-house with which I had been threatened, and which I approached with trepidation; but my trunk was not opened, and nothing was examined except my writing box, which the officers would have unlocked. A seal was, however, set on my trunk, which I hoped would have

[1] Surely a mistake: the Danube is at this point the international boundary, but the right bank belongs to Austria and the left to Bavaria.

enabled me to pass on to Vienna, without further plague, and then I expected to pay for all.

Thus far the Danube runs between two high mountains, and sometimes it is so compressed and shut up, as to be narrower than the Thames at Mortlake. The descent is often so considerable, that the water cannot be seen at the distance of a quarter of a mile, and sometimes the noise against rocks is as violent, and as loud as a cataract.

At the entrance into Austria the value of money is lowered; so that a silver piece, worth twelve *kreuzers,* in Bavaria, is instantly lowered to ten; a florin, of sixty kreuzers, becomes only worth fifty; a ducat of five florins, is lowered to four florins, twelve kreuzers; and a sovereign of fifteen florins, to twelve florins thirty kreuzers; a louis d'or, from eleven to nine florins, twelve kreuzers; and a great crown to two florins.

We went upwards of eight leagues, between two mountains, and stopped for the night, at a wretched place, which afforded no kind of refreshment; though I had indulged the hope of supplying myself here for two days to come, which being Friday and Saturday, among Austrian Catholics, I knew would be kept strictly *maigre*.

I had now filled up the chinks of my cabin with splinters, and with hay; got a new button to the door, reconciled myself to my filthy blanket, and made a pair of snuffers out of a chip of deal; but alas! the essential failed: this was all external, and I wanted internal comfort! the last bit of my cold meat was fly-blown, to such a degree, that, ravenous as I was, I threw it into the Danube; bread too, that staff was broken! and nothing but

Pumpernickel [1] was to be had here; which is so black and sour, as to disgust two senses at a time.

Friday morning, August 28th. This river continues running through the same woody, wild, and romantic country; which, to pass through, is pleasant and entertaining, to a stranger, but produces nothing, except firing, to the poor inhabitants. For fifty miles not a corn field or pasture is to be seen. Sheep, oxen, calves, and pigs, are all utter strangers in this land. I asked what was behind these mountains, and was answered, huge forests. At Ashach the country opens a little.

What an aggregate of waters is here! river after river, comes tumbling into the Danube, and yet it grows rather more deep than wide, by these accessions; but many small rivers detach themselves from it, and islands are frequently formed in the middle and sides of this world of waters: before we arrived at Linz, however, a flat fenny country appeared, with high mountains, covered with trees, at a distance.

The approach to this town (Linz), by water, is very beautiful. There is a road on each side the Danube, at the foot of high mountains and rocks, covered with trees, by which the river is again bounded. The castle is seen at a distance, and houses and convents, upon the summit of some of the highest hills, have a fine appearance. There is a bridge over the Danube of twenty very wide arches. The town is built on the summit and sides of high hills, and in situation much resembles Passau. The churches were shut up, as it was twelve o'clock when we arrived; however, I obtained permission to

[1] Rye bread.

enter the collegiate church, where I found a large organ.

There is such an appearance of piety here, as I never saw before in the most bigoted Catholic countries. All along the Danube, near any town, there are little chapels erected, at only twenty or thirty yards distance from each other, sometimes on the sides of these mountains, and in places too narrow for a footpath; [1] and I saw not a house in Linz that had not a Virgin or a saint, painted or carved, upon it.

I walked about the town for near two hours. It was market day, though but for poor stuff; as nothing eatable appeared, perhaps, because it was Friday, but " Brod ", vile cheese, bad apples, pears, and plums; and of other wares, only tape, toys, ordinary missals, and wretched prints of virgins and saints. I saw not a good shop in the town, though there are many showy and fine houses. Gable ends and pear-topped steeples, in the Bavarian style, are still in fashion here.

At Spielberg, which is only the shell of an old castle, upon a little island, is the first of the two waterfalls in the Danube, said to be so dangerous; however, now, there was nothing formidable in it but the noise.

Enns, a large city, is here in sight, upon the right hand; we went through an ugly country till it was dark; the river is sometimes like a sea, so wide that there is scarce any land in sight; at other times it is broken, and divided into small streams, by islands. The raft stopped at a hovel, on the left bank of the river, where the passengers landed, and spent the night. I remained in my

[1] These chapels are not sufficiently spacious to contain either persons or priest, they are only intended as receptacles for a crucifix or a Virgin. (Note by Dr. Burney.)

cabin, where, I believe, I was much better off, as to bed, than any of them; but, for provisions, we were all on a footing. Pierre, with great difficulty, clambered up the rocks, to a village, and procured me half a dozen eggs, with which he returned in triumph. But, alas! two of them were addled, and a third had a chicken in it; which, being fast day, I could not in conscience eat.

Saturday, we set off at five o'clock, but were stopped, after having gone three or four miles, by a violent fog, which rendered the navigation dangerous, among so many rocks, shoals, and islands. When this was dispelled, we soon reached Struden, which is situated in a wilder country than ever I saw in passing the Alps. Here is the famous waterfall and whirlpool, which the Germans so much dread, that they say it is the habitation of " der Teufel "; however, they had talked so much about it, that it appeared to me less formidable than I expected. The shooting London bridge is worse, though not attended with more noise.[1] The company prayed and crossed themselves most devoutly; but though it may, especially in winter, be a very dangerous pass in a boat, this raft may dip into the water, but it covers such a surface, that it cannot possibly either sink or be overset.

At Ips, a pretty town, with a new, handsome, and large *caserne*, or barrack, just by it, the country opens, and is very beautiful. Hereabouts they begin to make Austrian wine: the white wine is a pretty, pleasant sort, but small.

At Mölk, on the right of the Danube, is a most mag-

---

[1] Old London Bridge had twenty narrow arches, under which highly dangerous rapids formed. The present bridge was not opened till 1831.

nificent convent of Benedictines; it seems to cover two thirds of the town; the architecture is beautiful, and it has the appearance of being but lately built: here are vines all along the shore, on the left hand. Harvest was quite got in hereabouts; indeed there is but little appearance of agriculture in this wild country. I believe I remarked before, that the quantity of useless woods and forests, in several parts of Germany, indicate a barbarous and savage people; and, to say the truth, except in the great trading towns, or those where sovereign princes reside, the Germans seem very rude and uncultivated.

The country becomes more and more wild, as far as Stein. The rocks were often so high, on each side, as to prevent us from seeing the sun at two or three o'clock in the afternoon. At Stein there is a wooden bridge of twenty-five or twenty-six very wide arches, which leads to Krems, where the Jesuits have a most sumptuous college, beautifully situated on a hill; it has more the appearance of a royal palace, than anything that we can boast of in England. Stein is on the left, and Krems on the right hand of the Danube, going down. Here our float anchored for the night, though it was but five o'clock: indeed it had not stopped, except early in the morning, for the fog, the whole day. We had now near fifty miles to Vienna; and the scoundrel " Flossmeister " or waterman, assured me, and everybody at Munich, that we should certainly be there on Saturday night.

At Krems there is an immense organ, in the Jesuits' church. Here, and all the way to Vienna, the common people, in the public houses, and the labourers, at their work, divert themselves with singing in two, and sometimes more parts. Near Ips there was a great number of Bohemian women, whom we should call gipsies, on a pilgrimage to St. Mary " Tafel ", a church placed on the summit of a very high mountain, facing the town of Ips, on the other side of the Danube. No one could inform me why it was called St. Mary " Tafel "; but, in all probability, it had this appellation from the form of the mountain on which it is placed, which resembles a *table*. These women, however, did not sing in parts, like the Austrians, but in *canto fermo* [1], like the pilgrims that I heard in Italy, who were going to Assisi; the sound was carried several miles, by the stream and wind, down the river, upon· whose smooth surface it passed, without interruption.

Dr. Burney gives further instances of part singing among the soldiers and peasants, who were walking along the water-side, and the skill with which they performed:

It is not easy to account for this facility of singing in different parts, in the people of one country, more than in those of another: whether it arises in Roman Catholic countries, from the frequency of hearing music sung in parts, in their churches, I cannot say; but of this I am certain, that in England it costs infinite trouble, both to the master and scholar, before a young practitioner in singing is able to perform, with firmness, an under part to the most simple melody imaginable; and I never remember hearing the ballad singers, in the streets of London, or in our country towns, attempt singing in two different parts.

Had Dr. Burney less of the national habit of self-depreci-

[1] That is, plain-song, sung, of course, in unison.

ation, he would have mentioned in this connexion that his countrymen, two centuries earlier, in the palmy days of the Elizabethan madrigal composers, had been unrivalled in their ubiquitous talent for part singing. The England of Handel's day, however, had forgotten its ancient glories, and it would be unfair to expect from Dr. Burney an appreciation of the sixteenth century madrigal writers, when we of the twentieth century are only just beginning to assess them at their true value.

Sunday, August 30. This day was trifled away without getting to Vienna with the float, as I had been fully made to expect: an officer on board, tried with me to procure a land carriage for that purpose, but in vain. As we approached Vienna, the country became less savage. There are vineyards on the sides of all the hills, and large islands innumerable which divide the Danube.

Tulln is a little fortified town, with a *fine* church, and a *fine* convent, which, with a *fine* custom-house, usually constitute all the *finery* of Austria.

At Korneuburg, there is a very strong citadel, on the summit of an extreme high hill, which commands the river and city.

At Nussdorf, a village within three miles of Vienna, with nothing in it but a church and a custom-house, I was quite out of patience, at being told, that the float could not, as it was Sunday, on any account, enter Vienna. It was now but five o'clock, and the seventh day of my being immured in a sty, where, indeed I might have grown fat if I had had anything to eat; but that not being the case, hunger as well as loss of time, made me very impatient to be released; and after an hour lost in trying to procure a chaise, I at last got a miserable boat to carry me and my servant to Vienna.

This voyage added but little to my knowledge of German music, but a great deal to that of the people, and country through which I passed: indeed I had an opportunity of landing at every considerable town in the passage, where I visited the churches, though I had not time to make acquaintance with musical people, or to collect historical materials; but as to *national music*, perhaps the rude songs which I heard sung by the boors and watermen, gave me a more genuine idea of it, than is to be acquired from the corrupted, motley, and Italianized melody, to be heard in the capitals of this extensive country.

.   .   .   .

The approach to Vienna from the river, is not very unlike that of Venice, though there is much less water, for the Danube divides itself into three streams, about a mile and a half above the town; forty or fifty towers and spires may be seen from the water.

The custom-house did not disappoint my expectation of its being remarkably troublesome, particularly, in the article of *books*; all are stopped there, and read more scrupulously than at the inquisition of Bologna, in Italy; and mine, which, except music, were merely geographical and descriptive, were detained near a fortnight before I could recover them; and his excellency Lord Viscount Stormont, his majesty's ambassador at this court, afterwards told me, that this was the only thing in which it was not in his power to assist me. On entering the town, I was informed, that if a single book had been found in my *sac de nuit*, or travelling satchel, its whole contents would have been forfeited.

CHAPTER VI

Vienna

The sixteen days which Dr. Burney spent in Vienna rival in interest the period of his stay in Munich. Fully a third of the first volume of his second Journal is devoted to Vienna and its musical activities. Though Vienna had not attained the pre-eminence in music which it subsequently enjoyed in the days of Schubert and Beethoven, it was already distinguished by reason of the musical celebrities who had made it their home. Mozart was still living in Salzburg, and Joseph Haydn was away at Esterház, but Dr. Burney was fortunate enough to meet Gluck, by far the most original musical pioneer of the age, and further Metastasio, the famous poet, whose biographer he was to become. No less interesting to Dr. Burney were Hasse, one of the most popular opera composers of the century, and his wife, Faustina, the great operatic singer of Handel's day, whose rivalry with Cuzzoni wrought London society up to such a pitch of partisanship that opera for some years became impossible.

By way of prelude Dr. Burney entertains us with a few general remarks regarding Vienna:

This city, the capital of the empire, and residence of the imperial family, is so remote from England, has been so imperfectly described, by writers of travels, and is so seldom visited by Englishmen, that I should have presented my readers with a minute account of its public buildings and curiosities, if it had not furnished me with ample materials for a long article, relative to my principal subject, music, to which every other must give place. . . .

The streets are rendered doubly dark and dirty by their narrowness, and by the extreme height of the houses; but, as these are chiefly of white stone, and in a uniform, elegant style of architecture, in which the Italian taste prevails, as well as in music, there is something grand and magnificent in their appearance, which is very striking; and even many of those houses which have shops on the ground floor, seem like palaces above. Indeed the whole town and its suburbs, appear, at the first glance, to be composed of palaces, rather than of common habitations. . . .

The emperor's prerogative of having the first floor of almost every house in Vienna for the use of the officers of his court and army, is as singular in itself, as it is inconvenient to the inhabitants. The houses are so large, that a single floor suffices for most of the first and largest families in the city.

The inhabitants do not, as elsewhere, go to the shops to make purchases; but the shops are *brought to them*; there was literally a fair, at the inn where I lodged, every day. The tradespeople seem to sell nothing at home, but, like hawkers and pedlars, carry their goods from house to house. A stranger is teased to death by these chapmen, who offer to sale wretched goods, ill manufactured, and ill fashioned. In old England, it is true, things are very dear, but if their goodness be compared with these, they are cheap as dirt.

I must observe, that I have never yet found, in any country on the Continent, that the tradespeople, like many in England, could be trusted, without beating them down, and fixing the price of what is purchased of them, previous to possession. In London there is little danger of being charged unreasonably for anything that is had from a reputable shop, though the price is not asked, when the goods are sent for, nor paid, till the bill is brought in, perhaps a year after.

The British ambassador, Viscount Stormont [1], took a lively interest in Dr. Burney and his project, and was able to render him considerable assistance in the way of introductions. M. de Visme of Munich had prepared Lord Stormont for Dr. Burney's arrival, and explained to him the special nature of Dr. Burney's travels. Lord Stormont's help was of a practical nature: he had Dr. Burney to dinner on six occasions during his short stay, and offered him letters of introduction for Dresden, Berlin, and Hamburg. Further, Lord Stormont himself conducted Dr. Burney to the public library and presented him to the librarians, so that he received permission to go into the library at any time, even when it was shut to the public. The success of Dr. Burney's stay in Vienna was in a large part due to the kindly interest of his noble protector.

As ever, the theatre was Dr. Burney's first goal. He had intended to be present at an Italian burletta which the emperor and the Austrian archduchesses were to attend, but by mistake he went to the wrong theatre and witnessed a performance of Lessing's " Emilia Galotti " [2] instead. He was very disappointed that there was no singing in this piece, and seemed rather puzzled and shocked by the violence of the writing, little realizing that he was witnessing a masterpiece which was helping to revolutionize the German theatre and pave the way for the Romantic movement of the early nineteenth century; his comments are therefore interesting:

[1] David Murray, seventh Viscount Stormont (1727–1796), became second Earl of Mansfield on the death of his uncle, the great judge, in 1793. After being ambassador in Vienna, Stormont was transferred to Paris, and later held various appointments in the Government at home.

[2] Lessing (1729–1781) published "Emilia Galotti" in 1772; it was therefore a new play when Dr. Burney witnessed it.

I should suppose this play to have been well acted; there were energy and passion, and many speeches were much applauded; but I was so young at German declamation, that I could only catch a sentence now and then. However, I made out the drift of the piece, which very much resembles, in the catastrophe, that of Virginia.

After relating the plot of the play, Dr. Burney gives an extract from Lady Mary Wortley Montagu's description of a comedy at the same theatre in the year 1716, in the first volume of her letters, in which she comments unfavourably on the ribaldry of the actors and the licence of the author, and concludes as follows:

This ribald taste has taken another turn, and in tragedy seems now to exhale itself in impious oaths and execrations; for, in the piece of to-night, the interlocutors curse, swear, and call names, in a gross and outrageous manner. I know not, perhaps, the exact ideas annexed by the Germans to the following expressions, of " Bei Gott "; " Gott verdamm' ihn ", &c., but they shocked my ears very frequently. However, there is an original wildness in the conduct and sentiments of this piece, which renders it very interesting.

A large orchestra provided the overture and incidental music with admirable effect, employing compositions by Haydn amongst others:

This theatre is lofty, having five or six rows of boxes, twenty-four in each row. The height makes it seem short, yet, at the first glance, it is very striking; it does not appear to have been very lately painted, and looks dark; but the scenes and decorations are splendid. The stage had the appearance of being oval, which, whether it was produced by deception or reality, had a pleasing effect, as it corresponded with the other end of the theatre, which was rounded off at the corners, and gave an elegant look to the whole.

The indefatigable Dr. Burney went to the theatre again the next night, in spite of a tiring day. He visited the French theatre, and witnessed a German comedy,

or rather a farce of five acts: however, I should not suppose the piece to be without merit, as the natives seemed much pleased with it. This theatre is not so high as that at which I had been the night before, but it is still better fitted up; here the best places seem to be in the pit, which is divided in two parts, and all the seats are stuffed, and covered with red baize; the scenes were seldom changed during the piece; but the principal, that is, the scene of longest continuance, was flat in front, where there were two large folding doors, as in the French theatres, for the entrance and exit of the principal characters. At each side there was an elegant projection, in the middle of which there was likewise a door, used chiefly by the servants, and inferior characters. The comedy was often too grossly farcical; but there were scenes, as well as characters, of real humour, and one or two of the *Comédie larmoyante* kind, that were truly pathetic.

Premiums are now no longer given, as heretofore, in this theatre, to actors who voluntarily submit to be kicked and cuffed, for the diversion of the spectators. It is but a few years since, that bills were regularly brought in, at the end of each week; " So much for a slap on the face ";

" So much for a broken head; and so much for a kick on the breech ", by the comic actors. But, in process of time, the effect of these wearing out, it became necessary to augment their number, and force, in order to render the pleasure of the spectators more exquisite; till the managers, unable any longer to support so intolerable an expense, totally abolished the rewards of these heroic sufferings.

And now, since this *active wit* has ceased to be practised, it is observed that the theatre is not only more seldom crowded than formerly, but the audience is become more difficult to please. Indeed the consequences seem to have been so fatal, that many attribute the frequent bankruptcies of the managers to the *insufferable* dullness and inactivity of the performers.

To which Dr. Burney in a footnote adds the pious hope:

In consideration of their great utility, it is hoped that the worthy managers of our theatres do not let " the spurns and patient sufferings " of our pantomime clowns, go unrewarded at the end of the week.

Dr. Burney has again occasion to praise the performance of the theatre orchestra and the merit of the music which it played. At the end of the performance there was " a very spirited and entertaining dance ", in which the four principals particularly distinguished themselves.

Three large boxes are taken out of the front of the first row, for the imperial family, which goes frequently to this theatre; it was built by Charles the Sixth [1]. The empress queen [2] continues in weeds, and has appeared

[1] 1685–1740.
[2] Maria Theresa (1717–1780 , who reigned jointly with her son, Joseph II.

in no public theatre since the death of the late emperor [1].

On the occasion of Dr. Burney's second visit to the German
theatre, he was fortunate enough to see the imperial family.
The opera, which started at 6.30 p.m., was by Salieri, and
Dr. Burney was delighted to find in the principal woman
singer one of the Baglioni sisters, whom he had heard both at
Milan and Florence on his previous tour. Her voice seemed
greatly improved,

but I cannot attribute all the improvement I now found
in her voice to time; something must be given to the
difference of theatres; those of Florence and Milan, are
at least twice as big as this at Vienna, which is about the
size of our great opera house, in the Haymarket [2]. . . .

The size of this theatre may be nearly imagined, by
comparing with any one of our own, the number of
boxes and seats in each. There are in this five ranks of
boxes, twenty-four in each; in the pit there are twenty-
seven rows of seats, which severally contain twenty-four
persons.

The emperor [3], the archduke Maximilian, his brother, [4]
and his two sisters, the archduchesses Marianne, and
Mary Elizabeth [5], were all at this burletta. The box, in
which they sat, was very little distinguished from the
rest; they came in and went out with few attendants,
and without parade. The emperor is of a manly fine
figure, and has a spirited and pleasing countenance; he

[1] Her husband, Francis I, whom she married in 1736. He died in August, 1765.
[2] Erected in 1702 and rebuilt in 1767.
[3] Joseph II (1741–1790). Michael Kelly says: "He (Joseph) was passionately fond
of music, and a most excellent and accurate judge of it."
[4] Maximilian (1756–1801) subsequently became Elector of Cologne.
[5] Marianne was the eldest daughter of the Empress Maria Theresa. She was
appointed head of an abbey in Prague which had been founded and largely endowed
by her mother. Elizabeth was the third daughter, and at one time was regarded as
a possible second wife for Louis XV.

often changes his place at the opera, to converse with different persons, and frequently walks about the streets without guards, seeming to shun, as much as possible, all kinds of unnecessary pomp. His imperial majesty was extremely attentive during the performance of the opera, and applauded the Baglione several times very much.

Dr. Burney furnishes some interesting details regarding the prices of admission to the theatre:

The admission into this theatre is at a very easy rate; twenty-four *kreuzers* only are paid for going into the pit; in which, however, there are seats with backs to them. A *kreuzer* here, is hardly equal to an English halfpenny; indeed, part of the front of the pit is railed off, and is called the amphitheatre; for places there, the price is doubled, none are to be had for money, except in the pit and the slips, which run all along the top of the house, and in which only sixteen *kreuzers* are paid. The boxes are all let by the season to the principal families, as is the custom in Italy.

Dr. Burney only appears to have had time for one more visit to the opera, and of this he says very little, complaining bitterly of the custom in Germany of omitting the names of the singers in the Italian operas from the programmes. Towards the end of his stay he attended an afternoon performance of " Romeo and Juliet "

new written, by M. Weisse [1]. The first act was almost over when I arrived; but I soon found that it was not a translation of Shakespear, by the small number of characters

---

[1] Christian Felix Weisse (1726–1804). He " remodelled " both " Romeo and Juliet " and " Richard III " to conform with the fashionable French classical drama of the day.

in it; there being only eight in this tragedy, and in the English one of the same name, there are upwards of twenty.

The personages introduced by M. Weisse are Montecute, Capulet, lady Capulet, Romeo, Julie, Laura a Confidant, instead of the Nurse, Benvoglio a physician, who supplies the place of Friar Laurence, and Peter a servant to Romeo, instead of Balthasar.

Though the speeches and scenes were long, the four first acts were very affecting; but the performance both of poet and actors in the last act was abominable. There was no procession; but Juliet, dead at the end of the fourth act, is found buried at the beginning of the fifth. The tomb scene was bad, ill written and ill acted; and there was so much confusion, at last, that it was impossible to find out whether Romeo lived or died. He swallowed poison, indeed, which had racked, tortured and deprived him of his senses; but, as the doctor plied him well with drops, and a smelling bottle, he recovered just enough to say " Juliet! Oh, my Juliet "—" *Julie! Oh meine Julie!*" and the curtain dropped.

Dr. Burney was greatly impressed by the fact that there was no serious opera in Vienna either at the court or in the public theatres, though he admits the city " to be, among German cities, the imperial seat of music, as well as of power ". But this strange defect in so musical a city was of recent origin:

Lady Mary Wortley Montagu mentions an opera that was performed in the open air, when she was at Vienna, the decorations and habits of which cost the emperor thirty thousand pounds sterling; and, during the reigns of the late emperors, from the first years of Leopold [1], to the middle of the present century, there used to be operas at the expense of the court, written, composed, and performed, by persons of the greatest abilities that could be assembled from all parts of Europe: but the frequent wars, and other calamities of this country,[2] have so exhausted the public treasure, and impoverished individuals, that this expensive custom is now,

> " To my mind,
> More honoured in the breach, than the observance ".

For though I love music very well, yet I love humanity better.

There are several further interesting references in Dr. Burney's Journal to the imperial family and the important part which its members played in musical Vienna. Of Maria Theresa herself he writes as follows:

M. L'Augier told me that the empress queen had been a notable musician. Some years ago he had heard her sing very well; and in the year 1739, when she was only twenty-two years of age, and very handsome, she sung a *duo* with Senesino [3], at Florence, so well, that by her voice, which was then a very fine one, and graceful and steady manner, she so captivated the old man, Senesino, that he could not proceed without shedding tears of satisfaction. Her imperial majesty has so long been a performer, that, the other day, in pleasantry, she told the

---

[1] Leopold I (1640–1705).
[2] Notably the War of the Spanish Succession (1701–1713) and the struggle with Prussia, culminating in the Seven Years' War (1756–1763).
[3] (c.1680–1750). The great male soprano, who sang in many of the London performances of Handel's operas under the composer's direction.

old Faustina [1], the wife of Hasse, who is still living, and upwards of seventy years of age, that she thought herself the first, meaning the oldest, *virtuosa* in Europe; for her father [2] brought her on the court stage, at Vienna, when she was only five years old, and made her sing a song.

Dr. Burney's informant, M. L'Augier,

in despite of uncommon corpulency, possesses a most active and cultivated mind. His house is the rendezvous of the first people of Vienna, both for rank and genius; and his conversation is as entertaining, as his knowledge is extensive and profound.

He was very attentive to Dr. Burney, and besides arranging a musical party expressly for him, of which more anon, he was able to give Dr. Burney a good deal of valuable first-hand information regarding contemporary musicians:

He has been in France, Spain, Portugal, Italy, and Constantinople, and is, in short, a living history of modern music. In Spain he was intimately acquainted with Domenico Scarlatti [3], who, at seventy-three, composed for him a great number of harpsichord lessons which he now possesses, and of which he favoured me with copies. . . . They were composed in 1756, when Scarlatti was too fat to cross his hands as he used to do, so that these are not so difficult, as his more juvenile works, which were made for his scholar and patroness, the late queen of Spain, when princess of Asturias.

---

[1] (1700–1783). Another of Handel's great singers, and at one time the rival of Cuzzoni for the favour of the London patrons of opera.

[2] The Emperor Charles VI.

[3] 1685–1757. A great harpsichord player, and one of the first composers to exploit the possibilities of the instrument.

The interest in music displayed by Maria Theresa was equally evident in her children, and her son Joseph, who succeeded her, was for some time the patron of Mozart: indeed the whole imperial family was musical,[1]

the emperor perhaps just enough for a sovereign prince, that is, with sufficient hand, both on the violoncello and harpsichord, to amuse himself, and sufficient taste and judgment to hear, understand, and receive delights from others. A person of great distinction told me, that he saw, some years ago, four archduchesses of Austria, the emperor's sisters, appear at court in the opera of *Egeria*, written by Metastasio, and set by Hasse, expressly for their use. They were then extremely beautiful, sung and acted very well, for princesses, and the grand duke of Tuscany [2], who was likewise very handsome, danced, in the character of Cupid.

During his stay in Vienna, Dr. Burney received a visit from Signor Mancini of Bologna, who was singing-master to the imperial court and family:

He has taught eight of the archduchesses to sing, most of whom, he says, had good voices, and had made a considerable progress, particularly the princess of Parma [3], and the archduchess Elizabeth [4], who have good shakes, a good *portamento*, and great facility of executing swift divisions.

Dr. Burney had very few opportunities of seeing the Emperor, as the court moved on 4th September to Laxenberg

---

[1] There were five boys and eleven girls.
[2] Leopold (1747–1792) succeeded Joseph II as Emperor in 1790. He became Grand Duke of Tuscany on the death of his father, the Emperor Francis I, in 1765.
[3] Who, before her marriage in 1769 to Duke Ferdinand of Parma, had been the Archduchess Amelia of Austria.
[4] See footnote 5 to page 153.

for a month, where the Emperor's mother, the Empress Queen, was in residence:

On this occasion, almost all the first people of Vienna were preparing to follow him. The night before his departure, at a kind of riding-house in the suburbs, there was a species of tilts and tournaments, which the Germans call *Carrousel, ein Thurnier zu Pferd, oder Ringelrennen*. The emperor himself was one of the combatants on this occasion; after which his imperial majesty gave fireworks on the Danube, at which he was likewise present.

The churches of Vienna naturally received a full share of Dr. Burney's attention. Architecturally they were for the most part distasteful to him:

The churches and convents are chiefly of Gothic architecture; however, the Jesuits' college is an extensive and elegant modern building; and the church of St. Sophia, built on the model of St. Peter's at Rome, but upon a much smaller scale, is a beautiful copy of that structure in miniature; as is the Austin Friars, of the chapel of Loretto. . . .

The first time I went to the cathedral of St. Stephen, I heard an excellent mass, in the true church style, very well performed; there were violins and violoncellos though it was not a festival. The great organ at the west end of this church has not been fit for use these forty years; there are three or four more organs of a smaller size in different parts of the church, which are used occasionally. That which I heard in the choir this morning is but a poor one, and as usual, was much out of tune;

it was played, however, in a very masterly, though not a modern style. All the responses in this service, are chanted in four parts, which is much more pleasing, especially where there is so little melody, than the mere naked *canto fermo* used in most other Catholic churches; the treble part was sung by boys, and very well; particularly, by two of them, whose voices, though not powerful, had been well cultivated. . . .

The church is a dark, dirty, and dismal old Gothic building, though richly ornamented; in it are hung all the trophies of war, taken from the Turks and other enemies of the house of Austria, for more than a century past, which gives it very much the appearance of an old wardrobe.

Dr. Burney attended vespers in the cathedral one afternoon and high mass on the Festival of the Nativity of the Virgin, at which the orchestra was reinforced by a number of extra instruments: the music was " well written and well executed, except that the hateful sour organ poisoned all whenever it played ".

Dr. Burney examined the organ in the church of St. Michael with great interest

on account of the singular disposition of its keys. This instrument has no front, the great pipes are placed, in an elegant manner, on each side of the gallery, and there is a box only in the middle, of about four feet square, for the keys and stops; so that the west window is left quite open.

There are a number of interesting sidelights in the Journal on life in Vienna during the latter half of the eighteenth century.

The diversions for the common people of this place are such as seem hardly fit for a civilized and polished nation to allow.   Particularly the *combats*, as they are called, or baiting of wild beasts, in a manner much more savage and ferocious than our bull-baiting, throwing at cocks, and prize-fighting of old, to which the legislature has so wisely and humanely put a stop.[1]

These barbarous spectacles are usually attended by two or three thousand people, among whom are a great number of ladies!

In a footnote Dr. Burney gives a literal translation of a handbill, " such as is distributed through the streets every Sunday and festival ":

" This day, by imperial licence, in the great amphi-theatre, at five o'clock will begin the following diversions.

1st. A wild Hungarian ox, in full fire (that is, with fire under his tail, and crackers fastened to his ears and horns, and to other parts of his body) will be set upon by dogs.

2nd. A wild boar will in the same manner be baited by dogs.

3rd. A great bear will immediately after be torn by dogs.

4th. A wolf will be hunted by dogs of the fleetest kind.

5th. A very furious and enraged wild bull from Hungary will be attacked by fierce and hungry dogs.

6th. A fresh bear will be attacked by hounds.

7th. Will appear a fierce wild boar, just caught, which

---

[1] Bull-baiting was, however, not finally abolished in England until 1835, cock-fighting only in 1849.

will now be baited for the first time by dogs defended with iron armour.

8th. A beautiful African tiger [1].

9th. This will be changed for a bear.

10th. A fresh and fierce Hungarian ox.

11th. And lastly, a furious and hungry bear, which has had no food for eight days, will attack a young wild bull, and eat him alive upon the spot; and if he is unable to complete the business, a wolf will be ready to help him.''

The Viennese of that day were as much addicted to processions as to wild-beast shows. On one Sunday morning during Dr. Burney's stay in the city he was held up in the streets

by a procession of, literally, two or three miles long, singing a hymn to the Virgin, in three parts, and repeating each stanza after the priests, in the van, at equal distances; so that the instant one company had done, it was taken up by another behind, till it came to the women in the rear, who, likewise, at equal distances, repeated, in three parts, the few simple notes of this hymn; and even after them it was repeated by girls, who were the last persons in the procession. When these had done, it was begun again by the priests. . . . There were five or six of these processions this morning; and yet it is observed, that they are much less frequent than formerly.

Nevertheless, not a day passed while Dr. Burney was in Vienna without one or more processions to churches and convents in the vicinity. He characteristically remarks that " all

[1] An early instance of the habitual exaggeration of the advertiser. " Tygers ", as Dr. Burney calls them, are peculiar to Asia.

this helps to teach the people to sing in different parts " and
leaves it at that.

On another Sunday, whilst he was in Vienna,

there was a procession through the principal streets . . .
as an anniversary commemoration of the Turks having
been driven from its walls in 1683, by Sobieski king of
Poland, after it had sustained a siege of two months.[1]
The Emperor came from Laxenberg to attend the cele-
bration of this festival, and walked in the procession,
which set off from the Franciscans' church, and proceeded through the principal streets of the city to the
Cathedral of St. Stephen.

After the Te Deum had been sung to the accompaniment
of a large orchestra,

the whole was finished by a triple discharge of all the
artillery of the city, and the military instruments were
little less noisy now, than the musical had been before.

It was not, however, only in processions that the religious
feelings of the Viennese found vent. The ordinary church
services were crowded. On one occasion Dr. Burney went
into a church while a low mass was in progress. A band was
playing,

but the music was bad, and the performance worse;
however, I was hemmed in by the crowd, and forced to
stay and hear it for near an hour, before I could get out
decently.

Though the music in the churches was generally of so
indifferent a quality, it was the multiplicity of musical services which tended, in Dr. Burney's opinion, to make the
Viennese so musical. He is constantly alluding in the Journal

[1] 12th September, 1683.

to street singing, and makes some interesting observations thereon which merit quotation.

(One) night two of the poor scholars of this city sung, in the court of the inn where I lodged, duets in *falsetto*, *soprano* and *contralto*, very well in tune, and with feeling and taste. I sent to enquire whether they were taught music at the Jesuits' college, and was answered in the affirmative. Though the number of poor scholars, at different colleges, amounts to a hundred and twenty, yet there are at present but seventeen that are taught music.

After this there was a band of these singers, who performed through the streets a kind of glees, in three and four parts: this whole country is certainly very musical. I frequently heard the soldiers upon guard, and sentinels, as well as common people, sing in parts. The music school at the Jesuits' college, in every Roman Catholic town, accounts in some measure for this faculty; yet other causes may be assigned, and, among these, it should be remembered, that there is scarce a church or convent in Vienna, which has not every morning its *mass in music*: that is, a great portion of the church service of the day, set in parts, and performed with voices, accompanied by at least three or four violins, a tenor and bass, besides the organ; and as the churches here are daily crowded, this music, though not of the most exquisite kind, must, in some degree, form the ear of the inhabitants. Physical causes operate but little, I believe, as to music. Nature distributes her favours pretty equally to the inhabitants of Europe; but moral causes are frequently very powerful in their effects. And it seems as if *the national music of a country was good or bad, in*

proportion to that of its church service; which may account
for the taste of the common people of Italy, where indeed
the language is more musical than in any other country
of Europe, which certainly has an effect upon their vocal
music; but the excellent performances that are every
day heard for nothing in the churches, by the common
people, more contribute to refine and fix the national
taste for good music, than any other thing that I can at
present suggest. . . .

There was music every day, during dinner, and in the
evening at the inn, where I lodged, which was the Golden
Ox; but it was usually bad, particularly that of a band of
wind instruments, which constantly attended the ordinary. This consisted of French horns, clarionets, oboes,
and bassoons; all so miserably out of tune, that I wished
them a hundred miles off.

In general I did not find that delicacy of ear among
the German street musicians, which I had met with in
people of the same rank and profession in Italy. The
church organs being almost always out of tune here,
may be occasioned by the parsimony or negligence of
the clergy, bishop or superior of a church or convent;
but the being, or stopping, in or out of tune, among
street musicians, must depend on themselves, and on
their organs being *acute* or *obtuse*.

It is perhaps not easy to determine what kind of air
is most fit for the propagation of musical sound; whether
thick or thin, moist or dry; and if this were determined,
it might still be doubted in what kind of air music would
be heard to the greatest advantage, because, possibly,
that air which is most favourable to the transmission of

sound, abstractedly considered, may render the organs, by which it is perceived, less acutely sensible.

But more interesting to Dr. Burney than Vienna were the distinguished people whom he found living there; his account of the visits which he paid them will be considered in the following chapter.

CHAPTER VII

Vienna (continued)

There is a certain melancholy interest in the list of distinguished Viennese composers which Dr. Burney appends to the account of his stay in the city. Joseph Haydn alone lives to-day with undiminished reputation, and him Dr. Burney unfortunately did not meet. Of the nine bracketed with Haydn as having " greatly distinguished themselves as composers ", Gluck alone is still honoured, though his music is undeservedly neglected; Hasse, Salieri, and Ditters are mere names to any but the musical antiquary, and the rest " are become as though they had not been born ", though three of them are singled out with Haydn and Ditters as the composers of symphonies and string quartets which " are perhaps among the first full pieces and compositions, for violins, that have ever been produced ". And yet

Vienna is so rich in composers, and encloses within its walls such a number of musicians of superior merit, that it is but just to allow it to be, among German cities, the imperial seat of music, as well as of power.

Had Dr. Burney couched this statement in the future tense by way of a prophecy of Vienna's future greatness, its truth would have been amply proved by the musical history of the city during the subsequent century. So far as the period of Dr. Burney's visit is concerned, his claim for Vienna, based as it is, except for Haydn and Gluck, on a collection of nonentities, can only be conceded in view of the general barrenness of musical talent elsewhere in the empire.

There is little, therefore, of interest to the reader of to-day in the detailed accounts of visits and conversations which occupy quite three-quarters of the lengthy section in Dr. Burney's Journal allotted to Vienna, although with the public for whom he was writing a flood of memories would have been let loose at the mention of a name such as Faustina, whilst the reforms initiated by Gluck in opera must have been one of the chief topics of conversation wherever musicians fore-gathered.

Through the intervention of Lord Stormont and his friend, the Countess Thun, Gluck was induced to receive Dr. Burney, though he was reported to be " as formidable a character as Handel used to be: a very dragon, of whom all are in fear ". The interview passed off successfully, Gluck being soon got into a good humour. His little niece, accompanied by her uncle on a very bad harpsichord, sang Dr. Burney a number of his compositions, and finally Gluck himself was prevailed upon to sing, " and, with as little voice as possible, he contrived to entertain, and even delight the company, in a very high degree ". He played Dr. Burney almost the whole of " Alcestis ", and amongst other things portions of

a French opera, from Racine's *Iphigénie*, which he had just composed. This last, though he had not as yet committed a note of it to paper, was so well digested in his head, and his retention is so wonderful, that he sung it nearly from the beginning to the end, with as much readiness as if he had had a fair score before him.

Dr. Burney met Gluck again at a musical party given by Lord Stormont and sat next to him during dinner. During the evening Gluck's little niece sang arias from her uncle's operas and some Haydn string quartets were played. When the music was over, Dr. Burney and his host with most of the guests adjourned to M. L'Augier's house and stayed till twelve o'clock listening to a Florentine poet, the Abate Casti, recite his own verses from memory for several hours on end!

Before leaving Vienna Dr. Burney paid a farewell visit to Gluck, and though it was nearly eleven in the morning he found the composer still in bed. Gluck gave him manuscript copies of several of his compositions and parted from him on excellent terms.

Dr. Burney devotes pride of place in his Journal to his meetings with the Italian poet, Metastasio, whom he praises extravagantly, crediting him with more originality than Racine! To-day he is only remembered as a writer of opera libretti, which were set over and over again by different court composers of the eighteenth century.[1] Metastasio had been over forty years in Vienna, and had for long been the imperial poet laureate and an excellent example of the species.

When the emperor, empress, or any one of the imperial family orders it, he sits down and writes, two hours at a time only, just as he would transcribe a poem written by anyone else; never waiting for a call, invoking the Muse, or even receiving her favours at any other than his own stated periods.

Doubtless the fact that Metastasio was compelled to translate the whole of the works of Homer into Italian verse, before he had reached the age of fourteen, induced in him a secret abhorrence of poetry and killed any inspiration which he may have possessed! Dr. Burney's description of his mode of life is a striking contrast to the conventional idea of the habits of poets, and is worth quotation:

The whole tenor of his life is equally innoxious with his writings. He lives with the most mechanical regularity, which he suffers none to disturb; he has not dined from home these thirty years; he is very difficult of access, and equally averse to new persons, and new things; he sees, in a familiar way, but three or four people, and them, constantly every night, from eight o'clock till ten; he abhors writing, and never sets pen to paper but by

---

[1] Visitors to Assisi may remember a tablet to the memory of Metastasio in the wall of the house where he was born.

compulsion: as it was necessary to bind Silenus, before
he would sing; and Proteus, to oblige him to give oracles.

It only remains to say that Metastasio was a person of
fixed and unalterable prejudices: he believed the Psalms to
be in rhyme, and thought " that Milton's *Paradise Lost* cannot
be a perfect poem because it is written in *blank verse*, though
all the narrative parts of his own dramatic pieces are in
measured prose ".

Metastasio laughs at all poetic inspiration, and makes
a poem as mechanically as another would make a shoe,
at what time he pleases, and without any other occasion
than the want of it.

Dr. Burney had been warned before leaving England that
it would be useless to take letters of recommendation to
Metastasio, as he was " averse to society on all occasions ":

A person of very high rank assured me, that he had
been five years in Vienna before he could get acquainted
with Metastasio, or even into conversation with him;
and, after that time, but three visits had been exchanged
between them in several years.

However, thanks to the good offices of Lord Stormont,
Metastasio consented to receive Dr. Burney, and a visit was
accordingly arranged, to which Dr. Burney looked forward
with lively anticipation. The acute condition of the housing
problem in eighteenth century Vienna was demonstrated in
the previous chapter.

This great poet is lodged, as many other great poets
have been before him, in a very exalted situation, up no
less than four pair of stairs. Whether modern bards
prefer the sublimity of this abode, on account of its
being somewhat on a level with Mount Parnassus, nearer

their sire Apollo, or in the neighbourhood of gods in
general, I shall not determine; but a more plain and
humble reason can be assigned for Metastasio's habitation being " twice two stories high ", if we consider
the peculiar prerogative which the emperor enjoys at
Vienna, of appropriating, to the use of the officers of his
court and army, the *first floor* of every house and palace
in that city, six or eight privileged places only excepted.
On this account, princes, ambassadors, and nobles,
usually inhabit the second stories; and the third, fourth,
and even fifth floors, the houses being very large and
high, are well fitted up, for the reception of opulent and
noble families;. and our poet, though he occupies that
part of a house, which, in England, is thought only fit
for domestics to sleep in, has, nevertheless, an exceeding
good and elegant apartment, in which an imperial laureate
may, with all due dignity, hold dalliance with the Muses....

His pension is about five hundred pounds sterling a year,
which, with his regular life and economy, enables him to
live in a very reputable, though not splendid manner.

That the poet lived in some style was further borne out by
the elegance of the carriage in which he went to mass,

which I rejoiced to see: his talents and his virtues merit
all that can be done for him.

During his first visit Dr. Burney had a long talk with
Metastasio, which he reports in detail. The conversation was
mainly concerned with the poet's own works, but general
musical subjects were discussed and, to Dr. Burney's disgust,
for some time politics held the field, owing to the arrival that
morning of news of a revolution in Sweden.[1]

[1] The revolution of 19th August, 1772, which caused a considerable stir in Europe
at the time. It was engineered by Sprengtporten and Toll with the connivance of

Dr. Burney lost no time in paying his respects to Metastasio for a second time, and attended the poet's levée the next morning, where he met the governor of the city and was entertained with music. He paid two further visits to the poet, and, when taking leave, was rewarded by an embrace and a request for his book when it was published.

Dr. Burney paid three visits to the composer Hasse, and his wife, Faustina, the great singer, both of whom in their respective spheres of activity held positions second to none in the esteem of their contemporaries. Hasse and Gluck headed two of the largest musical cliques in Vienna, the former representing the traditional view, the latter pioneering the new movement, which was revolutionizing the opera. Dr. Burney was careful to steer a middle course between the opposing factions.

The spirit of party, in musical matters, runs high everywhere; and I everywhere found that it was wished that I should hear, or at least like, none but the friends of my friends. However, I soon saw, and *heard* through all this, and seldom suffered myself to be the dupe of partial decisions. For I was not contented with hearing music in fine houses, theatres, and palaces, but visited cottages, and garrets, wherever I could get scent of a good performer, or a man of genius.

Dr. Burney was anxious to secure a complete list of Hasse's compositions. He was noted for the fertility of his talent, even in that age of prolific composers, and admitted that his smaller compositions for voice or for instruments

were so numerous, that he should not know many of them again, if he was either to see or hear them. He

the king, Gustavus III, who was thereby enabled to force a new constitution on Sweden and to put an end to the political factions which were ruining the country. This conversation took place on 8th September. The news had therefore taken seventeen days to reach Vienna! It was conveyed to the company by Lord Stormont, who might reasonably have been expected to receive the earliest tidings of a political event of such importance.

modestly compared himself to animals of the greatest
fecundity, whose progeny were either destroyed during
infancy, or abandoned to chance; and added, that he,
like other bad fathers, had more pleasure in producing,
than in preserving his offspring. . . .

He is going, next spring, to Venice, the birthplace of
Signora Faustina, and it seems as if they both had determined to spend the rest of their days there.[1]

It does not appear that Signor Hasse has at present
either pension or employment at Vienna. He had great
losses during the last war [2]; all his books, manuscripts,
and effects were burned at the bombardment of Dresden,
by the King of Prussia,[3] to a very considerable amount.
He was going to print a complete edition of all his works;
the late King of Poland [4] promised to be at the expense of
paper and press; but after M. Breitkopf [5], of Leipzig,
had made a beginning, and got together materials for the
whole impression, the war broke out, and put an end to
all his hopes from this enterprise, and to those of the
public. He, however, does great justice to the musical
talents of the King of Prussia; and is even so candid, as
to say, that he believes, if his majesty had known that
contingencies would have obliged him to bombard
Dresden, he would previously have apprised him of it,
that he might have saved his effects.

---

[1] They did; Faustina dying in 1783, Hasse soon after, but they did not leave Vienna
until 1775.
[2] The Seven Years' War (1756–1763).
[3] Dresden was bombarded by Frederick the Great, King of Prussia, on 12th July,
1760.
[4] Augustus III (1696–1763), who was likewise Frederick August II, Elector of
Saxony.
[5] Johann Gottlob Immanuel Breitkopf (1719–1794), the great music publisher,
and son of the founder of the famous firm now known as Breitkopf und Härtel.

Dr. Burney paid several visits to Wagenseil, to whom some erroneously attributed the authorship of the tune of Handel's so-called "Harmonious Blacksmith" variations. He, poor man, had for the past seven years been confined to his room, his right thigh being withered. However, a harpsichord was wheeled to him, and Dr. Burney was able to hear him play. He was nominally music master to the archduchesses, and received a pension of fifteen hundred florins a year from the court, which he augmented by teaching at home and composing,

and, as he is luckily a single man, and Vienna not a dear place for the natives to live in, he may be supposed in easy circumstances.

Gassmann, the imperial Capellmeister, was of great assistance to Dr. Burney in securing admission to the music library of the imperial theatre and chapel.

I found in it (says Dr. Burney) an immense collection of musical authors, but in such disorder, that their contents are, at present, almost wholly unknown. However, M. Gassmann has begun a catalogue, and is promised by the Emperor, a large and more commodious room for these books, than the present, in which they are promiscuously piled, one on another, in the most confused manner imaginable. Yet I found a great number of curious things from the beginning of counterpoint to the present time. Indeed the quantity of music here, of the Emperor Leopold's[1] collecting, which is uniformly bound, in white vellum, with his arms on the back, is almost incredible; it seems to be all that Italy and Germany had then produced: and for operas, in score, and parts, the list of such only as have been performed at this court, would fill a folio volume.

[1] Leopold I (1640–1705).

Gassmann took a note of Dr. Burney's London address, and promised to send him details of anything noteworthy which might crop up during the compilation of the catalogue. Before Dr. Burney left Vienna, he was favoured by a long visit from Gassmann, who brought with him a complete list of his own works and copies of a great number of his manuscript quartets, evidently with a view to securing adequate representation in Dr. Burney's projected *History of Music*.

Though Dr. Burney was principally occupied in Vienna, as elsewhere, with music and musicians, he had ample opportunity, thanks to the introductions with which he was furnished, of seeing something of the social life of the imperial city. He went with Lord Stormont to a reception at the house of the Danish Minister, and was introduced to the whole diplomatic corps. He was greatly assisted in his work by the secretary to the papal nuncio, who was well acquainted with the people in Vienna with whom Dr. Burney was most anxious to converse. He also introduced Dr. Burney to the Bishop of Ephesus, who was at that time the papal nuncio at the imperial court and incidentally a member of the famous Milanese family Visconti. The nuncio granted Dr. Burney a long interview, and subsequently honoured him with an invitation to dinner.

Second only to the British Ambassador, Lord Stormont, in their endeavours on Dr. Burney's behalf, were the Countess Thun, an honoured name in the musical annals of Vienna, and M. L'Augier, one of the principal physicians of the imperial court, of whom we have already had occasion to make mention.

Countess Thun, who had

nothing about her that reminds one of the pride or heaviness attributed by travellers to the Germans,

was chiefly instrumental in securing Dr. Burney an interview with Gluck. She had unfortunately to leave Vienna for Laxenberg some time before Dr. Burney's departure, which was

an afflicting circumstance, as her house was always open

to me, and she did everything in her power to procure me entertainment and services.

On paying her a final visit of farewell, Dr. Burney found her surrounded by her friends, who, though they were not in my situation, but were sure of seeing her again very soon, either here, or at Laxenberg; yet they had almost tears in their eyes, at the thoughts of losing her, only for a few days. During this visit she was so kind as to produce all her musical curiosities, for me to hear and see, before we parted. Her taste is admirable, and her execution light, neat and feminine; however, she told me that she *had* played much better than at present, and humorously added, that she had had six children, and that " every one of them had taken something from her ". She is a cheerful, lively, and beneficent being, whom everyone here seems to love as a favourite sister. She is niece to the once handsome prince Lobkowitz [1], who was in England in 1745 and '46, and much connected with the famous count St. Germain [2], who made so much noise at that time, not only with his fiddle, but his mysterious conduct and equivocal character. This prince is now retired from the world, and will not see even his relations and best friends for many months together. He had cultivated music so far, as not only to play and to judge well, but even to compose in a superior manner;

[1] Ferdinand Philip Lobkowitz (1724–1784) was the patron of Gluck, who accompanied him to London, where they both remained for two years. His son was the friend and benefactor of Beethoven, and the name is enshrined in the dedication of the third, fifth, and sixth symphonies.

[2] The Comte de St. Germain (*c.* 1710–*c.* 1780) was the famous alchemist who invented an elixir of life; under the cloak of charlatanism he probably concealed his activities as an international intriguer. He was in England in 1743, when he was arrested as a Jacobite spy, and again in 1760.

and his niece gave me several of his pieces, which had great merit and novelty, particularly a song for two orchestras, which no master in Europe need be ashamed of.[1]

L'Augier was a great traveller, and his house was a rendezvous for all the most notable people in Vienna. He too, being in the service of the court, was obliged to retire to Laxenberg, but before his departure he gave a large musical party for Dr. Burney, which was one of the finest assemblies the latter had ever seen, and attended by a large number of the nobility of the city. The concert consisted of a recital on the pianoforte by a little girl of eight or nine years old, who played so well and with so much expression that Dr. Burney inquired

upon what instrument she usually practised at home, and was answered, " on the Clavichord ". This accounts for her expression, and convinces me, that children should learn upon that, or a pianoforte, very early, and be obliged to give an expression to lady Coventry's Minuet, or whatever is their first tune; otherwise, after long practice on a monotonous harpsichord, however useful for strengthening the hand, the case is hopeless.

After this there were harp solos, played on the single harp, without pedals,

which renders it a very difficult instrument, as the performer is obliged to make the semitones by brass rings with the left hand, which being placed at the top of the harp, are not only hard to get at, but disagreeable to hear, from the noise, which by a sudden motion of the hand they occasion. The secret of producing the semi-tones by pedals, is not yet arrived at

[1] There is a letter in the British Museum from Dr. Burney to Sir Robert Murray Keith, dated 9th November, 1784, in which Dr. Burney desires that his respects be conveyed to " my musical patroness and St. Cecilia of Vienna, the Countess Thun, by whose remembrance I should be extremely flattered ".

Vienna; and the double harp is utterly unknown there.[1]

The concert concluded with some trios for stringed instruments.

Dr. Burney's last days were spent in a round of farewell visits, which occupied him until the evening prior to his departure. He then

flew home, to pack, and to pay; here, among other things (he writes), I was plagued with copyists the whole evening; they began to regard me as a greedy and indiscriminate purchaser of whatever trash they should offer; but I was forced to hold my hand, not only from buying bad music, but good. For everything is very dear at Vienna, and nothing more so than music, of which none is printed.

As it was, I did not quit Vienna till I had expended ten or twelve guineas in the purchase of music; which, with what had been given me, what I had transcribed myself, and the printed books I had collected, rendered my baggage so unwieldy, as to cost me an additional horse to my chaise, all the way to Hamburg.

Dr. Burney had already explained in his Journal that

as there are no music shops in Vienna, the best method of procuring new compositions, is to apply to copyists; for the authors, regarding every English traveller as a *milord*, expect a present on these occasions, as considerable for each piece, as if it had been composed on purpose for him.

On Monday, 13th September, Dr. Burney left Vienna for Prague, on his way into northern Germany.

---

[1] Yet the first pedal harp had been invented as long before as 1720, though the evolution of the harp, as we know it to-day, was not completed until 1810.

CHAPTER VIII

The Journey through Bohemia

On quitting Vienna, Dr. Burney's first objective was Prague. His graphic account of the journey through Bohemia, devastated during the Seven Years' War, is worth quoting in full:

My journey through this country, was one of the most fatiguing I ever took in my life; for though the road, in general, is very good, for a German road, yet my want of time, which obliged me to travel night and day; the excessive heat and cold of the weather, occasioned by the presence and absence of the sun; together with bad horses, and diabolical wagons, used as chaises, exhausted both my spirits and my patience.

The country is flat, naked, and disagreeable to the eye, for the most part, all the way through Austria, Moravia, and Bohemia, as far as Prague, the situation and environs of which are very beautiful.

The dearness and scarcity of provisions, of all kinds, on this road, were now excessive; and the half-starved people, just recovered from malignant fevers, little less contagious than the plague, occasioned by bad food, and by no food at all, offered to view the most melancholy spectacle, I ever beheld.

No refreshments of any kind were to be found, till I

arrived at Kolin, a village rendered famous, by the battle fought near it in the last war [1]; here a pigeon, and half a pint of miserable sour wine, cost me three or four shillings; till now I had subsisted on bread and water, except one pint of milk, which I obtained with difficulty, and which cost me fourteen *kreuzers*, about sevenpence English.

I had frequently been told, that the Bohemians were the most musical people of Germany, or, perhaps, of all Europe; and an eminent German composer, now in London [2], had declared to me, that if they enjoyed the same advantages as the Italians, they would excel them.

I never could suppose effects without a cause; nature, though often partial to individuals, in her distribution of genius and talents, is never so to a whole people. Climate contributes greatly to the forming of customs and manners; and, it is, I believe, certain, that those who inhabit hot climates, are more delighted with music than those of cold ones; perhaps, from the auditory nerves being more irritable in the one than in the other, and from sound being propagated with greater facility: but I could, by no means, account for climate operating more in favour of music upon the Bohemians, than on their neighbours, the Saxons and Moravians.

I crossed the whole kingdom of Bohemia, from south to north; and being very assiduous in my enquiries, how the common people learned music, I found out at length,

---

[1] The battle of Kolin or Kollin (Dr. Burney calls the place Colin) took place on 18th June, 1757. Frederick the Great was defeated there by the Imperial troops and withdrew his army from Bohemia.

[2] Most probably John Christian Bach (1735–1782), eleventh son of the great John Sebastian, who had come to London in 1762 and, save for short periods, remained there until his death. He was an intimate friend of Dr. Burney.

that, not only in every large town, but in all villages, where there is a reading and writing school, children of both sexes are taught music.

Dr. Burney visited the schools of various places through which he passed, and gives the following description of the school at Časlau[1], a little to the south of Kolin, and " within a post " of that place, where the organist and principal violinist of the parish church served likewise as the two schoolmasters.

I went into the school, which was full of little children of both sexes, from six to ten or eleven years old, who were reading, writing, playing on violins, oboes, bassoons and other instruments. The organist had in a small room of his house four clavichords, with little boys practising on them all: his son of nine years old, was a very good performer.

The organist took Dr. Burney into the church and played to him; though he complained that he was out of practice, Dr. Burney considered him one of the best performers whom he had heard on his travels. The poor man pleaded

that he had too many learners to instruct, in the first rudiments, to be allowed leisure for study, and that he had his house not only full of other people's children, but his own;

" Chill penury repressed his noble rage:"

which is the case of many a musician, whose mind and talents are superior to such drudgery! yet, thus circumstanced, there is no alternative, but a jail.

Dr. Burney at length arrived in Prague, which was still suffering from the effects of Frederick the Great's victory of 20th June, 1757.

[1] Where Frederick the Great defeated an Austrian army in 1742.

This city is extremely beautiful, when seen at a distance. It is situated on two or three hills, and has the river Moldau running through the middle of it. It is divided into three different quarters, or districts, which are distinguished by the names of " Alt' Stadt ", " Neue Stadt ", and " Kleine Stadt ", or Old Town, New Town, and Little Town; the Kleine Stadt is the most modern, and the best built of the three. The houses are all of white stone, or stucco, in imitation of it, and all uniform in size and colour. The hill of St. Laurence, the highest about the town, commands a prospect, not only of the whole city, but of all the adjacent country: the declivity of this hill is covered with wood, consisting chiefly of fruit trees, and vineyards. A great part of the town is new, as scarce a single building escaped the Prussian batteries, and bombardment during the blockade, in the last war. A few churches and palaces only, that were strongly built, and of less combustible materials than the rest, were proof against their fury; and in the walls of these, are still sticking innumerable cannon balls, and bombs, particularly, in the superb palace of count Czernin, and in the Capuchins' church. This palace, which is of the Ionic order, and built of white stone, has thirty windows in front; the chapel, at the Capuchins, is an exact copy, in stone, of that at Loretto, in marble.

The inhabitants are still at work throughout the city, in repairing the Prussian devastations, particularly at the cathedral and imperial palace, which were both almost demolished; these are situated on a high hill, facing that of St. Laurence.

Dr. Burney took an early opportunity of calling on the organist of the cathedral,

but the messenger I sent in before me, in order to negotiate the visit, returned quite pale with fear, telling me, that it would be very dangerous for me to enter the house, as M. Wolfe was ill of the malignant and contagious fever, which had lately raged with so much violence, and swept off such a number of the inhabitants of this city. . . .

An itinerant band of street musicians came to salute me at the inn, the " Einhorn ", or Unicorn, during dinner; they played upon the harp, violin, and horn, several minuets and polonaises, which were, in themselves very pretty, though their performance of them added nothing to the beauty of the compositions; and it will, perhaps, appear strange to some, that this capital of so musical a kingdom, in which the genius of each inhabitant has a fair trial, should not more abound with *great* musicians.[1] It is not, however, difficult to account for this, if we reflect, that music is one of the arts of peace, leisure, and abundance; and if, according to M. Rousseau, arts have flourished most in the most corrupt times, those times must, at least, have been prosperous and tranquil. Now, the Bohemians are never tranquil long together; and even in the short intervals of peace, their first nobility are attached to the court of Vienna, and seldom reside in their own capital; so that those among the poorer sort, who are taught music in their infancy, have no encouragement to pursue it in riper

[1] This criticism is as true to-day of the country as a whole as it was when Dr. Burney made it. There has been only one great composer of Czech nationality, Antonin Dvořák (1841–1904), though Smetana, who founded the national school of composers of which Dvořák was the culmination, won a position of great esteem within the confines of his own country.

years, and seldom advance further than to qualify themselves for the street, or for servitude.

Indeed many of those who learn music at school go
afterwards to the plough, and to other laborious employments; and then their knowledge of music turns to
no other account, than to enable them to sing in their
parish church, and as an innocent domestic recreation,
which is, perhaps, the best and most honourable use, to
which music can be appropriated.

It has been said by travellers; that the Bohemian
nobility keep musicians in their houses; but, in keeping
servants, it is impossible to be otherwise, as all the children of the peasants and tradespeople, in every town and
village throughout the kingdom of Bohemia, are taught
music at the common reading schools, except in Prague,
where, indeed it is no part of school learning; the musicians being brought thither from the country. . . .

The Bohemians are remarkably expert in the use of
wind instruments, in general; but . . . the instrument
upon which their performers are most excellent, on the
Saxon side the kingdom, is the oboe; and on that of
Moravia, the tube, or clarion.

Dr. Burney derived this and most of his information about
Prague and Bohemian music from the organist of the convent
of the Holy Cross in Prague, who could speak Italian; the
language difficulty was a very real problem, as he found
German of very little use, the " Sclavonian dialect " being
the normal medium of conversation. He heard no music in
Prague, having missed by one day a big concert in the church
of the convent of the Holy Cross.

There have been no operas here lately; however,
German and Sclavonian plays are performed three times

a week, which are, at present, the only public exhibitions at Prague, of any kind. The nobility were now, for the most part, out of town; but in winter, they are said to have great concerts frequently at their hotels, and palaces, chiefly performed by their own domestics and vassals, who have learned music at country schools.

Dr. Burney left Prague for Dresden on Thursday morning, 17th September,

after many delays and plagues, incident to travellers in a foreign country; among the rest, my good landlord at the " Einhorn ", instigated the postmaster's servant to insist on my having an additional horse to my post wagon; and threw all the difficulties in my way, he possibly could, in hopes of keeping me longer in his *sponging* house. After these squabbles were over, and I had run the gauntlet through the gates and barriers, where my baggage was narrowly ransacked, by custom-house inquisitors, I got away about seven o'clock.

The first post, to Sdieps [1], I travelled through a mountainous country, and cold thick fog; the second, to Weltrus, through a good road, and level, though naked country; here the weather was again very hot. Sour milk, and black sour bread, " Pumpernickel ", were thus far, all the refreshments that could be obtained.

At Budin, the next stage, I found a music school; and heard two of the poor boys perform in the street, one on the harp, and the other on the triangles, tolerably well.

---

[1] Dr. Burney's spelling of the names of places, particularly in this section of the Journal, is very erratic. Whenever possible the correct or customary version of the spelling has been inserted in the text without comment. In a few instances, as is the case here, the spelling is so corrupt that identification is impossible.

At Lobositz,[1] two or three stages from the confines of Saxony, there is likewise another school, with more than a hundred children, of both sexes, of which number all learn music who choose it. I visited the church, which is small and neat, with a little plain organ in it; here the children, vocally and instrumentally, perform. I heard a considerable number of the boys practising on the fiddle, at school, but in a very coarse manner.

I hope I shall be excused, if I here relate a few of the hardships which I underwent, in the course of my journey through these parts of Germany; as the account of them may put future travellers on their guard, or, at least, prevent surprise, under similar circumstances.

And first, I must inform them that I did not meet with a chaise, or carriage, of any kind, that had a top, or covering, to protect passengers from heat, cold, wind, or rain, in my whole journey; and so violent are the jolts, and so hard are the seats of German post wagons, that a man is rather kicked than carried from one place to another. Yet, for these wretched conveyances, when I travelled in them alone, *extra-poste*, as it is called, it cost me frequently at the rate of eighteen pence for each English mile: so great is the number of fees and taxes on this occasion: " Postgeld ", Wagengeld ", " Schossegeld ", " Schwagergeld ", " Schmiergeld ", " Barriergeld ", and " Trinkgeld ", to hundreds, but particularly to the " Stall-knecht ", for getting " Pferde ", horses, ready in somewhat less than three hours.

[Dr. Burney here adds the following footnote in explanation

[1] Where the first battle of the Seven Years' War was fought on 1st October, 1756—a victory for Frederick the Great.

of these unfamiliar terms, which for picturesqueness may be compared with the catalogue of feudal taxes given by Arthur Young in his *Travels in France*:

For such of my readers as may be unacquainted with the language of their progenitors, the Saxons, it may be necessary to translate the names of the imposts above mentioned, into their English equivalents, of *horse-hire*, *chaise-hire*, *turnpikes*, *postilion*, *greasing wheels*, *toll at the gates*, on both sides of each town, as well as *drink* to the ostler, and a swarm of helpers, who, in removing baggage, steal cordage, straps, and everything which they can carry off undiscovered.]

But such as are provided with a comfortable carriage, with beds, provisions, and a number of servants, and are so indifferent about expense, that they calmly submit to all kinds of impositions, as things of course, may be utterly ignorant of the sufferings of others who dread expense; and who are exposed to all the plagues of bad vehicles, bad horses, bad inns, and worse provisions, or who are unable to find either inns or provisions of any kind.

The excellent roads, inns, and carriages, throughout Great Britain, make an Englishman very unfit to encounter such hardships; but indeed they exceed those of most other countries in Europe so much, that to travel with a *Vetturino*, a *Procaccio*, or a *Corriere*,[1] through the worst *Italian* roads, is ease and luxury, compared with what is suffered in Germany.

At Lobositz, which is situated on the Elbe, I quitted the chaise, and hired a boat down that river to Dresden,

---

[1] That is, a coachman, a postboy, or a courier.

in order to escape two or three terrible posts, and indeed postilions, for every German " Schwager " is such a friend to surgery, that I always wished to get out of his hands; and, besides personal safety, the country is so mountainous, and road so full of holes, and great loose stones, that both carriage and baggage frequently suffer. It was now six o'clock in the evening, when I arrived at the waterside; I was much disturbed at seeing the boat, in which I was to perform the voyage; it was long, narrow, and quite open at the top. There was straw to lie on, but nothing to cover me or my baggage in case of rain; at this time, indeed, the weather was hot, and I nestled into my straw, accommodating myself to my circumstances as well as I could.

The boat moved so very slow, there being only one waterman, that it frequently seemed to stand still. The weather as yet continued calm, but as we proceeded lower down the river, through an amazingly wild and rocky country, there were frequent waterfalls that made a violent noise, and seemed very likely to overset our little boat; about midnight it grew totally dark, and began to rain; I protected my head as well as I was able, with a *parapluie*, or small umbrella, but was very wet elsewhere.

The rain continued till daybreak, after which, the wind got up, and became quite furious, just in our teeth; in this kind of hurricane, the boat could make no way. Distress on distress! the *parapluie*, my only defence, was forced from my hands, in a violent gust of wind, and blown into the river, where it instantly sank; and we tried in vain, a considerable time, to fish it up: I was now wet, cold, hungry, and totally helpless; for the boat-man himself was in despair of ever getting to Dresden during this storm!

At length, however, we reached Königstein, a village and castle, on one of the highest rocks in Europe; this was but half-way from Lobositz to Dresden. I sent my servant and the boatman to try if they could procure a chaise, a cart, a wheelbarrow, or anything, to carry me to Pirna, the first post-town, and after keeping me shiver-ing with cold and wet, more than an hour, they returned with the news of having procured a wagon.

Here I got some bread, which revived me a little, and enabled me to clamber up this terrible rock, on foot, to warm myself; which it did as effectually, before I reached the summit, as if I had had recourse to a warm bed and sudorific. After this I had twelve English miles to Pirna, through the most stony and jumbling road I ever travelled.

At Pirna, the place where the King of Prussia took all the Saxon troops prisoners, at the beginning of the last war,[1] I was detained two hours before I could get horses, for each of which, by a new *reglement*, or regulation, I was obliged to pay a rixdollar, instead of a florin, the usual price. . . .

The road from Pirna to Dresden is good; the country on the left hand is flat, naked and unpleasant to the eye, when the grain is off the ground; but on the right, the hills, covered with vines and houses, all along the banks of the Elbe, are delightful.

Throughout his journey in these parts, Dr. Burney availed himself of every opportunity for inspecting the schools, where

[1] The battle of Pirna took place on the 28th September, 1756.

he found music taught on an equal footing with reading and
writing, though the standard of execution was everywhere
low. Most of the pupils

are intended for servants, and mean employments; and
as, in many parts of Bohemia and Saxony, the Gothic
power over vassals still subsists, these people have seldom
any ambition to excel in music, as they have no opportunities of mending their condition by it; now and then,
indeed, a man of genius among them, becomes an admirable musician whether he will or no; but when that
happens, he generally runs away, and settles in some
other country, where he can enjoy the fruit of his talents.

Upon the whole, however, it is manifest from these
schools, that it is not *nature*, but *cultivation*, which makes
music so generally understood by the Germans; and it
has been said by an accurate observer of human nature,
who has long resided among them, that " if innate genius
exists, Germany certainly is not the seat of it; though it
must be allowed, to be that of perseverance and application ".

CHAPTER IX

Dresden

Dr. Burney does not give the date of his arrival in Dresden, but it may be inferred to be 18th September. He appears to have spent five days in the city, which were fully occupied in investigations relating to his quest. His description of Dresden, ruined during the Seven Years' War, is of more than ordinary interest.

The approach to this city through the Elector's Gardens, by a beautiful *Château*, or Villa, and pavilions, in a very good taste, is extremely striking; but the city itself has suffered so much in the last war, that it is difficult for a stranger to imagine himself near the celebrated capital of Saxony, even when he sees it from the most favourable eminence in the neighbourhood, so few of its once many cloud-capped towers are left standing; only two or three remain entire, of all the stately edifices which formerly embellished this city; so that here, as well as at Prague, the inhabitants are still repairing the ravages of the Prussians; of whom it is remarkable, that though, during the last war, they ruined many a noble city, they never took one by a regular siege.

They were in possession of Dresden three years: it was taken from them during the absence of the king of Prussia, by the prince of Deux-ponts, who commanded the army of the empire.[1] In 1760, that monarch invested it again, and did incredible damage by his batteries, and bombardments, till it was relieved by General Lacy.[2]

The river Elbe divides the city into two parts, which are called Old and New Town; these have a communication by one of the finest bridges in Europe, built of white stone, and consisting of eighteen arches; it is 540 feet long, and 36 broad. There is a rule observed in passing this bridge, worthy of imitation; one side being appropriated to the use of those who are going to the Old Town, and the other to those who are going to the New; so that each passenger moves without interruption, and has his right hand constantly next the parapet wall. . . .

Everyone here is in the utmost indigence; . . . most of the nobility and gentry are too much impoverished, to be able to afford to learn, or to let their children learn music.

The Saxons of old, so remarkable for patience, industry, and probity, are now reduced to knavery and chicane, beyond the inhabitants of any other country. Dresden is at present a melancholy residence; from being the seat of the Muses, and habitation of pleasure, it is now only a dwelling for beggary, theft, and wretchedness. No society among the natives can be supported; all must

[1] This was on 4th September, 1759. Charles, Duke of Zweibrücken (or Deux-ponts) became heir-presumptive to the Bavarian Electorate on the accession of Charles Theodore, Elector Palatine, in 1778, and the efforts which were made to establish his claim resulted in the war of the Bavarian Succession.

[2] Frederick the Great invested Dresden again on 13th July, 1760. Lacy, who was in command of the Austrian troops stationed at Pirna, really contributed very little to the relief of the city, which was effected by Field-Marshal Daun on 22nd July. Count Franz Moritz Lacy (1725-1801), who afterwards remodelled the administration of the Austrian army, was at this period Daun's Quartermaster-General.

retrench; the court is obliged to abandon genius and talents, and is, in turn, abandoned by them!

Except the wretched comic opera, there is no one spectacle, but that of misery, to be seen at Dresden; no *guinguette*, no public diversion in the city or suburbs, for the people, and not a boat or vessel either of pleasure or business can be descried on the river Elbe, which is here nearly as wide as the Thames at London Bridge. The Saxon traffic *up* this fine river, is said to be ruined by some commercial disputes with Austria; and *down* it, by the king of Prussia not permitting a single vessel from Dresden to pass by his fortress of Magdeburg; so that besides paying heavy duties, all goods must be removed into Prussian vessels before they are suffered to proceed to Hamburg.

The horses in this Electorate have had no corn allowed them, nor the soldiers powder for their hair, these three years; but though every species of economy seems now put in practice, yet, it is thought with little effect, as to restoring the inhabitants and state to their ancient affluence and splendour.

During the reign of Augustus the Third [1] this city was regarded by the rest of Europe, as the Athens of modern times; all the arts, but particularly, those of music, poetry, and painting, were loved and cherished by that prince, with a zeal and munificence, greater than can be found in the brightest period of ancient history; but, perhaps, some part of the late and present distresses of this country, have originated in this excessive magnificence.

---

[1] Of Poland, who was Frederick August II, Elector of Saxony (1696–1763), and grandfather of the reigning Elector.

The gardens of the late minister, count Brühl [1], which are situated on the banks of the Elbe, and open to the public, command a delightful prospect of that river, of its hilly and fertile banks, towards Pirna, and of the New Town, and beautiful bridge, leading to it.

A most magnificent and elegant temple in these gardens was reduced to a heap of rubbish, in which it still lies, during the Prussian bombardment; and the Saxons accuse his Prussian majesty of carrying personal resentment against their minister so far, as to order his engineer to point his artillery at the temple and other buildings, as well as statues in these gardens. However this may have been, not a street of this once charming city has recovered the devastations of the last war.

The present Elector [2] is a great encourager of honesty and good morals in his subjects; and has manifested himself to be susceptible of the tender feelings of humanity, by the abolition of racks and tortures, to which criminals were exposed in his dominions, during former reigns.

Dr. Burney's first objective in Dresden was the house of the British Minister, Mr. Osborn, who outvied his colleagues in the attentions which he showered upon the distinguished traveller. Mr. Osborn entertained Dr. Burney at dinner, and afterwards took him to visit the other members of the diplomatic corps. On another occasion he arranged a large dinnerparty, followed by a private concert, attended by all the foreign Ministers.

[1] Heinrich, Count von Brühl (1700–1763), was the notorious favourite and Prime Minister of the Elector, Frederick Augustus II, and was largely responsible for the disastrous policy which involved Saxony in the Seven Years' War. He embezzled the public funds and his extravagance was proverbial: he employed twelve tailors and wore a new suit every day. Dr. Burney met his eldest son, who was then living in Dresden.

[2] Frederick August III (1750–1827), known as " the Just ": became the first King of Saxony in 1806, and as such is known as Frederick August I.

Mr. Osborn also introduced Dr. Burney to Count Sachen, the Minister for foreign affairs, who invited him to dinner.

This nobleman gives a public dinner once a week to the foreign ministers, to persons of condition, and to strangers, in a truly hospitable and splendid manner; and though his appointment is not great, so considerable is his private fortune, that he is able to support the dignity of his office at his own expense, without aggravating the present miseries of the people, by appropriating the public money, either to enrich himself or maintain magnificence.

The count's entertainment was one of the most sumptuous I ever saw; the company consisted of near forty persons, of both sexes, most of whom were of high rank and condition; each course was served on the most elegant plate, and beautiful Dresden china.

The climax of these social activities, however, was reached by Dr. Burney's presentation at the electoral court by Mr. Osborn:

At noon Mr. Osborn carried me to court, where, after waiting about an hour, in the drawing-room, among the ambassadors and great officers of state, for the arrival of the Elector, I had the honour of being presented to his highness as soon as he entered: he was pleased to enquire, "from whence I came last?" I answered, from Vienna; but Mr. Osborn informed his highness, that I had been at Munich, and had had the honour of being presented to the Electress-Dowager, his mother [1], and added something concerning my musical enquiries; this seemed to awaken curiosity. "You love music?" "Yes, Sir."

[1] See p. 125.

" Have you been in Italy?" and upon my answering in
the affirmative, his Electoral highness appeared to be
pleased, and desirous of entering into a more particular
conversation; but, throwing his eyes around, and seeing
the foreign ministers, officers of state, and a number of
strangers, and people of condition eager for notice, and
expecting their share of his attention, he turned about,
and spoke two or three words to prince Beloselsky, the
Russian minister; then one or two to the Prussian and
Austrian ministers, after which he retired. . . .

When the Elector quitted the drawing-room, everyone
hastened up another pair of stairs, to the apartment of
the Electress. I had the honour of being presented to
her highness, as she passed by, in her way to dinner; she
was a princess Palatine of Deuxponts [1], and born in 1752;
she is tall and thin, of a fresh rosy complexion, and has
strong indications of good humour in her countenance.

Her husband, the Elector, was two years her senior, and
therefore only twenty-two years of age. He was reported to
be

so good a musician as to accompany readily, and in a
masterly manner, on the harpsichord, at sight; but was
so shy of playing before company, that even the Electress,
his consort, had hardly ever heard him. His favourite
amusement is dancing, and, to oblige him, his subjects
and courtiers are dancing for ever.

On another occasion Dr. Burney attended the court in the
evening,

where the Electoral family, with their principal atten-

---

[1] Zweibrücken: once a duchy and now for the most part incorporated in Bavaria.

dants were at cards. I here had the honour of being presented to the Elector's three brothers; prince Charles Maximilian, presumptive heir to the Electorate, born in 1752; prince Anthony Clement, born in 1755, intended for the church [1]; and prince Maximilian Emanuel [2], born in 1759. The eldest of these princes has the misfortune to be so lame, that he is obliged to wheel himself about in a chair; having not only lost the use, but almost the appearance of his legs; he seems, however, very intelligent and curious in conversation. The other two are far from robust.

The next day I was presented to the two princesses, sisters of the Elector; the eldest, though but fifteen, is formed, and perfectly well-bred; she honoured me so far as to speak a considerable time to me concerning the Electress-Dowager, her mother, whom Mr. Osborn had told her, I had seen frequently at Munich. The youngest sister, about twelve years of age, is very pretty, and has a sharp and intelligent countenance; she spoke but little, however that little was pertinent and obliging.

Dr. Burney paid one visit to the opera in company with Mr. Osborn. Salieri's *L'Amore innocente*, a burletta, was performed, which was throughout " tranquil, unmeaning, and as truly soporific as a nurse's lullaby ". The Electoral family came from the country to attend this performance, which took place in the little theatre; the seating accommodation here consisted of four rows of boxes, nineteen in each row. The large theatre was shut up for reasons of economy;

No money was ever taken for admission into this

---

[1] But lived to succeed his eldest brother as the second King of Saxony, reigning from 1827 until 1836.
[2] The father of King Frederick Augustus II, who reigned from 1836 until 1854. Maximilian himself had resigned the succession.

theatre, which is nearly as large as that at Milan [1]. It has five rows of boxes, thirty in each, is of an oval form, like the theatres of Italy, and has an orchestra capable of containing a hundred performers.

In the year 1755, the late King of Poland [2] had in his service, for this theatre, ten *soprano* voices, four *contralto*, three tenors, and four basses. . . . The instrumental performers were of the first class, and more numerous than those of any other court in Europe; but, now, not above six or eight of these are to be found at Dresden.

It was from the dispersion of this celebrated band, at the beginning of the last war, that almost every great city of Europe, and London among the rest, acquired several exquisite and favourite performers.

This theatre, once the scene of the triumphs of Hasse and Faustina, had not been in use since the wedding celebrations of the reigning Elector, three years previously.

Dr. Burney found time for two visits to the picture gallery, and rhapsodizes at length over the Correggios there. He tells us, in connexion with the famous Nativity, that

the King of Prussia stopped half an hour to admire it, when he first entered Dresden. The Electress Queen offered it to him, but he declined taking it; however, he had a fine copy made of it by Dietrich, at a very high price.

The lovely Sistine Madonna of Raphael, now considered one of the chief treasures of the gallery, is dismissed with the remark that it " has suffered greatly in the colouring; the heads, however, are charming ".

Dr. Burney attended service on the Sunday morning at

[1] See p. 31.
[2] Augustus III, who was also Elector of Saxony, and reigned from 1733 to 1763.

the Lutheran Frauenkirche: the "decent and respectable" congregation numbered nearly three thousand, and greatly impressed him by their unison singing of the chorales:

the people being better musicians here than with us, and accustomed from their infancy to sing the chief part of the service, were better in tune, and formed one of the grandest choruses I ever heard. . . .

The King of Prussia, in his last bombardment of Dresden [1], tried every means in his power to beat this church, as well as the other public buildings, about the ears of the inhabitants, but in vain, for the orbicular form of the dome threw off the balls and shells, and totally prevented their effect: however, he succeeded better in five or six other churches, which he totally demolished.

Dr. Burney paid a second visit to this church in order to hear and examine the organ. Through the good offices of the British Minister he was likewise permitted to hear the organ in the electoral chapel; "the multiplicity of stops in this organ, amounting to 54, only augments noise, and adds to the weight of the touch". Indeed the poor organist,

when he had done, was in as violent a heat with fatigue and exertion, as if he had run eight or ten miles, full speed, over ploughed lands in the dog-days.

That night Dr. Burney went to the house of the organist

to see the ruins of the famous *Pantaleone*. This instrument, and the performance upon it, at Paris, in 1705, gave birth to a very ingenious little work, under the title of *Dialogue sur la musique des Anciens*, by the Abbé Chateauneuf: the inventor went by the name of his

[1] On 12th July, 1760.

instrument ever after; it is more than nine feet long, and had, when in order, 186 strings of catgut. The tone was produced by two *baguettes*, or sticks, like the dulcimer; it must have been extremely difficult to the performer, but seems capable of great effects. The strings were now almost all broken, the present Elector will not be at the charge of furnishing new ones, though it had ever been thought a court instrument in former reigns, and was kept in order at the expense of the prince. M. Binder (the organist) lamented, that he could not possibly afford to string it himself, as it was an instrument upon which he had formerly employed so much of his time.

During divine service in Dresden the gates of the city were shut. This custom dated from the Reformation,

for the citizens having been observed to go in great numbers to walk in the fields while the public prayers were performing, rather than assist at them, the gates were ordered to be shut, to prevent the inhabitants from going out, and they were forced to church by the soldiers then in garrison. At present, the army is never made use of for that purpose, for the Saxons are now as strongly attached to the tenets of Luther, as they were then to the Roman Catholic religion.

Another ancient institution, which still survived in the city, was the establishment of singing boys or poor scholars:

Even at the common boarding schools of this city, children are taught to sing hymns in parts. The school singers who frequent the streets, not excepting the little boys, wear a black undertaker-like uniform, and large grizzle wigs; and as every house pays annually something towards their support, the ambassadors generally give them a crown a quarter, for *not* singing at *their* doors. . . .

The method prescribed to them to follow and observe, is this: the town is divided into certain wards; when they begin to sing, the first of the month, for instance, before the doors of the principal ward, they sing the second of the month at the next; and so on, till they have successively made their singing rounds over all the wards of the city, which they commence again in a perpetual rotation.

Besides the usual turn, it is customary with families of distinction, and some citizens who maintain the strictest appearance of devotion, to appoint these scholars to sing before their houses once or twice in the week, for which they receive extraordinary payment, and although that is discretionary, yet it is so far regulated, that no one should give them less than two *groschen*, or four pence for every canticle they sing. Some families employ them to sing gay genial airs on birthdays and name-days; and they are frequently engaged to sing mournful ditties and dirges at night, with lighted torches in their hands, before the houses of the rich and opulent, when they die; and they accompany the funerals to the place of interment, singing the *neniæ*, in the same manner the *præficæ*, or weeping women, at the burials of the ancients, used to do.

It is to be observed, that besides the laborious way of singing in the streets during the whole winter, in a severe climate, they are obliged to sing in different churches every Sunday and festival. They are generally divided into troops of sixteen or eighteen together, and what they collect during the whole week, is put into a common box, which is opened every Saturday by the rector of the school, and what remains over and above their necessary expenses, he divides into small sums among them, in proportion to their musical merit; for when he that leads the vocal band gets a dollar to his share, the next that excels gets but a florin, or two-thirds of a dollar. These shares are not entrusted into their own hands immediately, but are kept for them by the rector, till they have also finished their classics, and then, at their quitting the school, they respectively receive their savings.

From their ranks were recruited the village schoolmasters of the electorate, who also served as organists in the parish churches. The best of the singing boys were sent to the Leipzig and Wittenberg universities, where over three hundred were at this time enjoying a free education.

Dr. Burney's stay in Dresden coincided with that of a fellow-countryman called Tunnerstick,

who was born at Poole, in Dorsetshire, but brought up in France, and who, last summer, in several parts of Germany, had undertaken to perform a very curious experiment: it was no less, than to drive a nail through the brain of a horse, by which he would be, to all appearance dead; but, after extracting the nail, and pouring into the wound a chemical liquor prepared by himself for that purpose, the horse in five or six minutes' time, was to recover sufficiently to carry any one of the spectators.

Mr. Tunnerstick was at Vienna at the same time as myself, and performed before thousands of spectators;

but the account of the operation seemed to me so extraordinary, that imagining there was some quackery or
deception in it, I would not make one of the number.
However, upon my arrival at Dresden, I found that he
had repeatedly performed the same thing there, before
physicians, anatomists, and the whole court; one of the
horses that had undergone this singular operation, and
was recovered, had been killed by command of the
Elector, in order, by dissection to ascertain the fact,
whether the nail had really penetrated the brain; and
it was allowed by all the physicians and surgeons of the
place, to have passed through the most dangerous part
of it. Another horse that had been *assassinated* in the
same barbarous manner, at the same time and place,
was recovered, and continued perfectly well, when I left
Dresden.

The Elector wishing to have this medicine turned to
some useful account, and not merely employed in healing
wounds made through wanton cruelty, had asked this
equestrian operator, whether it would be equally efficacious
if applied to fresh wounds in other parts of the body?
Dr. Tunnerstick answered in the affirmative; but afterwards, pretending to take offence at some doubts, that
had been expressed, concerning the success of this second
experiment, evaded making it, and went away in a
pet.

Dr. Burney appears to have quitted Dresden on 23rd September; he was in any case in Leipzig on 24th September.

CHAPTER X

Leipzig and Berlin

Dr. Burney stopped for two days in Leipzig. There was very little of musical interest in the city to occupy his attention.

This city (he writes) has not yet recovered (from) its rigorous treatment during the last war; and its celebrated fair, which used to be the rendezvous of the rich, the gay, and the industrious citizens of every quarter of the globe, as well as an assembly of the sovereign princes and nobility of all the northern parts of Europe, seems now dwindled into a common mart, or quarterly fair, such as is held in a small English market town.

He found a warm friend in Johann Hiller (1728–1804), the inventor of the " Singspiel " and virtual founder of the famous Gewandhaus concerts. Hiller hardly quitted Dr. Burney from his arrival to his departure. On the first evening he dragged the poor weary traveller to his box at the opera, where a touring company from Berlin was performing.

The performers did not charm me, either by their singing or acting; all were out of tune, out of time, and vulgar. I hardly ever was more tired; but indeed, after travelling all night in an open wagon, a better performance would with difficulty have kept me awake.

The next morning Hiller took Burney to hear one of his own " Singspiele " rehearsed.

The overture, and one song, had been performed when we entered, but all was begun again. I found this music very natural and pleasing, and deserving of much better performers than the present Leipzig company can boast; for, to say the truth, the singing here is as vulgar and ordinary as our common singing in England among those who have neither had the advantage of being taught, nor of hearing good singing. . . . The instrumental parts went ill; but as this was the first rehearsal, they might have been disciplined into good order, if M. Hiller had chosen to bounce and play the tyrant a little; for it is a melancholy reflection to make, that few composers are well treated by an orchestra, till they have first used the performers roughly, and made themselves formidable.

Dr. Burney attributes the low standard of singing in Leipzig to its distance from an Italian opera, staffed by Italian singers! The memory of John Sebastian Bach, the great Cantor, who had died in Leipzig twenty-two years before, was still green. It is, however, as an organist and a theorist that Dr. Burney hymns his praises, having

united in himself the talents of many great men: deep science, a fertile and lively genius, an easy and natural taste, and the most powerful hand that can be imagined.

His greatest talent was then hardly recognized, the compositions singled out for praise being remarkable rather for the display of technical ingenuity than for the measure of inspiration attained.

Hiller took Dr. Burney through the Leipzig book-shops.

It seems, by the catalogues published in this city, at

the two great fairs of Easter and Michaelmas, that more books are printed in Germany, than in any other country of Europe: and perhaps Leipzig has a greater share in these publications, than any other city of Germany.

One of the first visits which Dr. Burney paid was to Johann Gottlob Immanuel Breitkopf (1719–1794), the son of the founder of the great music publishing house subsequently known as Breitkopf und Härtel, and the most eminent member of his family. Dr. Burney expected much from his interview with Breitkopf,

but I found him rather taciturn than communicative. He claims the honour of being the inventor of musical types,[1] and seems entitled to it, as he has, for thirteen or fourteen years, furnished his own country, as well as other parts of Europe, with a prodigious quantity of music from his press, of all kinds, by the greatest composers of the present age,[2] of which he prints catalogues quarterly; he seems likewise to have been the first who gave to his catalogues an index *in notes*, containing the *subjects*, or two or three first bars, of the several pieces in each musical work;[3] by which a reader is enabled to discover not only whether he is in possession of an *entire* book, but of any part of its contents.

Besides *printed* copies of works of the most celebrated composers of all nations, he sells in manuscript, at a reasonable price, single pieces of any work already printed, as well as of innumerable others which have never been published.

[1] Hardly the inventor, the type printing of music dating from the end of the fifteenth century. Breitkopf did much to improve the process.
[2] Notably Carl Philipp Emmanuel Bach.
[3] Called in modern parlance, a thematic catalogue.

On another occasion Dr. Burney was shown over the Breitkopf printing works

and found a great number of presses at work, of various kinds, for his publications are not confined to music. Among the several questions which my curiosity put to the workmen, one was, how many different characters were used for letterpress, and what proportion they bore in their number to the types used in printing? and I was much surprised to find, that the different characters employed in the music press, were upwards of three hundred and that there were not more than one hundred used in common printing.

Dr. Burney visited a number of the Leipzig churches, which were generally very dirty, and discovered several fine organs, though there was no worthy successor of J. S. Bach to perform upon them. With regard to the internal decorations of the churches, he writes:

In Charles the fifth's[1] time, before religious disputes were adjusted, a kind of truce was agreed on between the Catholics and Reformers, under the title of *Interim*, which stipulated, that the ornaments and vestments of the church, as well as some of the ceremonies, should remain in *statu quo*, till, by a general council, religious peace was finally concluded; and this *Interim* was afterwards adopted in some of the free cities, where the churches, though still in the possession of Lutherans, retain all the ancient ornaments of the Roman Catholic times.

From Leipzig Dr. Burney passed on to Berlin:

After suffering the usual hardships of bad fare, bad

[1] 1500–1558.

roads, bad carriages, and bad horses, for two days and a night, in my way from Leipzig to Berlin; and being obliged, during that time, to wait three or four hours, either in my open vehicle, or the open air, at each post-house, while horses were sought and fed with straw, wheels greased, and inevitable squabbles about the number of horses which I was to have, were adjusted, I arrived at Schwarmuth[1], within one post of Berlin.

When a traveller comes to a post-house, in this part of the world, with two horses, he is rudely teased to go out with *three*; and if he arrive with three, *four* are forced upon him, if possible, at his departure, and so on, *crescendo*, let the first number be what it will; and all this is transacted on the part of the post-master and his people, with an insolence and brutality so determined, that reasoning and remonstrating operate no otherwise than in rendering them more obstinate and malevolent. It seems a thing of necessity, for postilions, in every part of the world, to be greater brutes than those they drive: here, it is the case, *par excellence*; and so insatiable in their demands and expectations, are these sworn foes to man and beast, that I have frequently tried to part in peace and good humour with them, by more than doubling their stated and accustomed fees, but in vain: each claim was a hydra.

I quitted Schwarmuth at seven o'clock in the evening, in hopes of getting to Berlin before midnight. The weather was now extremely disagreeable; rain was coming on, with a cold and furious north wind full in my face. The wagon with which I had been furnished, at

[1] ? Saarmund.

the last post-house, was the worst and most defenceless that I had hitherto mounted; before nine o'clock, it rained violently, and became so dark, that the postilion lost his way, and descended from his place, in the front of the wagon, in order to feel for it with his hands; but being unable to distinguish any track of a carriage, he mounted again, and, in driving on, at a venture, got into a bog, on a bleak and barren heath, where we were stuck fast, and obliged to remain from eleven o'clock at night, till near six the next morning; when daylight enabled us to disentangle the horses and carriage, and discover the road to the capital of Brandenburg. It had never ceased raining and blowing the whole night; the cold was intense; and nothing could be more forlorn than my condition.

When I arrived at the gates of this city (Berlin), about nine o'clock in the morning, September 28th, I had hopes that I should have been suffered to pass peaceably to an inn, having received a passport at Treuenbrietzen, the first Prussian town I entered on the Saxony side, where I had submitted to a thorough rummage of my baggage, at the persuasion of the custom-house officers, who had assured me that it would prevent all future trouble upon entering Berlin. But this was merely to levy fees upon me, for, notwithstanding my passport, I was stopped three-quarters of an hour at the barrier, before I was taken into the custody of a sentinel; who mounting my post-wagon, with his musket on his shoulder, and bayonet fixed, conducted me, like a prisoner, through the principal streets of the city, to the custom-house. Here I was detained in the yard more than two hours, shivering with cold, in all my wet garments, while everything was taken out of my trunk and writing box, and examined as curiously as if I had just arrived at Dover, from the capital of France.

Dr. Burney appears to have spent some ten days in Berlin, of which three were passed at Potsdam, where the court was in residence. He entered upon his inquiries with lively anticipation, Frederick the Great (1712–1786) being equally famous among his contemporaries as a patron of art and letters and as a great military commander. He adopted the same attitude in either capacity: uniformity was straitly enjoined upon all his subjects, and any variation from the standard of taste set them by the sovereign was regarded as *lèse-majesté*. Dr. Burney was therefore somewhat disappointed: most of the music which he heard was dull and old-fashioned, and was played in a rough and mechanical manner, devoid of light and shade. Of all the composers in the service of His Prussian Majesty, only two had dared to show originality; the rest were content to copy the models approved by their royal master. The favourite composers of the King were old Capellmeister Graun, who had been dead for some years, and Quantz, the royal flute master:

the one is languid, and the other frequently common and insipid, . . . and yet, their names are *religion* at Berlin, and more sworn by, than those of Luther and Calvin.

There are, however, schisms in this city, as elsewhere; but heretics are obliged to keep their opinions to themselves, while those of the establishment may speak out: for though a universal toleration prevails here, as to different sects of Christians, yet, in music, whoever dares to profess any other tenets than those of Graun and Quantz, is sure to be persecuted.

Even the repertoire at the opera house was confined to the

works of three composers, although relief was afforded by the performance of Italian operas at carnival time.

And, in the opera house, as in the field, his majesty is such a rigid disciplinarian, that if a mistake is made in a single movement or evolution, he immediately marks, and rebukes the offender; and if any of his Italian troops dare to deviate from strict discipline, by adding, altering, or diminishing a single passage in the parts they have to perform, an order is sent, *de par le Roi*, for them to adhere strictly to the notes written by the composer, at their peril. This, when compositions are good, and a singer is licentious, may be an excellent method; but certainly shuts out all taste and refinement.[1]   So that music is truly stationary in this country, his majesty allowing no more liberty in that, than he does in civil matters of government: not contented with being sole monarch of the lives, fortunes, and business of his subjects, he even prescribes rules to their most innocent pleasures.

And yet Frederick was an able musician and a composer of some merit. During the lifetime of his father, Frederick William I, he was not only forbidden to study and practise music, but even to hear it. His mother, Sophia Dorothea of Hanover, encouraged his musical tastes and procured musicians to instruct him,

but so necessary was secrecy in all these negotiations, that if the king his father had discovered that he was disobeyed, all these sons of Apollo would have incurred the danger of being hanged. The prince frequently took

[1] It must be remembered that Dr. Burney was writing in the age of "graces" and "ornaments", when it was a universal custom for singers and players to embellish the music which they were performing with cadenzas and appoggiaturas: however reprehensible a practice, it was generally countenanced by composers.

occasion, to meet his musicians a-hunting, and had his concerts either in a forest or cavern.

Frederick had the greatest antipathy to any form of church music, and this species of music was therefore not cultivated in Berlin. To such a pitch was this prejudice carried that the secular works of any composer who had dared to write an anthem or oratorio were for ever suspect, and impatiently dismissed by the King as savouring of the Church. His well-known feeling against native artists is illustrated by the following remark, which was occasioned by the request that he should hear a German singer: " A German singer? I should as soon expect to receive pleasure from the neighing of my horse." On this occasion he had, as a matter of fact, to admit an error of judgment.

Frederick's habits of life resembled the clockwork precision of his soldiers when on parade. He was rarely in Berlin except at carnival time, from the middle of December onwards into January:

When his majesty and the court arrive at Berlin, every day of the week, except Saturday, which is a day of rest, has its particular amusements allotted to it, according to the following regulations.

On *Sunday*, the Queen [1] has a great court. On *Monday*, there is an opera. *Tuesday*, a ridotto, or masqued ball, in the opera house. *Wednesday*, a French play, at the court theatre. *Thursday*, the princess dowager [2] has a drawing room; and on *Friday*, there is another opera.

At other times, his majesty's usual residence is at Sans-Souci, a palace near Potsdam, five German miles

---

[1] Formerly the Princess Elizabeth Christina of Brunswick Bevern. She was noted for her charity and was also endowed with certain literary gifts. She lived on until 1797.

[2] Louisa Amalie was a sister of the Queen of Prussia and the widow of Augustus William, younger brother of Frederick the Great, who had died in 1757. Her son was heir-presumptive to the throne, and became king on the death of his uncle in 1786.

from Berlin, where he is attended by his musicians in ordinary, who are there in monthly waiting, by turns.

At Potsdam the same rigorous regime was observed:

His majesty's hour of rising, is constantly at four o'clock in the morning, during summer, and at five in winter; and from that time till nine, when his ministers of different departments attend him, he is employed in reading letters, and answering them in the margin. He then drinks one dish of coffee, and proceeds to business with his ministers, who come full fraught with doubts, difficulties, documents, petitions, and other papers, to read. With these he spends two hours, and then exercises his own regiment on the parade, in the same manner as the youngest colonel in his service.

At twelve o'clock he dines. His dinner is long, and generally with twelve or fourteen persons; after this he gives an hour to artists and projectors; then reads and signs the letters, written by his secretaries, from the marginal notes which he had made in the morning. When this is over, he thinks the *business* of the day is accomplished; the rest is given to amusement; after his evening concert, he gives some time to conversation, if disposed for it, and his courtiers in waiting constantly attend for that purpose; but whether that is the case or not, he has a lecturer to read to him, every evening, titles and extracts of new books, among which he marks such as he wishes to have purchased for his library, or to read in his cabinet. In this manner, when not employed in the field, reviewing his troops, or in travelling, he spends his time: always retiring at ten o'clock, after which, however, he frequently reads, writes, or composes music for his flute, before he goes to bed.

Dr. Burney's first act in Berlin was to present his letters of introduction. In spite of his sufferings during the journey, he hurried straight away from the custom-house to see Mr. Harris, the British envoy-extraordinary at the Prussian court, who received him with great politeness and gave him much excellent advice regarding the methods which he should pursue in making his inquiries. During his stay in Berlin Dr. Burney visited two pupils of J. S. Bach: J. F. Agricola (1720–1774), who had succeeded Graun as court composer. He was reputed to be the finest organist in Berlin and the best teacher of singing in Germany. "Though he was indisposed, and had just been blooded", he sat down and played to Dr. Burney on a "fine *piano forte*". The other was J. P. Kirnberger (1721–1783), the theorist, who at this time was so engrossed in mathematical studies that he appeared "to be more ambitious of the character of an algebraist, than of a musician of genius". He took Dr. Burney to visit "the house of Hildebrand, the best maker of harpsichords, and pianofortes, in Berlin". More interesting than either to Dr. Burney was Friedrich Wilhelm Marpurg (1718–1795), the eminent critic and writer, "who had so long laboured in the same vineyard" as Dr. Burney, and was himself the author of a history of music. Marpurg was, however, at this time director of the royal lottery and had been invested with the title of Councillor of War, so his services were lost to music. However, Dr. Burney derived much pleasure and profit from his conversation during the three visits which he paid him. Marpurg gave him a description of a machine which had been invented in Berlin for recording extemporized music and voluntaries—an instrument which had a counterpart in England and had long been of great interest to Dr. Burney.

Dr. Burney attended a performance at the French theatre, where an opera was performed, which had "very little musical merit", and on this occasion the singers "contrived to make that little, still less". He went over the large opera house, and was much impressed by its exterior decorations.

A considerable part of the front of this edifice forms a hall, in which the court has a repast on ridotto days; the rest is for the theatre, which, besides a vast pit, has four rows of boxes, thirteen in each, and these severally contain thirty persons. It is one of the widest theatres I ever saw, though it seems rather short in proportion. . . .

The king being at the whole expense of this opera; the entrance is *gratis*, so that anyone, who is decently dressed, may have admission into the pit. The first row of boxes is set apart for the royal family and nobility; the boxes that are even with the pit, and those of the second and third row, are appropriated to the use of the ministers of state, foreign ministers, and persons of rank, who have offices about the court; and a stranger of distinction, by application to the baron Pölnitz, chamberlain and director of public spectacles, is sure of being accommodated with a place in the theatre, according to his rank.

The performance of the opera begins at six o'clock; the king, with the princes, and his attendants, are placed in the pit, close to the orchestra; the queen, the princesses, and other ladies of distinction, sit in the front boxes; her majesty is saluted at her entrance into the theatre, and at her departure thence by two bands of trumpets and kettledrums, placed one on each side the house, in the upper row of boxes.[1]

The king always stands behind the *maestro di capella*, in sight of the score, which he frequently looks at, and

[1] In a footnote Dr. Burney expatiates on the love of noise which was at this time so marked a characteristic of the German courts. " There is scarce a sovereign prince in Germany, who thinks he can dine comfortably, or with proper dignity, without a flourish of drums and trumpets."

indeed performs the part of *director-general* here, as much as of *generalissimo* in the field.

The establishment of the Berlin opera house and the composition of the orchestra are of great interest. The band was arranged according to the custom at Dresden, and consisted of about fifty performers, the proportions being as follows (the order and nomenclature are Dr. Burney's): eleven violins, five violoncellos, two double basses, two harpsichord players, one harp, four tenors, four flutes, four oboes, four bassoons, and two French horns. It must have been a very "reedy" orchestra. Attached to the opera were two composers, a "concert-master", a ballet-master and a poet. Among the principal singers was a lady, seventy-two years of age: Dr. Burney drily observes that this is "a time of life, when nature seldom allows us any other voice, than that of complaint, or second childhood". The opera chorus consisted of twenty-four singers, and in addition there was of course a ballet.

There were also performances of Italian comic operas

at the expense of the king, for which two women, and three men singers, are in salary. The instrumental performers are drawn from his majesty's band, as are the dancers, from his serious opera; the singers, male and female, reside at Potsdam. These operas are performed at no fixed time, but depend upon the king's pleasure to command them, in one of the theatres of his palaces, at Potsdam, Berlin, or Charlottenburg.

The King was not alone in his patronage of music:

The queen, and the princess dowager of Prussia, frequently give concerts at Berlin, to which the entrance is open and general. At these performances, the principal singers of the opera, and musicians of his majesty's band, are employed.

Fashions in dances were as variable then as now:

In assemblies, except minuets, the dances are almost constantly English,[1] the Polonaises, so much in vogue formerly, are now no longer practised, but they still, sometimes, make use of French dances.[2]

Dr. Burney visited all the Berlin churches which were reputed to have good organs, but

found the organs of Berlin large, coarse, and crowded with noisy stops, which, if they had been in tune, would have produced no pleasing effects; but as it was, such a number of dissonant and ill-voiced pipes, more tortured than tickled my ears. . . .

I enquired in vain of musical people in that city, whether they knew of any such machine, as a swell, worked by pedals, in any of their organs; no such contrivance had ever been heard of, and it was difficult to explain it.

In the garrison church, built in 1722, Dr. Burney discovered an organ case "in the old Teutonic taste and extremely curious", which he dismisses contemptuously as an "ecclesiastical puppet-show ":

At each wing is a kettledrum, which is beat by an Angel placed behind it, whose motion the organist regulates by a pedal; at the top of the pyramid, or middle column of pipes, there are two figures, representing Fame, spreading their wings, when the drums are beat, and raising them as high as the top of the pyramid; each of these figures sounds a trumpet, and then takes its flight.

---

[1] Probably the "contre-danse" or "country-dance", which arrived via Paris.
[2] Such as the "Rigaudon"

There are likewise two suns, which move to the sound of cymbals, and the wind obliges them to cross the clouds; during which time, two eagles take their flight, as naturally as if they were alive.

Apart from the performances of organists, Dr. Burney does not appear to have heard much music in Berlin. He attended two private concerts, but neither the music nor the playing were to his taste. Of the music of the people we hear very little. Singing was taught in some of the schools, and there still existed in the city a choir of children, twenty-four in number, who, clothed in a grey uniform and cloaks, sang in the streets, and collected money, which was divided amongst them. Otherwise the streets of Berlin were quiet, except for the song of the night watchmen:

The night watch here, consists of a certain number of armed men, who are distributed in the several streets, throughout the city. They cry the hour in a kind of *chant*, with the sound of a horn, which is likewise the custom throughout Germany.

The custom persists in Rothenburg up to the present day, but is chiefly familiar to us by reason of its appearance in the second act of Wagner's music drama, " Die Meister-singer von Nürnberg ".

Dr. Burney probably left Berlin for Hamburg on 5th or 6th October: the chronology of his journey at this point is obscure, and he leaves us for a whole six days without dates. Before proceeding further, however, a digression is necessary to deal with his visit to Potsdam, an account of which will be found in the following chapter.

CHAPTER XI

Potsdam

Dr. Burney was at Potsdam during the period 30th September to 3rd October, and he can rarely have spent four days more strenuously than these. As the court was at Sans-Souci, all the musicians of importance in Berlin were in attendance at Potsdam; moreover, Dr. Burney was burning with curiosity to hear the King play the flute, and thus receive first-hand experience of his musical capability, which was renowned throughout Europe. The road to Potsdam reminded him of his journeys between London and King's Lynn.

The road from Berlin hither, is through a deep running sand, like the worst parts of Norfolk and Suffolk, where there are no turnpikes, till within a few miles of the town; and then it is through a wild forest of fir trees, with lakes frequently in sight. Upon a nearer approach, there is a fine opening on the left hand, to a very large piece of water, and a beautiful view of the town, in which three towers, of the same size and shape, only appear, but these are elegant. The rest of the way is through a wood, cut into walks and rides, which intersect each other, and lead to different towns and villas.

The examination at the gates of this city, is the most minute and curious, both in going in, and out, which I have ever experienced in my travels; it could not be more rigorous at the postern of a town besieged. Name, character, whence, where, when, to whom recommended, business, stay, and several other particulars, were demanded, to which the answers were all written down.

However, a stranger, upon his entrance into this city, is made some amends, by the variety and splendour of new objects, for the bad road, and difficulty of admission, which he has previously encountered.

The streets are the most regularly beautiful which I ever remember to have seen; the houses all seem to be built of white stone, though they are only of brick, stuccoed over, in imitation of stone. . . .

The number of houses in this city has been very much increased during the reign of his present majesty, and that of his father. At the beginning of this century, there were only two hundred houses, and at present there are at least two thousand, and seventeen thousand inhabitants, exclusive of the military, which amount to about eight thousand men.

Four battalions of foot guards, with the squadron of life guards, and the regiment of the prince of Prussia [1], compose the constant garrison of Potsdam. The uniform of the first battalion of foot guards, is blue, embroidered with silver, and turned up with red; the waistcoats are of pale yellow; the hats, which are extremely large, have a very broad silver lace, in imitation of *point d'espagne*, and are cocked in the old Khevenhuller fashion,[2] which, added to huge black whiskers, give the men a most formidable appearance. The fourth battalion, called the

---

[1] Who afterwards became Frederick William II, King of Prussia (1744–1797); he was a nephew of Frederick the Great.

[2] That is, looped in front and behind.

Lestewitz battalion, is formed of the remains of the late king's *tall* grenadiers.[1]

The squares, public buildings, and houses of individuals, in this city, are elegant and noble. . . . His majesty's present passion is for architecture, in which he is said to expend £200,000 a year. Potsdam is almost entirely new built, from his own designs, besides his new palace, near Sans-Souci, and innumerable houses and palaces in Berlin, constructed since the last war.[2] Whenever a citizen is about building a house, either in his capital, or at Potsdam, his majesty furnishes the design, and is at the expense of building the front. . . .

In visiting the principal streets and squares of this beautiful city, which is well built, well paved, magnificent, and new, I could not help observing, that foot passengers were here, as well as in every other city of Europe, except London, exposed to accidents from being mixed with horses and carriages, as well as from the insolence and brutality of their riders and drivers, for want of a *footpath* . . . and, perhaps, England is the only country, at present, where the common people are sufficiently respected, for their lives and limbs to be thought worth preserving.

The present rage for architecture, in his Prussian majesty, is carried on with such excess, that, in Potsdam, buildings which have all the external grandeur and elegance of palaces, are made the habitations of common soldiers, who rather exist than live in them, upon five *kreuzers*, twopence halfpenny, a day. However, this

---

[1] The guard of giants was the personal hobby of Frederick William I (1688–1740); it was gradually disbanded by his son, Frederick the Great.

[2] The Seven Years' War (1756–1763).

passion is hereditary, for the late king of Prussia made it a condition, in bestowing offices and employments about his court and person, that each incumbent should build a house; reserving to himself the pleasure of planning and constructing the front.

Dr. Burney's first action on arrival at Potsdam was to seek out Franz Benda (1709–1786), Konzertmeister to the king since the death of Graun, through whom he hoped to procure admission to the king's private concert. But Benda had already gone to the palace to perform his task of accompanying the king's flute playing. Although it was seven o'clock in the evening Dr. Burney drove out to Lord Marshal's [1] (sic) house in the suburbs, and presented the letter of introduction given him by Mr. Harris. The porter, " an honest Scotsman ", inquired whether Dr. Burney spoke English, and then informed him that Lord Marshal was " at home, but in his night gown ". So well did Lord Marshal and Dr. Burney get on with one another that the visit lasted three hours, the conversation ranging over a whole field of musical and other subjects. Though his advanced age made it impossible for him to attend court, Lord Marshal was on excellent terms with the King, who " kept a cover for him constantly at his table ", and whom he promised to interest in Dr. Burney's work. On two subsequent occasions during his visit Lord Marshal entertained Dr. Burney to dinner.

Dr. Burney visited Benda and interviewed old Quantz (1697–1773), the court composer and flautist, who instructed the King. He presented his letters of introduction to Colonel Quintus Icilius, a great connoisseur of the arts, whose real name was Guichard, Quintus Icilius being

only his *nom de guerre*, given to him, in pleasantry, by his

[1] George Keith, tenth Earl Marischal (? 1693–1778), brother of Marshal Keith (1696–1758), the great Prussian general. Both brothers were great favourites of Frederick the Great. George succeeded to the earldom in 1712, but was an ardent Jacobite. After the '15 he fled the country and went to Spain, subsequently entering the service of the Prussian king and acting as Prussian ambassador in Paris and elsewhere. He was pardoned by George II in 1759 and returned to his Scottish estates, but latterly returned to Berlin at the earnest request of Frederick the Great.

majesty, who, when he conferred upon him a command in a regiment, hastily raised and collected from the refuse of all nations, during the heat of the last war, honoured him with the appellation of the commander of Cæsar's tenth legion, a name which has since been adopted by the whole Prussian nation.

Dr. Burney also had letters to Colonel de Forcade, who was "court marshal" to the heir apparent, the Prince of Prussia[1], for whom Dr. Burney had a parcel of books from England. The Prince of Prussia invited Dr. Burney to supper:

At half an hour past six in the evening, I therefore went to the palace of the prince royal, where I expected to hear music; but cards, and conversation, filled up the time, till supper. At my first entrance, I had the honour of being presented to his princess[2], who is fair, rather tall, and possessed of that pleasing degree of plumpness, which the French call *l'embonpoint charmant*: with a person infinitely less agreeable than falls to the share of this princess, her uncommonly gracious and condescending address and manner would captivate everyone whom she honours with her notice. . . .

She plays the harpsichord well herself, as I was assured, and was very curious and conversible about music: even while at cards, she condescended to address herself to me very frequently, and at last asked me if I had known her brother, when he was in England?—I then recollected, and not before, that her royal highness was a princess of

---

[1] Afterwards Frederick William II (1744–1797), King of Prussia, the patron of Mozart and Beethoven.

[2] Frederika Louisa, daughter of Landgrave Louis IX of Hesse-Darmstadt. This was his second wife. He married Elizabeth Christina, daughter of Duke Charles of Brunswick, in 1765, but the marriage had been annulled in 1769.

Hesse-Darmstadt, and sister to that prince of Hesse-Darmstadt, who last year made the tour of England, and to whom I had had the honour of being presented in London.[1]

During this time, a young prince of two years of age,[2] and his sister of only a year old,[3] were brought into the card room to the princess their mother; and, not long after, the prince of Prussia entered, to whom I had the honour of being presented. His royal highness is tall, and of a manly, plain, natural, and agreeable character. At supper, he was so gracious as to make me sit down on his left hand, and to address the discourse to me almost the whole evening. He was cheerful and open, and seemed very well acquainted with the present state of the several countries of Europe, particularly England. Music had a considerable share in the conversation, and it was not difficult to discover that his royal highness is less strongly attached to old music, and to old masters, than his majesty.

Dr. Burney was not presented to Frederick the Great, but by means of the powerful introductions with which he was armed, he succeeded in the difficult task of winning admission to the King's private concert and hearing his Prussian Majesty play the flute. Prior to the concert Dr. Burney visited the new palace,

built since the last war. The ground on which it is erected, was a morass eight years ago, as was the whole country round it, which is a dead flat, and still very naked and

---

[1] Possibly Louis, first Grand-Duke of Hesse (1753–1830).
[2] Afterwards Frederick William III, King of Prussia (1770–1840).
[3] Wilhelmina, afterwards wife of William of Orange, who became William I, King of the Netherlands.

barren; it was however in consequence of the rapidity with which this palace was constructed, and the face of the country changed, that a German wit said, " it must be allowed, that his majesty performs miracles, though he believes none ".

It is not my design to give a minute description of this superb palace; I shall only observe, in general, that it appeared to me, one of the most elegant and perfect, which I had seen in Europe. It is constructed, as well as most of the magnificent buildings in Potsdam, from his majesty's own designs. . . .

The apartments are fitted up with the utmost magnificence and taste. There is a *suite* of rooms appropriated to almost every branch of the royal family. Those of the king, of his sister [1] princess Amelia, and the prince of Prussia, are the most splendid. In each of these apartments, there is a room dedicated to music, furnished with books, desks, a harpsichord, and with other instruments.

His majesty's concert room is ornamented with glasses of an immense size, and with sculpture, partly gilt, and partly of the most beautiful green varnish, by Martin of Paris [2]; the whole furniture and ornaments of this room, are in a most refined and exquisite taste. There is a *piano forte* made by Silbermann of Neuberg [3], beautifully varnished and embellished; and a tortoiseshell desk for

[1] More accurately " sister-in-law ".

[2] The inventor of " Vernis-Martin ", an Oriental lacquer which enjoyed a tremendous vogue during the reign of Louis XV; the secret of Martin's varnish is said to have been communicated to him by missionaries who had worked in Japan.

[3] Gottfried Silbermann (1683–1753), the most celebrated member of a famous family of organ builders. He constructed at least three pianofortes for Frederick the Great, upon one of which J. S. Bach played on the occasion of his visit to Potsdam in 1747. " Neuberg " should read Freiburg.

his majesty's use, most richly and elegantly inlaid with silver; on the table lay a catalogue of concertos for the *new palace*, and a book of manuscript *Solfeggi*, as his majesty calls them, or preludes, composed of difficult divisions and passages for the exercise of the hand, as the vocal *Solfeggi* are for the throat. His majesty has books of this kind, for the use of his flute, in the music room of every one of his palaces.

In another apartment, there is a most magnificent harpsichord, made by Shudi [1], in England; the hinges, pedals, and frame are of silver, the case is inlaid, and the front is of tortoiseshell; this instrument which cost 200 guineas, was sent to Hamburg by sea, and from thence to Potsdam, up the Elbe and the Havel, which, I was told, had injured it so much, that it has been useless ever since; however, it is natural to suppose, that some jealousy may have been excited by it, and that it has not had quite fair play from those employed to repair it; for I never heard of any one of the great number of harpsichords, which are annually sent from England to the East and West Indies by sea, receiving so much damage as this is said to have done, in a much shorter passage. . . .

There were innumerable things in and about this palace, which merited a minute examination; but I was obliged to hasten away, in order to be present at his majesty's evening concert, at Sans-Souci. I was carried thither between five and six o'clock in the evening, by an officer of the household, a privileged person, other-

---

[1] Burkat Shudi (1702–1773), the great harpsichord maker and founder of the firm of Broadwood. Frederick the Great acquired two Shudi harpsichords in 1766. It is recorded that Mozart, during his visit to London in 1765, played on an instrument which Burkat Shudi had made for Frederick the Great.

wise it would have been impossible for a stranger, like myself, to gain admission into a palace where the king resides; and even with my well-known guide, I underwent a severe examination, not only at going out of the gates at Potsdam, but at every door of the palace. When we arrived at the vestibule, we were met by M. de Catt, lecturer to his majesty, and member of the royal academy, to whom I had been furnished with a letter, who very politely attended my conductor and me the whole evening.

I was carried to one of the interior apartments of the palace, in which the gentlemen of the king's band were waiting for his commands. This apartment was contiguous to the concert room, where I could distinctly hear his majesty practising *Solfeggi* on the flute, and exercising himself in difficult passages, previous to his calling in the band.

Dr. Burney had a short talk with Quantz, who told him that the King, his scholar, "played no other concertos than those which he had expressly composed for his use, which amounted to 300, and these he performed in rotation". But this conversation was soon

interrupted by the arrival of a messenger from the king, commanding the gentlemen of his band to attend him in the next room.

The concert began by a German flute concerto, in which his majesty executed the solo parts with great precision. . . . I was much pleased, and even surprised with the neatness of his execution in the *allegros*, as well as by his expression and feeling in the *adagio*; in short, his performance surpassed, in many particulars, anything I had ever heard among *Dilettanti*, or even professors. His majesty played three long and difficult concertos successively, and all with equal perfection. . . .

M. Quantz bore no other part in the performance of the concertos of to-night, than to give the time with the motion of his hand, at the beginning of each movement, except now and then to cry out *bravo!* to his royal scholar, at the end of the solo parts and closes; which seems to be a privilege allowed to no other musician of the band. The cadenzas which his majesty made, were good, but very long and studied. It is easy to discover that these concertos were composed at a time when he did not so frequently require an opportunity of breathing as at present; for in some of the divisions, which were very long and difficult, as well as in the closes, he was obliged to take his breath, contrary to rule, before the passages were finished.

After these three concertos were played, the concert of the night ended, and I returned to Potsdam; but not without undergoing the same interrogatories from all the sentinels, as I had done in my way to Sans-Souci.

The musical taste of the King was conservative in the extreme, and Dr. Burney could find little good to say of the compositions of Quantz, which he played: the publication of these pieces, which were specially composed for the King and appropriated to his use, was not permitted, and Dr. Burney sagely remarks that

it is with music as with delicate wines, which not only become flat and insipid, when exposed to the air, but which are injured by time, however *well kept.*

He observed the same conservatism and lack of originality

in the music of the military bands in Potsdam, when he visited the parade ground " in hopes of hearing military music, as well as of seeing military discipline, in its utmost perfection ".

The parade at Potsdam is in a field, enclosed by a wall, where no stranger is permitted to enter, without leave from the captain of the guard. With respect to music, the same stability of style, and of taste, is observable here as at court; and I did not find that the Prussians, in their marches, had advanced a single step towards novelty, or refinement, since the first years of his present majesty's reign; for neither the airs that were played, nor the instruments that played them, had any peculiar merit: however, the old-fashioned march, of *dot and go one*, is perhaps, best calculated to mark the time, and to regulate the steps of the soldiers.

CHAPTER XII

Hamburg—Bremen—Groningen

Dr. Burney appears to have reached Hamburg on 8th October:

The entrance into this city, is free from examination, or custom-house embarrassments, the name only of a traveller being demanded at the gates. The streets are ill built, ill paved and narrow, but crowded with people who seem occupied with their own concerns; and there is an air of cheerfulness, industry, plenty, and liberty, in the inhabitants of this place, seldom to be seen in other parts of Germany.

Hamburg was of special interest to Dr. Burney on account of its associations with Handel, and as being the domicile of Carl Philipp Emanuel Bach (1714–1788), third son of the great John Sebastian and brother of Dr. Burney's friend John Christian Bach. Philipp Emanuel Bach was a notable pioneer, and laid the foundations upon which the immortal school of Viennese composers—Haydn, Mozart, Beethoven, Schubert—built up the great tradition which dominated music for nearly a century. As a composer he was soon superseded by his immediate successors; he strove, perhaps almost self-consciously, to break away from the style of his father, but succeeded in winning an independent reputation for himself among his contemporaries.

The story of Handel's sojourn in Hamburg as a young man and his rivalry with Mattheson is too well known to bear repetition here. Music in Hamburg at the time of Dr. Burney's visit was at a low ebb, and bore but little trace of these past glories. Bach indeed greeted him with the remark: "You are come here fifty years too late." However, Dr. Burney considered Bach himself quite sufficient "musical temptation" to visit Hamburg, as he "had long contemplated with the highest delight, his elegant and original compositions".

Dr. Burney's first visit in Hamburg was to M. Eberling, with whom he had been for some time in correspondence. Eberling had undertaken the German translation of the Journal of Dr. Burney's Italian Tour, which was published in Hamburg in 1772; a few loose sheets of this German translation were already in Dr. Burney's hands. Eberling, as soon as he was apprised of the projected tour in Germany,

carried his zeal so far as to write to several of his friends, and to able professors in the different cities of my route, pressing them, in the most urgent manner, to afford me all possible information and assistance in my enterprise.

Eberling was "a man of letters, and an extremely well informed *dilettante* in music". He showed Dr. Burney "his excellent collection of music, and musical writers", introduced him to Bach, having previously prepared the latter for Dr. Burney's visit by showing him the German translation of the Journal of the Italian Tour. He also took Dr. Burney to the house of M. Busch,

professor of mathematics, at whose house, and with whose family, I spent a most agreeable evening; which, indeed, was productive of no musical event, or new discovery; for I had long been convinced, that there is no harmony more enchanting, than that arising from the coincidence of hearts, and accord of sentiments in society.

M. professor Busch, and M. Eberling are at the head

of the *academy of commerce*, established at Hamburg, in 1768, an institution admirably calculated for the education of young persons, intended for merchants, in the several parts of the world, where the German, English, French, Italian, and Dutch languages are required; with which the pupils are taught book-keeping, geography, and history, as far as it is connected with the commercial interests of the several inhabitants of the globe.

Messieurs Busch and Eberling are assisted in this undertaking, by nine different masters, two of whom are experienced merchants, skilled in every branch of trade. I visited the young students while they were receiving their instructions from the several masters, and never before saw so much order, decorum, and application among young persons, who seemed under so little restraint. The society at present is numerous, and consists of young gentlemen from Spain, France, England, Holland, Russia, and different parts of Germany; two years only are required for completing the course of their mercantile studies, at the end of which, with a tolerable genius, they will have acquired a sufficient knowledge in languages and traffic, to be usefully employed in a counting house. The same care that is taken in forming these young persons for commercial concerns, is likewise bestowed in preparing them for the commerce of the world, by rendering them intelligent and amiable members of society; seventy pounds a year, includes every expense of lodging, board and instructions.

One evening during Dr. Burney's stay in Hamburg, Eberling organized a private concert for him, which was attended by all the Hamburg musicians and lovers of music, C. Ph. E. Bach presiding. Portions of one of his " Passions " were performed:

a pathetic air, upon the subject of St. Peter's weeping, when he heard the cock crow, was so truly pathetic as to make almost every hearer accompany the saint in his tears.

One of the most wonderful passages in his father's " St. Matthew Passion " is concerned with the same incident.

Dr. Burney was greatly assisted in his researches by C. Ph. E. Bach. Bach had for nearly thirty years been attached to the court in Berlin, and

had alone the honour to accompany his majesty upon the harpsichord in the first flute piece that he played at Charlottenburg, after he was king.

But the fact that Bach's originality did not find expression in compositions for the flute relegated him to a subordinate position at court:

A style of music prevailed, totally different from that which he wished to establish: his salary was inconsiderable, and he ranked below several that were greatly inferior to him in merit.

Although he had many opportunities of moving to a more congenial sphere of activity, Bach

could not obtain his dismission: however, his salary, after many years' service, was augmented.

Indeed, as M. Bach was not a subject of Prussia, it seems as if he might have quitted Berlin whenever he pleased; but as he had married during his residence there, and had issue by that marriage, it is supposed that his wife and children, being all subjects of his Prussian majesty, could not retire out of his dominions without his permission.

Eventually in 1767 he was allowed, "after repeated solicitations and petitions", to accept a vacant position in Hamburg, and had been there ever since with his family.

Dr. Burney has a great deal to say about Bach and his music which falls outside the scope of this volume. But he gives us an estimate of this great man, which probably coincides with the general contemporary judgment of him, and is therefore worth reproducing. Though C. Ph. E. Bach is now completely overshadowed by his famous sire, there was a time when an opposite opinion prevailed.

. . . Bach's style . . . has been imitated and adopted by the performers upon keyed instruments in every other part of Germany. How he formed his style, where he acquired all his taste and refinement, would be difficult to trace; he certainly neither inherited nor adopted them from his father, who was his only master; for that venerable musician, though unequalled in learning and contrivance, thought it so necessary to crowd into both hands all the harmony he could grasp, that he must inevitably have sacrificed melody and expression. Had the son chosen a model, it would certainly (have) been his father, whom he highly reverenced; but as he has ever disdained imitation, he must have derived from nature alone, those fine feelings, that variety of new ideas, and selection of passages, which are so manifest in his compositions. . . .

He is learned, I think, even beyond his father, whenever he pleases, and is far before him in variety of modulation; his fugues are always upon new and curious subjects, and treated with great art as well as genius.

Dr. Burney thought that C. Ph. E. Bach had "outstripped his age", which complained that his music was "long, difficult, fantastic and far-fetched". That Dr. Burney should compare the father unfavourably with his son is not surprising. Taste had changed since the days of J. S. Bach, though even in his lifetime his music had never been in any sense popular. But little of J. S. Bach's music was available at this time, and the very existence of his greatest works was forgotten. Dr. Burney's disparagement, based solely on the scant material then existing, is probably therefore pardonable.

C. Ph. E. Bach confided his philosophy of life to Dr. Burney on the way home from a church which they had attended to hear some of his music "very ill performed and to a congregation wholly inattentive". He told Dr. Burney

that, if he was in a place, where his compositions could be well executed, and well heard, he should certainly kill himself, by exertions to please. "But adieu music! now," he said, "these are good people for society, and I enjoy more tranquillity and independence here, than at a court; after I was fifty, I gave the thing up, and said, let us eat and drink, for to-morrow we die! and I am now reconciled to my situation; except, indeed, when I meet with men of taste and discernment, who deserve better music than we can give them here; then, I blush for myself, and for my good friends, the Hamburghers."

Bach entertained Dr. Burney to dinner at his house:

I found with him three or four rational, and well bred persons, his friends, besides his own family, consisting of Mrs. Bach, his eldest son, who practises the law, and his daughter. The instant I entered, he conducted me upstairs, into a large and elegant music room, furnished with pictures, drawings, and prints of more thar a hundred and fifty eminent musicians: among whom, there are many Englishmen, and original portraits in oil, of his father and grandfather [1]. After I had looked at these, M. Bach was so obliging as to sit down to his *Silbermann clavichord*, and favourite instrument,[2] upon which he played three or four of his choicest and most difficult compositions, with the delicacy, precision, and spirit, for which he is so justly celebrated among his countrymen. In the pathetic and slow movements, whenever he had a long note to express, he absolutely contrived to produce, from his instrument, a cry of sorrow and complaint, such as can only be effected upon the clavichord,[3] and perhaps by himself.

After dinner, which was elegantly served, and cheerfully eaten, I prevailed upon him to sit down again to a clavichord, and he played, with little intermission, till near eleven o'clock at night. During this time, he grew so animated and *possessed*, that he not only played, but looked like one inspired. His eyes were fixed, his under lip fell, and drops of effervescence distilled from his countenance. He said, if he were to be set to work frequently, in this manner, he should grow young again. He is now fifty-nine, rather short in stature, with black hair and eyes, and brown complexion, has a very animated countenance, and is of a cheerful and lively disposition. . . .

He played to me, among many other things, his last

[1] Johann Ambrosius Bach (1645–1695) of Eisenach, a violinist.
[2] As it was of his father. C. Ph. E. Bach wrote a textbook on the method of playing this instrument.
[3] It being the only keyboard instrument capable of producing the " vibrato " effects of a string instrument.

six concertos, lately published by subscription, in which he has studied to be easy, frequently I think at the expense of his usual originality; however, the great musician appears in every movement, and these productions will probably be the better received, for resembling the music of this world more than his former pieces, which seem made for another region, or at least another century, when what is now thought difficult and far fetched, will, perhaps, be familiar and natural.[1] . . .

M. Bach showed me two manuscript books of his father's composition, written on purpose for him when he was a boy, containing pieces with a fugue, in all the twenty-four keys,[2] extremely difficult, and generally in five parts, at which he laboured for the first years of his life, without remission. He presented me with several of his own pieces, and three or four curious ancient books and treatises on music, out of his father's collection; promising, at any distant time, to furnish me with others, if I would only acquaint him, by letter, with my wants.

Bach took Dr. Burney round the Hamburg churches to see the organs. In the church of St. Michael he saw the organ designed by Handel's old rival, Mattheson (1681–1764), the construction of which was a condition in his will whereby he bequeathed all his possessions to Hamburg. This organ was reputed to be " the largest and most complete in Europe " and cost about £4000: " the keys are covered with mother-of-pearl, and tortoiseshell; the front is curiously inlaid, and the case richly ornamented ".

---

[1] A sagacious judgment of general application, equally effective to-day.

[2] The " Forty-eight Preludes and Fugues " or " Das Wohltemperirte Klaver " the first part completed in 1722, the second in 1744. They were not printed until 1800. The books may have been compiled by J. S. Bach expressly for his son's use, but the works which they contained were of course not specially composed for him.

M. Mattheson's picture is placed in the front of the organ, and in the front of the gallery there is a fine old-fashioned Latin inscription, giving an account of his benefaction: this good man had more pedantry and nonsense about him, than true genius. In one of his vocal compositions for the church, in which the word *rainbow* occurred, he gave himself infinite trouble to make the notes of his score form an *arch*.

Mattheson was for many years secretary of legation to the English Resident in the city. Another condition of his will provided for the performance of an anthem of his composition; "but it was fairly laughed at, when heard in its old-fashioned guise ".

Dr. Burney was taken to see Klopstock (1724–1803), the German epic poet and author of the "Messias ", whom his contemporaries called the German Milton. Dr. Burney

had the pleasure of conversing with him, and several persons of learning and discernment, for a considerable time; during which, many curious subjects were started and discussed,

but he gives no report of the conversation, and cautiously admits that he is " unable to speak of M. Klopstock's poetical abilities ".

Dr. Burney was diligent in visiting the Hamburg book-shops, and makes his " acknowledgments to M. Bode, an eminent printer and publisher, and a good musician ", who rendered him great service and later translated his Journal of the German Tour into German. Bode (1730–1793) was the editor of a newspaper in Hamburg and printed Lessing's great *Hamburgische Dramaturgie*, which revolutionized the German drama. He spent a long time at Westphal's " musical warehouse ":

As M. Westphal is in correspondence with all the great printers and publishers of music in Europe, his catalogue is not merely local, and confined to Hamburg, or even the German empire; but is general, and that of all Europe: besides compositions that are printed and engraved, he has a great collection of manuscript music, which he disposes of, at a very fair and reasonable price. I was now unable to examine half the contents of his catalogue.

Westphal had a private concert at his house, which Dr. Burney attended. The music was chiefly supplied by amateurs, many of whom were promising.

This kind of concert is usually more entertaining to the performers than the hearers. . . . In these meetings, more than others, anarchy is too apt to prevail, unless the whole be conducted by an able and respectable master.

We need only add that Dr. Burney received every attention from Mr. Mathias, the British Resident at Hamburg, to whom he carried letters of introduction,

and who countenanced and honoured me with the same notice as His Majesty's ministers had bestowed upon me in other parts of Germany.

Mr. Mathias took Dr. Burney to spend the day at the villa of Mr. John Hanbury, " where true English hospitality reigns ". On the way back,

in the evening, on the Altona side of the city, there were such crowds of people walking and sauntering up and down the road, it being Sunday, that carriages could, with infinite difficulty, approach the gates. It gave me a great idea of the populousness of Hamburg: and, upon enquiry, I was assured that it contains 120,000 inhabitants,

within the walls, and 80,000 without.[1]   The common
people were to-day clean, and looked free from want;
a sight not very frequent in the other parts of Europe
through which I had lately passed.

The time had now arrived for Dr. Burney to undertake
his journey homewards. He had visited almost every German
capital and

from my first landing on the continent, steering from
west to east, and from south to north, I made an angle
through Flanders, Brabant, and the German empire, of
near two thousand miles, before I entered Holland, in
my way back to England. . . .
With respect to Germany, if I have been unable to
penetrate into several parts of it which were well entitled
to my attention, or have omitted to mention musicians
of abilities in others, I hope it will be remembered, that
to have visited every province, court, and city, of this
vast empire, and to have stayed as long in each as would
have been necessary to hear *all* the best performers,
during carnival time, as was frequently recommended to
me, would have required the life of a Patriarch.

He probably quitted Hamburg on 14th October, and on
his way to Amsterdam stopped for a few hours in Bremen.
" It contained no musical incitement sufficiently powerful
to encourage a longer residence."   However, Dr. Burney
visited the Lutheran cathedral,

where I found the congregation singing a dismal melody,
without the organ. When this was ended, the organist
gave out a hymn tune, in the true dragging style of

---

[1] By 1910 the population of Hamburg had increased to 1,015,707, of which 932,078
lived in the city itself.

Sternhold and Hopkins.[1] The instrument is large, . . . but the playing was more old-fashioned, I believe, than anything that could have been heard in our country towns, during the last century. The interludes between each line of the hymn were always the same. . . .

After hearing this tune, and these interludes, repeated ten or twelve times, I went to see the town, and returning to the cathedral, two hours after, I still found the people singing all in unison, and as loud as they could, the same tune, to the same accompaniment. I went to the post-office [2], to make dispositions for my departure; and, rather from curiosity than the love of such music, I returned once more to this church, and, to my great astonishment, still found them, vocally and organically performing the same ditty, whose duration seems to have exceeded that of a Scots Psalm in the time of Charles I.

But seeing that Bremen lacked those two essentials, a court and a theatre, without which music in the eighteenth century was almost unthinkable, Dr. Burney was hardly surprised that music was in a low state of cultivation there.

Dr. Burney inspected the organ of the principal church of Groningen on his way through the town, and visited the organist. Here in Groningen

I again found myself in a country of *carillons*; I had indeed heard some slight attempts made at Bremen, but in this place every half hour is measured by chimes.

On 20th October Dr. Burney arrived in Amsterdam.

[1] The *Whole Booke of Psalmes*, by T. Sternhold, I. Hopkins, and others, appeared in 1562.
[2] Where arrangements were made for post horses, carriages, &c.—a word which has since acquired an entirely new meaning.

CHAPTER XIII

Amsterdam and the Low Countries
The Home-coming

Dr. Burney appears to have devoted three days to Amsterdam, though there was but little of musical interest to detain him there.

In my way from Groningen hither, having crossed the Zuyder Zee, I approached this city by water, which affords one of the finest spectacles that can be imagined; such a noble port, and so crowded with ships of all sizes and countries I had never before seen at one glance; I entered the town in great tranquillity, without a single question concerning myself or baggage. The streets through which I passed to the Bible [1], in the Warmorstraat, were narrow, but clean, and well paved, with a brick footpath, though not raised, as in London; the shops were well furnished, and there was all the appearance of a brisk commerce, and an affluent people. . . .

There has been no theatrical exhibition in this city, since the playhouse was burnt down, except at the fair, in an occasional booth; nor is the theatre likely to be soon rebuilt, as the ground is not yet fixed upon, where it is to be constructed. Perhaps the fatal accident by

---

[1] The inn, where (he writes) " I retreated to the first bed which I had seen since my departure from Hamburg ".

which the former playhouse was burnt down, is regarded by the magistrates, as a *warning*; for, many years ago, when the steeple of the New Kerk was destroyed by lightning, before it was near finished, supposing that heaven was averse to steeples, they would never resume the work. . . .

The French company of comedians, who acted here while there was a theatre, are not yet dismissed, but are kept on half pay. . . . The inhabitants at present seem to have no places of amusement in the evening, except their shops and counting houses. . . . Upon the whole, Amsterdam does not seem to be a very amusing residence for idle people; there is so little for them to see in the way of pleasure, and so much for the mercantile part of the inhabitants to do in the way of business, that they seem very unfit company for each other.

The British agent in Amsterdam introduced Dr. Burney to the blind organist of the Oude Kerk:

he was deprived of his sight, at seven years old, by the smallpox; and this misfortune first suggested to his friends the thought of making music, which hitherto had afforded him no pleasure, his profession; and it afterwards became his darling amusement. . . .

He is married, and has children; and though not young and totally blind, he runs up and down the narrow steps of the organ loft, as nimbly as if he were but fifteen, and had the perfect enjoyment of his sight: he likewise pulls out, and puts in the stops of the organ himself, with wonderful dexterity, which, from their being so numerous, would be a difficult task, and require practice,

in one that could see . . . ; the touch of this instrument
is the heaviest that I ever felt, each key requiring almost
a two pound weight to put it down.

However, the organist played " with as much lightness and
rapidity, as if it were a common harpsichord ". He was also
carilloneur to the town, and took Dr. Burney up into the
tower of the Stad-huys while he performed:

It is a drudgery unworthy of such a genius; he has
had this employment, however, many years, having been
elected to it at thirteen. He had very much astonished
me on the organ, after all that I had heard in the rest of
Europe; but in playing those bells, his amazing dexterity
raised my wonder much higher; for he executed with
his two hands passages that would be very difficult to
play with the ten fingers. . . .

He began with a Psalm tune, with which their High
Mightinesses are chiefly delighted, and which they
require at his hands whenever he performs, which is on
Tuesdays and Fridays; he next played variations upon
the Psalm tune, with great fancy, and even taste: when
he had performed this task, he was so obliging as to play
a quarter of an hour extempore, in such a manner as he
thought would be more agreeable to me than psalmody. . . .

But surely this was a barbarous invention, and there
is barbarity in the continuance of it: if M. Pothoff (the
performer) had been put into Dr. Dominicetti's hottest
human cauldron [1] for an hour, he could not have per-

---

[1] Cf. Horace Walpole's *Letters* under 26. x. 1781: " An alderman's son . . . is
proud . . . of having a few more words said to him at a levée than are vouchsafed
Dr. Dominicetti." Also Boswell's *Life of Johnson*, 26th October, 1769, where Dr.
Johnson condemns Dominicetti and his " medicated baths ", which had been established in Cheyne Walk, Chelsea, in 1765.

spired more violently than he did after a quarter of an hour of this furious exercise; he stripped to his shirt, put on his night cap, and trussed up his sleeves for this *execution*; and he said he was forced to go to bed the instant it was over, in order to prevent his catching cold, as well as to recover himself; he being usually so much exhausted, as to be utterly unable to speak.

By the little attention that is paid to this performer, extraordinary as he is, it should seem as if some hewer of wood, and drawer of water, whose coarse constitution, and gross habit of body, required frequent sudorifics, would do the business equally to the satisfaction of such unskilful and unfeeling hearers. . . .

Besides these *carillons à clavier*, the chimes here, played by clockwork, are much celebrated. The brass cylinder, on which the tunes are set, weighs 4474 pounds, and has 7200 iron studs fixed in it, which, in the rotation of the cylinder, give motion to the clappers of the bells. If their High Mightinesses' judgment, as well as taste, had not failed them, for half the prime cost of this expensive machine, and its real charge for repairs, new setting, and constant attendance, they might have had one of the best bands in Europe: but those who can be charmed with *barrel music*, certainly neither want, nor deserve better. . . .

This is truly the country of chimes; every quarter of an hour a tune is played by them at all the churches, but so indistinctly, on account of the confluence of sounds, that I was seldom able to discover what was played. . . . There is scarce a church belonging to the Calvinists, in

Amsterdam, without its chimes, which not only play the same tunes every quarter of an hour, for three months together, without their being changed; but, by the difference of clocks, one has scarce five minutes' quiet in the four and twenty hours, from these *corals for grown gentlemen*. In a few days' time I had so thorough a surfeit of them, that in as many months, I really believe, if they had not first deprived me of hearing, I should have hated music in general.

Dr. Burney visited several other Amsterdam churches and attended afternoon service in one, where he endured "two long and tiresome Psalms".

As every species of national music seemed to merit my attention, I went to the synagogue of the German Jews, in this city, to hear what the musical performance, during their religious rites, was, and how far it differed from that of other synagogues where I had heard singing in different parts of Europe. At my first entrance, one of the priests was chanting part of the service in a kind of ancient *canto fermo* [1], and responses were made by the congregation, in a manner which resembled the hum of bees.

After this, three of the sweet singers of Israel, which, it seems, are famous here, and much attended to by Christians as well as Jews, began singing a kind of jolly modern melody, sometimes in unison, and sometimes in parts, to a kind of *tol de rol*, instead of words, which, to me, seemed very farcical. One of these voices was a falsetto, more like the upper part of a bad *vox humana*

---

[1] Or plain-song melody.

stop in an organ,[1] than a natural voice.   I remember
seeing an advertisement in an English newspaper, of a
barber, who undertook to dress hair in such a manner
as exactly to resemble a peruke; and this singer might
equally boast of having the art, not of singing like a
human creature, but of making his voice, like a very bad
imitation of one. Of much the same kind is the merit of
such singers, who, in execution, degrade the voice into
a flute or fiddle, forgetting that they should not receive
law from instruments, but give instruments law.

The second of these voices was a very vulgar tenor,
and the third a baritone. This last imitated, in his accompaniment of the falsetto, a bad bassoon; sometimes
continued one note as a drone bass, at others, divided it
into triplets, and semiquavers, iterated on the same tone.
But though the tone of the falsetto was very disagreeable,
and he forced his voice very frequently in an outrageous
manner, yet this man had certainly heard good music
and good singing. . . . At the end of each strain, the
whole congregation set up such a kind of cry, as a pack of
hounds when a fox breaks cover.   It was a confused
clamour, and riotous noise, more than song or prayer.
However, this is a description, not a censure of Hebrew
music, in religious ceremonies. It is impossible for me
to divine what ideas the Jews themselves annex to this
vociferation, I shall, therefore, neither pronounce it to
be good nor bad in itself, I shall only say, that it is very
unlike what we Christians are used to in divine service.

[1] Elsewhere Dr. Burney confesses that, of all the " vox humana " stops he had
heard, " no one, in the treble part, has ever reminded me of anything human, so
much as of the cracked voice of an old woman of ninety, or, in the lower parts, of
Punch singing through a comb "

Dr. Burney, having lightened his purse at the Amsterdam music and book sellers, passed on, probably on 24th October, to Haarlem, where he inspected the famous organ:

Indeed, it is the *lion* of the place; but to hear this lion roar, is attended with more expense than to hear all the lions and tigers in the Tower of London.[1] The fee of the *keeper*, or organist, is settled at half a guinea; and that of his assistant keeper, or bellows-blower, at half a crown.

Leyden was the next halt:

In this city, which is one of the best built and most agreeable of the Low Countries, there is not only a celebrated university, but a theatre, where Dutch plays are exhibited two or three times a week. As there is no great commerce carried on here, it is the place to which the rich citizens of Amsterdam retreat, as well when their *plum* is full grown, as when age and infirmities have deprived them of the power of longer pursuing the Mammon of unrighteousness. . . .

As to music, mechanical chimes, every quarter of an hour; *carillons* at noon, two or three times a week; and huge organs, coarsely played, to more coarse psalmody, constitute all that Apollo and the Nine Muses have given to this place, in the way of harmony and melody, as far as I was able to discover.

At the Hague, "the residence of the Stadtholder[2], and the place where his court is constantly kept", Dr. Burney

---

[1] The menagerie at the Tower of London, from which the Lion gate in the Middle Tower received its name, existed until 1834.
[2] William V, born 1748, fled to England in 1795 and lived there in exile, dying in 1806.

attended a performance at the French theatre, which he drily remarks " is small, as was the company, and the merit of the performers ".

The Hague seems more calculated for birds of passage than natives. The want of variety in the company, and in the performers, makes them soon mutually tired of each other. It is common for German and Italian musicians, in their way to or from England, to visit, and stop a short time at the Hague, where, by concerts, they usually gain money sufficient to enable them to pursue their journey; but they seldom remain here longer than a ship which enters a port merely to wood and water. . . .

If my musical acquisitions and discoveries received but small augmentation at the Hague, I was amply rewarded for the trouble of going thither, by the notice with which I was honoured by his excellency, Sir Joseph Yorke [1], and the pains he kindly took with design to render me service.

Passing through Delft, where he heard a fine performance on the carillon, Dr. Burney at length reached Rotterdam, where he paid a visit to the organist; with the exception of the information culled from him,

the only discovery which I was able to make, relative to music, in this large and populous city, was, that it contained nothing more to be discovered: but this negative kind of knowledge is not without its use, as it assuages curiosity, and precludes all self reproach on the score of negligence.

[1] Sir Joseph Yorke (1724–1792) was the third son of the first Earl of Hardwicke, and afterwards became Lord Dover. He was British Minister at the Hague from 1751 until 1780.

At this point we leave Dr. Burney's Journal and resume the narrative in Madame D'Arblay's *Memoirs* of her father: [1]

After travelling by day and by night to expedite his return, over mountains, through marshes, by cross roads; on horse back, on mules, in carriages of any and every sort that could but hurry him on, he reached Calais in a December so dreadfully stormy, that not a vessel of any kind could set sail for England. Repeatedly he secured his hammock, and went on board to take possession of it; but as repeatedly was driven back by fresh gales, during the space of nine fatiguing days and tempestuous nights. And when, at last, the passage was effected, so nearly annihilating had been his sufferings from sea sickness, that it was vainly he was told he might now, at his pleasure, arise, go forth, and touch English ground; he had neither strength nor courage to move, and earnestly desired to be left awhile to himself.

Exhaustion, then, with tranquillity of mind, cast him into a sound sleep.

From this repose, when, much refreshed, he awoke, he called to the man who was in waiting, to help him up, that he might get out of the ship.

" Get out of the ship, sir?" repeated the man. " Good lauk! you'll be drowned!"

" Drowned?—What's to drown me? I want to go ashore."

---

[1] This incident is placed here by reason of the context in which it occurs in the *Memoirs* and because Madame D'Arblay expressly states that it took place on Dr. Burney's "last voyage home". If this be so, she must surely have mistaken the month. If the month be correct, the story would appear to relate to the Italian tour, but there is no reference to the double journey in the circumstantial account of the Channel crossing in the manuscript journal (cf. p. 84). The journal of the German tour ends abruptly at Rotterdam with no indication of the route by which Dr. Burney reached England.

" Ashore, sir?" again repeated the man; " why you're in the middle of the sea! There ar'nt a bit of ground for your toe-nail."

" What do you mean?" cried the Doctor, starting up; " the sea? did you not tell me we were safe in at Dover?"

" O lauk! that's two good hours ago, sir! I could not get you up then, say what I would. You fell downright asleep, like a top. And so I told them. But that's all one. You may go, or you may stay, as you like; but them pilots never stops for nobody."

Filled with alarm, the Doctor now rushed up to the deck, where he had the dismay to discover that he was halfway back to France.

And he was forced to land again at Calais; where again, with the next mail, and a repetition of his sea sickness, he re-embarked for Dover.

The exposures and privations to which Dr. Burney had been subjected during his long journey left their mark on his health, which finally broke down completely: " he became a prey to the merciless pangs of the acutest spasmodic rheumatism; which barely suffered him to reach his home, ere, long and piteously, it confined him, a tortured prisoner, to his bed ". He retired to Chessington, where he was nursed back to life and health by his wife and daughters, with the assistance of the family friend, Mr. Crisp.

The success of the Journal of the German Tour, when it was published, surpassed even that of its predecessor. Madame D'Arblay tells us, however, that her father was taken to task by one critic for exaggerating

the account drawn up of the expenses, the bad roads, the bad living, the bad carriages, and other various faults and deficiences upon which the travels in Germany had expatiated: all which this new correspondent was convinced were related from misinformation, or misconception; as he had himself visited the same spots without witnessing any such imperfections. He conjured the Doctor, therefore, to set right these statements in his next edition; which single amendment would render the journal of his Tour in Germany the most delightful now in print. . . .

Dr. Burney retorted that he could not be

the dupe of misrepresentation, for he had related only what he had experienced. His narrative was all personal, all individual; and he had documents, through letters, bills, and witnesses in fellow travellers, and in friends or inhabitants of the several places described, that could easily be produced to verify his assertions: all which he was most able and willing to call forth. . . .

The critic hastily withdrew his charge:

he took shame, he added, to himself, for not having weighed the subject more chronologically before he wrote his strictures; as he had now made out that his hasty animadversion was the unreflecting result of the different periods in which the Doctor and himself had travelled; his own German visit having taken place previously to the devastating war between the King of Prussia and the Empress Queen, which had since laid waste the whole country in which, unhappily, it had been waged.

Perhaps the most singular mark of " the quick-spreading favour with which the Tours were received; the celebrity which they threw around the name and existence of Dr.

Burney ", is to be found in the production of a parody of Dr. Burney's Journals by " Joel Collier ", which, we are told, " though executed with burlesque humour, whether urged or not by malevolence, was never reprinted; and obtained but the laugh of a moment, without making the shadow of an impression to the disadvantage of the tourist ".[1]   The anonymous scribe was content to pour ridicule on the technical phraseology of the Journals, which certainly sometimes lends itself to irreverent treatment, and no personal attack on the author was intended.

The crowning recognition of the value of Dr. Burney's work lay in his admission by a unanimous vote to the fellowship of the Royal Society in the year following his return from Germany; in the enjoyment of this well-deserved honour we take our leave of him.

---

[1] *Musical Travels through England,* by " Joel Collier, organist ", was sold for a shilling, and, in spite of Madame D'Arblay's statement to the contrary, was so successful that it ran into four editions.   They are all rare, as the Burney family is said to have done all in its power to suppress the book.   " Joel Collier " was one George Veal, who played in the orchestra at the Italian opera.

APPENDIX

(See page 43)

The only other reference to Mozart in Dr. Burney's Journals occurs at the conclusion of the second volume of the German Tour. In an appendix to the Journal proper, he gives short details of the state of music in those parts of Germany which he was unable to visit, culled chiefly by correspondence from various sources. He tells us that the notorious Hieronymus von Colleredo (1737–1812),

the archbishop and sovereign of Salzburg, is very magnificent in his support of music, having usually near a hundred performers, vocal and instrumental, in his service. This prince is himself a *dilettante*, and a good performer on the violin; he has lately been at great pains to reform his band, which has been accused of being more remarkable for coarseness and noise, than delicacy and high finishing.

He is only remembered to-day for his detestable treatment and vulgar abuse of Mozart, who remained in his service until he was literally kicked out in June, 1781. Mozart was in Salzburg in the summer of 1772 in connexion with the allegiance festival of Hieronymus, who had just been elected to the vacant archbishopric; Mozart was commissioned to compose an opera to celebrate the occasion.

The Mozart family were all at Salzburg last summer (1772); the father has long been in the service of that court, and the son is now one of the band; he composed an opera at Milan, for the marriage of the archduke, with the princess of Modena, and was to compose another at the same place for the carnival of this year,[1] though he is now but sixteen years of age.[2] By a letter from Salzburg, dated last November, I am informed, that this young man, who so much astonished all Europe by his infant knowledge and performance, is still a great master of his instrument; my correspondent went to his father's house to hear him and his sister [3] play duets on the same harpsichord; but she is now at her summit, which is not marvellous; " and," says the writer of the letter, " if I may judge of the music which I heard of his composition, in the orchestra, he is one further instance of early fruit being more extraordinary than excellent ".

As the judgment of a contemporary this is of great interest, and its gradual adoption by the world at large is the major factor in the tragedy of Mozart's life. Needless to say, posterity has completely reversed this adverse opinion, and now accords Mozart a position in the musical pantheon second to none.

[1] Both these commissions were the result of the Italian journey in 1770–1771, during which Dr. Burney met the Mozarts. The marriage of the Archduke Ferdinand and Princess Beatrice of Modena took place on 15th October, 1771. Mozart was commissioned by the Empress, Maria Theresa, to write a " dramatic serenata " not an opera. It was performed with great success on 17th October, and as a special reward the Empress sent Mozart a gold watch set with diamonds having her portrait on the back of the case. The new opera "Lucio Silla", composed for Milan, was produced there on 26th December, 1772.

[2] Mozart was born in 1756 and died in 1791.

[3] Maria Anna Mozart (" Nannerl "): 1751–1829.

INDEX